LITTLE ZION

SHELLY O'FORAN

LITTLE ZION

A Church Baptized by Fire

THE UNIVERSITY OF NORTH CAROLINA PRESS

Chapel Hill

© 2006 The University of
North Carolina Press
All rights reserved
Manufactured in the
United States of America
Designed by Jacquline Johnson
Set in Janson
by Keystone Typesetting, Inc.

The paper in this book meets the guidelines for
permanence and durability of the Committee on
Production Guidelines for Book Longevity of the
Council on Library Resources.

This book was published with the assistance of
the Z. Smith Reynolds Fund of the University of
North Carolina Press.

Unless otherwise noted, the photographs in this
book were taken by Mary Ann Gatty.

Library of Congress Cataloging-in-Publication
Data
O'Foran, Shelly.
Little Zion : a church baptized by fire / Shelly
O'Foran.
p. cm.
Includes bibliographical references and index.
ISBN-13: 978-0-8078-3048-2 (cloth: alk. paper)
ISBN-10: 0-8078-3048-8 (cloth: alk. paper)
ISBN-13: 978-0-8078-5763-2 (pbk.: alk. paper)
ISBN-10: 0-8078-5763-7 (pbk.: alk. paper)
1. Little Zion Baptist Church (Boligee, Ala.) —
History. 2. Boligee (Ala.) — Church history.
I. Title.
BX6480.B585O36 2006
286'.176142 — dc22

2006005199

cloth   10 09 08 07 06   5 4 3 2 1
paper   10 09 08 07 06   5 4 3 2 1

TO THE CHILDREN OF

Little Zion Baptist Church,

and to my children,

Kelly Erin O'Foran,

Carrie Megan O'Foran,

and Lan Yulin O'Foran

CONTENTS

ILLUSTRATIONS

PREFACE

On the evening of January 11, 1996, a small, rural African American church near Boligee, Alabama, caught fire, probably the work of arsonists. The burning of Little Zion Baptist Church was not discovered immediately, as the building stood far back from the road on a gravel path through the trees. When the fire department arrived, the damage had already been done. Unfortunately, the thoroughness of the burning probably destroyed any evidence that might have helped the Federal Bureau of Investigation (FBI) and the Bureau of Alcohol, Tobacco, and Firearms (ATF) determine who or what was responsible.

The burning of Little Zion, while tragic for its seventy or so members at the time, was part of a larger and even more disturbing pattern of African American church burnings that received media attention during 1996. In remote western Alabama, that pattern was already evident on January 11. Members of the Little Zion congregation shared the loss of their church with members of Mt. Zoar Baptist Church, a neighboring African American church also destroyed by fire that night. The grief was shared, too, by members of nearby Mt. Zion Baptist Church, who had lost their church by fire a few weeks earlier on December 22, 1995. By midsummer a fourth African American church, about thirty miles away in Greensboro, also would be destroyed.

As this book is being prepared for publication, a decade has passed since the 1996 burnings. The Little Zion case has not been solved, and arson against houses of worship remains a sad reality. In early 2006, many more Alabama churches burned suspiciously, some with primarily white congregations, others attended mostly by African Americans. Particularly disturbing, several black churches near Little Zion, including one in Boligee, caught fire. Little Zion's Rev. Willie C. Carter told a CNN reporter, "Oh, Lord Jesus, have mercy. . . . It be getting started one more time."[1] Although as of this writing three young men have been arrested and charged in federal court in connection with these nine fires, the damage done by such burnings poses a long-term challenge to the targeted congregations.

In 1996 Rev. W. D. Lewis, the ninety-two-year-old pastor[2] of Little Zion, stood among the ashes of his former church and said, "The one that did it, if he were to come here, I would forgive him." But of course he did not come. Nor was he brought in by local or federal authorities. So the tedious work of rebuilding began, as well as the difficult process of making sense of the violence.

I learned about the church burnings later that winter from an announcement made at the close of Sunday worship at the Adelphi, Maryland, Religious Society of Friends Meeting. Washington Quaker Workcamps, a local relief organization, sought volunteers for the rebuilding effort. My husband and I and our four-year-old daughter joined Quakers and people of many other faiths from across the country, and even as far away as Tanzania, in the reconstruction of Little Zion that summer.

The group of volunteers, which included predominantly white, suburban young people with resources to pay transportation and living costs for workcamp stints of one week to one month, joined the predominantly African American, rural, older community of church members and contractors in the rebuilding effort. My own family, of Irish American descent, living in College Park, Maryland, and enjoying middle-income paychecks, was unique among the rebuilding volunteers only in that we were at least a decade older than most and had begun raising children. Though mostly inexperienced in construction, the volunteers provided free, enthusiastic labor and, according to the general contractor, helped to shave significant time and money from the project.

My family participated in the effort from June 22 to July 6, 1996, hanging drywall in the new church. While measuring and cutting sheetrock, I came to understand that the church could not be contained by the structure of the building that had burned down. As I watched the transformation of the space from a construction site, where workers crushed their empty paper water cups beneath muddy boots, to a sacred place for Sunday shoes, I realized that Little Zion lived in its people's memories and inherited traditions, which they practice and teach to their children today to ensure the church's continued vitality tomorrow. I conceived the collection of this narrative as a way of tracing the outlines of a structure that exists beyond the physically tangible building, built solid of another kind of material — vulnerable perhaps to the passage of time and the process of forgetting, but certainly not to fire.

According to oral accounts, Little Zion began sometime in the mid-1800s, during slavery or just after emancipation. Mr. Dick Smaw,[3] the white landowner, donated a small piece of land, and the African American members of the new church built a brush arbor to shield them from weather during worship. Eventually, that structure was replaced by a log cabin and later by a frame church. In 1970 the frame church was torn down, the lumber used to build a nearby home for one of the church members, and a brick church was built. That was the building destroyed by fire in early 1996 and rebuilt later that year. On the holiday of Martin Luther King's birthday, one year after the burning, the new church was dedicated and became the fifth structure to stand on this spot as Little Zion Baptist Church.

After returning home from the rebuilding effort, I approached Rev. Lewis and other church members with a proposal to collect their memories of Little Zion, to tell its story as fully as possible in the voices of its members. The church generously embraced the idea, and I began the long process of collecting and reflecting on the approximately seventy-five hours of taped conversations and church events in which I was privileged to participate from 1996 to 2003.

I began with three words. During the rebuilding effort, on the back of the drywall near the baptismal pool, someone had written, "Baptized by Fire."[4] Facing the studs, those words are built into the church now. Though they can no longer be seen, they endure inside Little Zion, just below where Rev. Lewis signed: "Reverend Lewis, Pastor." This book is my attempt to understand the significance of those and other such sacred words in this community—especially the generations of oral narratives that hold the shape of Little Zion Baptist Church just as surely as the bricks and mortar of the building.

In one of those stories, told by Little Zion's current pastor Rev. Willie C. Carter, the church sits hidden from view on a remote hill in Greene County, Alabama. But in this place, God draws near, and in that communion the lines between the everyday world and the transcendent fall away. Rev. Carter goes to this hill to pray and meditate, anytime, day or night. He said of the rebuilt church:

I feel good in this new church, the same as I did in the old one. It's something about the hill it's built on, does something strange to me. You know I drive to the hill sometimes, don't go in the church. But I get out and pray right there on the hill. And I gets relief. If things aren't going right in my life, I just get good relief. Something is strange with the hill.

Most people don't like to come up here alone. They'll say, "Oh, you come up on the hill by yourself?"

I say, "Yeah, I come up on the hill by myself." I say, "What's up here? I mean the Lord is here. I believe He here."

I love it up there. I can go up there at the midnight hour; it don't bother me. I get consolation there. If I need to pray, I'm going. I believe the Holy Spirit has been there. I think of what the Lord told Solomon: When he get through building the temple, then the Lord gonna come and dedicate it. His name will be hung at Zion. (9/7/98)

In another of those narratives, Rev. Michael A. Barton said that the church building remains an empty shell without the people, living in the Spirit of God, who give it life. Pastor of Little Zion from mid-2000 to early 2004, Rev. Barton preached during Sunday school on July 20, 2003:

The physical construction of the church was complete./
But the church is not complete without the Spirit./
It is within the people of God/
That the Spirit of God abides./
And you can have a nice building,/
But if the people are not built,/
Then all you have is just a building./
We must understand that/
We don't *come* to the church./
We *are* the church.

In the collected memories that follow, I hope the observations about Little Zion Baptist Church continue to reveal something of its many meanings in this rural Alabama community.

Unless noted otherwise, quotations by church members used throughout this book are drawn from personal interviews included in the Works Cited list. I include a parenthetical citation only when necessary to distinguish between multiple interviews of the same person. In addition, since interviews with church members were conducted orally, spellings sometimes were uncertain. Whenever I was unable to confirm a correct spelling, I have included the note "[phonetic spelling]."

ACKNOWLEDGMENTS

I'd like to thank the members of the Little Zion Baptist Church family, without whom this project would not exist. I'd also like to thank my husband, Norman O'Foran, and my three daughters, who made this book a major priority in their lives for many years. Special thanks go to my mother, Mary Ann Gatty, for accompanying me on fieldwork trips and taking the photos that allow readers to get a glimpse of the community of people whose voices are heard in this project. Michael Gatty helped to convert many of those photos to a digital format.

At the University of Maryland, Professors Verlyn Flieger, Eugene Hammond, Shirley Logan, Sheri Parks, and especially Professor Barry Lee Pearson, gave me much needed advice and support in the construction and editing of the narrative that follows. Professor Audrey Kerr, my good friend and colleague for more than a decade, encouraged this project from the beginning and kept me focused throughout the writing of this book.

I'd like to offer additional gratitude to Professor Verlyn Flieger, who has been my mentor these many years, as well as to the many wonderful teachers I have been fortunate enough to encounter in my lifetime.

Finally, thanks to Senior Editor Elaine Maisner and the staff of UNC Press, who guided this book through the publication process.

Fieldwork was made possible, in part, by travel grants from the University of Maryland's Committee on Africa and the Americas and from the Department of English. Bob Gatty and Norman Foran donated many frequent-flier miles and airline tickets.

I feel blessed to have had the opportunity to do this work.

LITTLE ZION

Study to show thyself approved unto God, a workman that needeth not
to be ashamed, rightly dividing the word of truth.
— 2 *Timothy* 2:15

CHAPTER ONE

Introduction

The church that I belong to name Little Zion Baptist Church.
My grandmother told me about the founding of it; nobody else
knows the record of that early church. She couldn't remember
what year it was when Little Zion Baptist Church originated,
but it was under slavery. They felt like prayer had delivered
them from under slavery. She would tell me they couldn't afford to pray around the slave masters, because they didn't believe too much in that. But they [Deacon Carter's ancestors]
had a lot of feeling of belief in Jesus Christ, and the white folks
didn't bother with them long as they stayed together.

So they went out and got them limbs off the trees, and sawed
up some poles and made a arbor, brush arbor. Stood some
sticks up, and put more sticks on top of it, break small limbs
and put on top of that until they had a big arbor, covered over
with brushes. This arbor located on the old Small place. The
old man called Dick Small owned the land, give it to them for
to have their church service.

They went up under there and my grandma say they would
rock back and forth, groan and moan and rock. They had the
zeal, but they didn't know what should be done. This man
named Steve Burnett worshipped there, and he would pray,

and they had a lot of emotion with them, and they would get happy and shout.

They stayed under that brush arbor a long while, until they got where they could hew them out some logs. They build them a log cabin to go in and have service. So they have service in there and they come more to life, and they prospered more. So they go to work and they build them a frame structure. When they build that frame structure, then I had about come forward. I was born then.

I don't know what year the frame structure was built, but it was old when I was born in 1916. That was the third time it was built.

In 1970, we build a brick church. 1996 we build another brick church after the burning, and that's what's up there now. That church was built five times in the same spot. There's no telling how long that place has been worshipped at, though, before they got a record of it. The deed was recorded in nineteen twenty-something, but nobody really knows how old the church is.

— Deacon Ed Carter[1]

Take the Boligee, Alabama, exit off of Interstate 59 onto Route 20, and you will pass the BP gas station, where you can grab some southern fried chicken, beans, and greens at the lunch counter; Paramount High School, attended by an almost all-black population; fields of cotton, farmed for centuries by slaves and until the mid-1900s by sharecroppers; and catfish ponds, where many of Greene County's farmers are placing their economic hopes for the future. If you watch closely after a few miles and turns, you will see a small sign for Little Zion Baptist Church and a paved road to the left and up a hill. There you will find the beautiful brick church with stained-glass windows, rebuilt in 1996 after its destruction by fire earlier that year.

If you arrive at Little Zion outside of scheduled church events, chances are you will make the journey from the highway alone, passed only by a few cars. The occupants of those cars probably will wave to you, and you will be expected to wave back. Then you will suspect you have been noticed as an outsider to this region.

Deacon Ed Henry Carter shares his memories of Little Zion Baptist Church during an October 1996 interview.

In 1996 Linda Janet Holmes described her experience collecting the life story of midwife Margaret Charles Smith in Greene County:

> Everyone in Eutaw² can take advantage of the town square's set of hanging traffic lights to stare into passing cars. Experienced watchers don't need to look at license plates to identify newcomers. Relatives expecting guests get word from such watchers long before their visitors arrive.
>
> Several middle-aged to elderly black men greet one's entrance with solemn nods from their positions on milk crates outside the A & P. (I always need to get out at the A & P to use the pay phone to call Mrs. Smith for directions. I wonder if these men see my arrivals as the next episode of a soap opera, even though months go by between them.)³

When my family arrived as volunteers in Greene County for the 1996 church rebuilding project, we joined a group of outsiders to

Little Zion after its 1996 rebuilding.

this community. We stayed on a small campus run by the Federation of Southern Cooperatives, a farmers' aid organization a few miles from the post office, café, and one block of businesses that comprise Boligee's center. In search of hardware supplies and groceries, work-campers constantly confronted the many differences between our own lifestyles and those of Greene County—largely differences, as noted earlier, of race, income, and geography (that is, urban versus rural, southern versus northern experiences).[4] Most notably, we discovered in Boligee what Holmes called "reminders of segregation" everywhere.[5] In fact, a *Christian Science Monitor* article published during the rebuilding effort called Boligee, Alabama, "A Town With 'Two of Everything,'" pointing out:

> Greene County has a black and a white newspaper, a black bank and a white bank, a black public swimming pool, a predominantly white public pool, an all-white private country club, black public

schools, and a private all-white academy. Funeral homes and cemeteries are racially separate. Some doctors' offices still have separate
waiting rooms.

At the Boligee Café, blacks sit at the table to the right of the door
and whites to the left. . . .

Except for the tiny, 30-member Roman Catholic church, houses
of worship remain racially divided. "Eleven o'clock Sunday morning is the most segregated hour of the week," says Booker Cooke,
chief of staff of the Greene County Board of Commissioners.[6]

Of course, these "reminders of segregation" confirmed for many
workcampers — including me — a sense of racial tension in Boligee
we'd expected based on news reports of the church burnings. For two
African American churches in this small town to catch fire mysteriously on the same night, after another had been similarly destroyed
a few weeks earlier, strongly suggested racially motivated arson to us.
We came to Little Zion as part of an effort to right that perceived
wrong. We came as activists, attempting to change on some level the
culture we found here.

Though not conscious of it at the time, I also came to Little Zion as
a student of folklife, seeing the rebuilding effort through the interests
of my chosen field of Ph.D. study. Where some saw drywall installation, for instance, I saw the transmission of tradition among community members. Unlike the activist's stance, however, my scholarly
perspective never purposely included the desire to change the community I felt privileged to witness. Rather, I spent considerable effort
attempting to change my own awareness, making a few small steps
from the outsider perspective of the student-activist toward an insider
point of view as a Little Zion churchgoer.

Finally, I came to Little Zion as a Quaker and former Roman
Catholic, having grown up attending St. John the Baptist Catholic
Church in Silver Spring, Maryland, during the 1970s, and attended
Religious Society of Friends worship services regularly since 1991.
Since I learned about the burning of Little Zion in the context of
a Quaker worship service and joined a rebuilding project run by a
Quaker organization, it seems obvious that my religious perspective

would have had some bearing on my experiences at Little Zion. But it wasn't until much later that I realized how deeply my perceptions were influenced by the language and practices of my own religion.

This book grew out of what Quakers sometimes call a "leading," or sense of greater purpose in everyday actions. As an activist, I felt led to collect these oral narratives as a way of participating in the rebuilding effort. Trained as a writer, my drywall skills were lacking. The collection of narrative offered an alternative that church members embraced. As a folklife student, I saw this project as a way to help fulfill scholarly training requirements while working on something meaningful to a community beyond the academy. My goal for this work was simple: To write a life story of Little Zion Baptist Church told primarily in the voices of its members.

With the support and encouragement of many people at Little Zion, I hope that this project will be of interest to a broader audience. While grounded in recent folklife scholarship, this book speaks to anyone interested in religious or African American cultural traditions, and everyone concerned about the rash of African American church burnings that received extensive media coverage during the late 1990s. In the wake of more recent terrorist attacks and the wars in Afghanistan and Iraq, this book also addresses the many Americans struggling with issues of cultural identity, tolerance, and the role of religion in promoting or undermining understanding between demographic groups. *Little Zion* offers one community's negotiation of those concerns — told through immediate and compelling personal narrative. Targeted by a probable hate crime, Little Zion's members fold the burning into a long journey of faith and struggle for justice. They conduct the rebuilding effort, and even their subsequent participation in this book, through the language and practice of their religious beliefs. For readers who have visited or participated in rural black Baptist churches in the South, many of the narratives here will ring with a familiar power. For those new to churches in this worship tradition, the voices of Little Zion's members offer an introduction to a small but vibrant church at the center of the lives of several generations of believers.

I knew from the outset that writing a life story of Little Zion

Baptist Church would be a complicated task. Even if I removed my own voice from the narrative, my presence as the editor who pieces together a single tale from multiple sources could not be denied. Even if I were to present the interviews transcribed and unedited, asking the reader to bridge the gap between modes of oral and written communication unaided, my presence would still have asserted itself in the narratives themselves, influenced by the questions I asked — or didn't ask. So, like many others working along the lines of race and culture, I've settled for a somewhat self-reflexive accounting, assembling a story of the church out of the stories shared with me, acknowledging and exploring the ways that the form of the final narrative also reflects the trajectory of my own experience collecting in this community. I've kept my focus as much as possible on the lives of Little Zion's members, while admitting the limitations and possible biases of my perspective. Of course, detailing possible bias is like trying to get a good view of a blind spot; it can be managed only in glimpses around the edges.

I attempt a few of those glimpses here, outlining how my perspectives as an activist, folklife student, and Quaker provide a context for my impressions of this community — and how church members' attitudes toward my roles at Little Zion shaped the final writing of this book. I came away from this project with a sense that I can address my own limitations in the same way that church members and I practice our different forms of Christianity: through the purposeful use of language. At Little Zion, words carry tremendous power in the singing, preaching, testifying, and storytelling both inside and outside of worship services. At the Friends Monthly Meeting in Herndon, Virginia, to which I now belong, words might seem to an outsider to be far less central to the service. Herndon Friends sing three or four hymns before the official start of meeting for worship. Then the congregation settles into silent meditation, which is broken only occasionally when someone feels moved to speak and delivers a short message. Congregants believe those messages to be divinely inspired, however, and those who rise to speak do not make the decision to do so lightly.[7] (In fact, the word "Quaker" originally was a derogatory term referring to the "quaking" that many experienced in the face of the call to deliver a message.) So while words in an unprogrammed[8] Quaker meeting are few, they are charged with a sacred power that would be familiar to any participant in Little Zion's services. I believe Quakers, Baptists, other Christians, and people of most religious traditions worldwide share a respect for language as a sacred vehicle for naming that which is ultimately unnamable in our religious understanding. Thus, I deeply respect the sacred nature of the words shared with me in these narratives and hope to re-create that experience for readers through the form and content of this book.

As I began this project struggling to find ways of understanding community life at Little Zion, I turned to many types of informational sources. After the burning, I studied extensive news accounts to place this tragedy in the context of nationwide coverage of a rash of suspicious church fires. When detailing Little Zion's early history, I looked to archival sources for clues to how and when the church began. In considering members' descriptions of their spiritual journeys, I examined folklorists' explorations of belief and religious experience. But these sources — external to the experiences of those participating in Little Zion's activities — offered limited insight. And as my familiarity with this community grew, church members shared more openly and completely with me, and the relevance of outside sources diminished. So throughout these pages I've attempted to subordinate other material to church members' memories of and reflections on the significance of Little Zion in their lives.

This book begins with an early interest in Little Zion's connection with the outside world, exploring on both a large and small scale — from the national attention received by the burning to the local relationship between Little Zion and its Greene County neighbors (Chapter 2).[9] Later, the focus narrows to the events of church life, including Sunday services, weddings and funerals, elementary school classes, and much more (Chapter 4). Chapter 4 becomes pivotal in the collection context, as rituals and events seem visible to outsiders permitted to attend, but layers of meaning often remain obscured to the unfamiliar observer. Finally, the project considers individual religious experiences, which mostly remain internal events, accessible to outsiders only through the sharing of narrative by insiders. In Chapter 5, members detail spiritual journeys of conversion, baptism, the development of faith, occasional backsliding, and, for some men, the call to preach. In fact, the call encourages preachers to move outward again, spreading the Word and exhorting others to live their faith in the world. Thus, the book moves full circle, returning from individual perspectives to an emphasis on community.

But these multivoiced chapters cannot do justice to the oratorical power of the narrations themselves, as church members shared their memories of Little Zion for future generations. I have attempted to honor this purpose and to restore a sense of orality to the project by alternating the chapters featuring analysis with sections documenting church memories shared by a single storyteller. Chapter 3 features the uninterrupted narrative of Sister Rosie Lee Hendricks. Since much of this material also is quoted elsewhere, this chapter allows the reader to place Sister Hendricks's comments within both the interpretive discussion and that of the shared recollections. In Chapter 6, however, the narrative by Rev. Michael A. Barton consists almost entirely of material not quoted and analyzed in other chapters, allowing you to hear the preacher's voice somewhat unfiltered. Thus, you could move through the book in many ways, reading only the thoughts offered by Little Zion's members, or only the syntheses of many perspectives, or both.[10]

ONE ACTIVIST'S SENSE OF GREENE COUNTY HISTORY

I originally came to Little Zion as part of an effort to right the perceived wrong of racially motivated arson. Therefore, I saw racial tension everywhere I looked in Greene County, Alabama. In one courthouse visit, I saw it in the photographs lining the hallways with images of local civil rights movement confrontations. I saw it in the big dusty volumes of marriage records — until the 1960s bearing the separate labels "Marriage: Colored," "Marriage: White." And I saw it in the attitude of the African American clerk at the information desk, who upon hearing about my project, hastened to reassure me that blacks and whites in Greene County get along just fine and that any agitation is done by outsiders.

I also could not see beyond the issue of race because my very presence as a white visitor, especially given the circumstances of the burning, introduced it. Certainly, the largely segregated culture of this church flourishes mostly on its own, only occasionally brushing up against a nearby white culture in Greene County. To frame the generations of memories of these people with their relationship to white outsiders fails to recognize the strong traditions of a shared African American heritage at Little Zion. But of course everywhere I went I brought my own culture with me, transforming comfortable in-group interactions into more self-conscious conversations along the boundaries of race and ancestry.

I came to view Greene County as a region with two pasts: That of the white planters and their descendants, largely documented through the efforts of a local historical society,[11] and that of the African Americans, who almost universally arrived here as slaves and remained as farmers. Their stories, for the most part, remain much more inaccessible, with existing writings largely unpublished and available only as part of research collections.

Local publications paint Greene County as a romantic antebellum southern place of stately mansions and elegant society. *A Visitor's Guide to Historic Greene County*, a contemporary pamphlet distributed at the Visitor Center in Eutaw, called the antebellum years "the golden era" in Greene County's history:

> The Tombigbee and Warrior Rivers became lifelines for small communities developing along the banks and bluffs. Cotton was loaded on steamboats bound for Mobile, and there the boats reloaded for the return trip bearing supplies, dry goods and the extravagances available to this flourishing agrarian society of merchants and plantations upriver. This "golden era" spanned the years from 1840 to 1860 when a Planters' culture overshadowed the pioneer farmer and herdsman era of the early 1800's and Greene County became widely regarded for its prosperous, cultured and elegant communities.[12]

Census data provides another perspective, however, noting that while Greene County had become a major cotton producer by 1860, with its 57,858 bales that year, ranking fourth in the state, the labor was provided by slaves. Greene County planters averaged 21.2 slaves, second in the state and more than two times as many as the 10.3 average in slave states for 1860.[13] These laborers produced not only cotton but Indian corn, peas, beans, and potatoes.

Dear Master: Letters of a Slave Family, first published in 1978, offered a glimpse into the lives of a few of these slaves, who lived at the Hopewell and New Hope plantations in neighboring Hale County from 1840 to 1865 — around the time Little Zion's faith community is believed to have begun. John Hartwell Cocke, a Virginia planter, established these Alabama holdings in an attempt to turn a profit while preparing slaves for emancipation and colonization in Africa.[14] Cocke outlined five rules for slaves to live by in earning their freedom: " 'No leaving the plantation without a written pass;' 'No fighting;' 'No strange servants to be recd. without a pass;' 'Nor provoking language to be used one to another;' 'Unconditional submission to the authorities I set over [you].' "[15] Editor Randall Miller noted, however, that few slaves were freed under this covenant: "Only a handful of Cocke's slaves, ill-prepared for freedom he thought, ever realized the full promise of Hopewell."[16] Perceived rule breakers were whipped routinely, as detailed in letters to his master by slave driver George Skipwith:

> and I have whipped none without a caus the persons whome I have correct I will tell you thir name and thir faults.
>
> Suky who I put to plant som corn and after she had been there long anuf to hav been done I went there and she had hardly began it I gave her som four or five licks over her clothes I gave isham too licks over his clothes for covering up cotton with the plow.
>
> I put frank, isham, violly, Dinah, Jinny evealine and Charlott to Sweeping cotton going twice in a roe, and at a Resonable days worke they aught to hav plowed seven accers a piece, and they had been at it a half of a day, and they had not done more than one accer and a half and I gave them ten licks a peace upon thir skins I gave Julyann eight or ten licks for misplacing her hoe. That was all the whipping I have done from the time that I pitched the crop untell we comenced cutting oats.[17]

The Civil War and Reconstruction economically decimated the plantation system, leaving newly freed slaves struggling to make a living without land or assets and planters scrambling to farm their large holdings without free labor. Within a few years, sharecropping gained currency throughout the Black Belt, with tenants cultivating crops on planters' land in exchange for some portion of the harvest, depending on the extent to which planters provided for the workers' needs.[18] In 1905 Walter Fleming noted that the sharecropping system that developed following the war "has lasted almost without change,"[19] a statement that remained true throughout the first half of the twentieth century in Little Zion's surrounding community, according to church member reports.

Fleming's account rings with the resentment of the white planters who now had to pay a price to the laborers raising their crops:

> Emancipation destroyed the agricultural supremacy of the Black Belt. The uncertain returns from the plantations caused an exodus of planters and their families to the cities, and formerly well-kept plantations were divided into one- and two-house farms for negro tenants, who allowed everything to go to ruin. The negro tenant system was much more ruinous than the worst of the slavery system, and none of the plantations ever again reached their former state of productiveness. Ditches choked up, fences down, large stretches of fertile fields growing up in weeds and bushes, cabins tumbling in and negro quarters deserted, corn choked by grass and weeds, cotton not half as good as under slavery — these were the reports from travellers in the Black Belt, towards the close of Reconstruction.[20]

Members of Little Zion recalled the sharecropping system as another way to keep blacks economically disadvantaged while whites prospered. Mrs. Johnnie Busby Jackson noted, for example, that no matter how much cotton her family harvested, the landowner told them they had just managed to pay off the previous season's debt — with no profit to sustain them until the next season. So the cycle of debt and dependency began again every year.

By the late 1860s, Greene County blacks suffered from systematic, organized terror at the hands of the Ku Klux Klan, worse than in any other southern state — except possibly North Carolina, according to *White Terror*, published in 1971. Allen W. Trelease noted, "There were two major theaters of activity, which together embraced half of the state. The first consisted of several western counties, especially Greene and Sumter in the Black Belt."[21]

Whites in Eutaw reportedly resorted to arson to maintain political and economic supremacy, burning the courthouse down "to destroy accusations brought against citizens for their role in the Southern rebellion."[22] In fact, arson against black institutions began as soon as churches and schools were incorporated during Reconstruction. Trelease cited this example of white humor: "the paper [Tuscaloosa's *Independent Monitor*] facetiously noted the appearance of a great comet in Tuscaloosa and Greene counties, the tail of which dropped down one night and burned three or four Negro schoolhouses. 'The antics of the tail of this wonderful comet have so completely demoralized free-n—— education in these counties; for negroes are so superstitious that they believe it to be a warning for them to stick, hereafter to "de shovel and de hoe," and let their dirty-backed primers go.' "[23]

During the first half of the twentieth century, widespread peonage farms operated in this region, according to Pete Daniel in *The Shadow of Slavery*. Here, armed guards held indebted blacks captive and worked them virtually as slaves, routinely whipping and sometimes killing them, even though the system had been made illegal by federal law in 1867. Since peonage frequently was isolated in rural areas, and was accepted by many whites, Daniel continued, no firm estimates of its extent are available. He cites A. J. Hoyt, however, "who had spent years investigating . . . peonage" and concluded "in 1907 that in Georgia, Alabama, and Mississippi 'investigations will prove that 33⅓ per cent of the planters operating from five to one-hundred plows, are holding their negro employees in a condition of peonage, and arresting and returning those that leave before alleged indebtedness is paid.' " Daniel also asserted that "cases reported in Alabama from 1903 to 1905 show that peonage existed in nearly every county."[24]

One of the last slavery convictions in the United States was reportedly made against the Dial family in Sumter County, Alabama—bordering Greene County to the west—in 1954. According to a *Washington Post* reprint of newspaper accounts, Fred N. Dial and Oscar Edwin Dial, of Boyd, Alabama, were found guilty in Birmingham court of holding Coy Lee Tanksly and Hubert Thompson "in voluntary [*sic*] servitude by acts of violence."[25] The Dials were each sentenced to eighteen months in prison, according to the *Post* reprint of news accounts.

During the civil rights movement Greene County's African American population mobilized—largely through local churches like Little Zion—with voter registration drives to take political control of the county. In 1970, Greene became the first county in Alabama to elect a majority-black county commission, and since then the county's elected offices have been filled primarily with black citizens. In 1982, the U. S. Commission on Civil Rights attributed improvements in the lives of African Americans in Greene County to this political shift: "Since blacks have had political power, the county government has provided standard housing for displaced tenant farmers, helped to establish a health clinic for residents, and developed plans for county-wide transportation and sewage systems." The commission noted, however, that "many of these services in Greene were made possible with Federal financial assistance."[26]

But whites retained the economic upper hand in the county, according to census data. By 1980, the median African American family income of $7,765 represented about 40 percent of the comparable $19,447 for white families. That gap remained almost unchanged by 1999, when the median black family earned $20,340, or about 39 percent of the $51,648 brought home by white households.[27]

As of this writing, de facto segregation still seems to keep the experiences of African Americans and whites in this region separate, so that in many ways the stories of these citizens—about everything from education to employment to home and church life—do not blend into a sense of shared history and culture. Rev. James E. Carter, recording a family history video in 1987, posed this challenge for Greene County's black and white residents: "As time advances on, we must learn how important it is to be able to communicate with each other as human beings — so that we can live together in perfect harmony as God wants us to live."

ONE FOLKLIFE PERSPECTIVE ON LITTLE ZION

When I began collecting memories at Little Zion, I realized the project occupies a crossroads in the interests of folklife scholars.[28] A generation ago, folklorists certainly would have been attracted to this rural, African American community, since its demographics seem to fit an old stereotype of who were "the folk" in America. As Amy Shuman and Charles L. Briggs noted in 1993, "Folklorists were once content to accept the category of 'folk' as traditional, peasant, working class, rural, poor, self-trained or marginal."[29] But today, scholars have come to see "the folk" as any group — rich or poor, urban or rural, widespread or local — with shared traditions. Folklorists in the new millennium would question whether the concentration on Little Zion unconsciously promotes the field's historic bias in assuming tradition must be found in politically, socially, and/or economically "marginalized" communities.

But if scholars in the last generation would have automatically accepted Little Zion as a community of interest, they probably would have rejected the attempt to represent this church through the exploration of personal narrative. During a time when folklorists emphasized the classification of types of lore, individual conversations served mainly to reveal the larger patterns of religious expression, such as tales of conversion, of heaven and hell, even of hypocritical preachers, sinners, and backsliders. The interviews with community members would have been scrutinized — with details researched, categorized, and reported — but the personal details of the interactions probably would have been ignored as too subjective for scholarly analysis. Today, the field has largely abandoned the attempt to objectively classify traditions in the face of convincing arguments that all such representations remain, on a fundamental level, artificial constructs of the scholar's own imagination. Now, we focus on the context of the collection experience in the attempt to recognize our own biases and thereby minimize them.

That interest in context has pushed folklorists to redefine their profession in fundamental ways, most dramatically in the expansion of the field's own name: "Folklore" has embraced "folklife." Through the mid-twentieth century, folklore was commonly defined as the primarily verbal traditions of rural communities, passed down through the generations. By 1971, however, Dan Ben-Amos radically redefined the field with the succinct statement, "Folklore is artistic communication in small groups."[30] This new perspective gained immediate acceptance, becoming what Amy Shuman and Charles Briggs would call "an influential slogan" more than two decades later.[31] In defining folklore so broadly, Ben-Amos and the scholars that followed opened the field to forms of communication far beyond the "spoken and sung traditions" of rural communities. Folklorists now studied everything from urban myths to photocopied office cartoons to personal narrative. And with the explosion of electronic communications at the end of the millennium, scholars embraced new forms such as e-mail-lore, no longer requiring artistic communication to take place in face-to-face settings.

Some of the field's transformation from "folklore" to "folklife" has been driven by black scholars who entered the field in the latter third of the twentieth century and began challenging biases common among predominantly white collectors throughout the field's history. In 1978, Daryl Cumber Dance published *Shuckin' and Jivin:' Folklore from Contemporary Black Americans* with the assertion that "insight into the true meaning of much Black folklore is sometimes lacking even in many of the white folklorists who have provided a valuable service in preserving and presenting this folklore."[32] Dance set out "to present a more general and more fully comprehensive collection than can be found among other publications." "This book," she continued, "includes materials collected from both rural and urban areas, from informants of all ages, and from storytellers of all educational and economic levels."[33] In 1983 Adrienne Lanier Seward asserted that early folklorists showed a strong interest in only the "lore" of African Americans because they did not recognize the richness of African American culture. She argued that these collectors saw African Americans as bearers of artifacts, not as people participating in a rich and diverse culture. She called for African American folklore to lead a reassessment in the discipline, moving away from a lore-centered definition of folklore, toward one that embraces all aspects of folklife.[34] In 1993 John Roberts called on the discipline to continue to challenge earlier "simplistic notions of black culture and creativity" by focusing on African American cultural diversity.[35]

This book, set in rural Alabama among a population that outsiders might describe as "marginalized" in many ways, risks stereotyping the Little Zion community as therefore essentially a "folk" culture, filled with a timeless wisdom that has somehow survived the relentless press of change in the dominant, techno-savvy culture.[36] This project makes no such claims on behalf of the people who shared their memories of Little Zion Baptist Church. If the reader finds wisdom in places, let it be attributed to the personal experiences and reflections of these individual people, living near Boligee, Alabama, at the turn of the millennium. Let it not be generalized into "folk" wisdom or products of "the black experience." For, as John Roberts so eloquently argued, "The experiences of African Americans have always been diverse, and the ways in which they have represented these experiences in creative cultural traditions have always reflected this diversity. The simple truth is that our analytical tools have not been capable of capturing the complex nature of African American creative traditions." He asserted that a prize in the endless contest for cultural representation is "identity conceived as a fluid and ever-changing sense of who we are in relation to others.[37]

The occasion for this work, the burning of the church, provides an analogy for how the memories collected in the narratives that follow are treated. As is considered in some detail in Chapter 2, Little Zion burned during a national crisis of suspicious fires at predominantly black churches. In 1996 alone, the National Church Arson Task Force reported investigations under way at eighty-seven African American houses of worship significantly damaged or destroyed by suspected hate crimes — including arsons and bombings.[38] When I read those statistics, I felt moved to explore their meaning. I collected these memories as a way of looking at the importance of *one* of those eighty-seven churches to its culture.

It would be tempting to generalize from these narratives, to reason that Little Zion represents the many churches burned in America during this crisis. But that conclusion would reduce the church to a symbol — and the other burned churches to a mere projection of that symbol. The move would reveal little more than my own effort to create a way of reading and understanding an epidemic of violence. Rather, this book offers readers the chance to listen to the thoughts and opinions voiced by members of single community, connected to many other groups of people by a common crisis, but in no way representative of them.

In the same way, I do not feel qualified to generalize about the traditions of Little Zion Baptist Church as representative of twentieth-century African American religious practices.[39] As already suggested, readers familiar with rural black churches in the South will be acquainted with the language of spirituality used by members of Little Zion. The fact that the narratives resonate with a recognizable power in no way diminishes that power, as is evident especially in Chapter 3, where Sister Rosie Lee Hendricks details her spiritual journey. In fact, the sense that these narratives have been told from a broader context of black church traditions roots them in a soil deeper and richer than any that could be cultivated in any one place. But as an outsider to African American religious practices, I felt compelled to narrow my focus to the individual performances of tradition I recorded in this time and place.[40]

As I began my fieldwork, the Little Zion community embraced the project wholeheartedly. The church's history had never been recorded, and Rev. Lewis and other leaders welcomed the effort to preserve their recollections for future generations.[41] Of course, I had earned some level of trust in the Little Zion community first. During the rebuilding effort, the presence of our four-year-old daughter and my obvious pregnancy singled my family out of the hundreds of volunteers who worked on the church. Members of Little Zion's community had helped us find playmates for Kelly while my husband and I hung drywall, and had worried that the physical labor would hurt our developing baby. I believe these activities built rapport between us, as the willingness to work hard and the sharing of family concerns transcended some of the cultural and demographic barriers. When I returned to Greene County every summer for several years, church members expressed both surprise and delight that my interest in Little Zion had continued. The fact that I brought along a professional photographer who was also my mother added to the ties between my family and those at this church.

During the summers of 1996–2003, I made six fieldwork trips, each lasting from four days to one week. I also attended the January 1997 dedication service for the completed church. These visits allowed me to attend regular Sunday worship, special programs such as Choir Day and Youth Day celebrations, revival and baptismal ceremonies, and even a wedding. I conducted informal interviews with twenty-one adults and five children, spending from twenty minutes to several hours talking with each interviewee about his or her memories. My mother, Mary Ann Gatty, accompanied me to take photos whenever possible. Generally we met in people's homes, but occasionally we conducted interviews in the church sanctuary or kitchen, at someone's office, or even in a nearby restaurant. I interviewed several older church members more than once, as we needed extended conversations to document a lifetime of recollections. I also spent significant time socializing in the Little Zion community, stopping by for a glass of iced tea, meeting for lunch, or being privileged to share dinner in someone's home.[42]

I tape-recorded all interviews and church events, attempting to capture this story in the words of the people whose story it is to tell. To that end, I asked only general questions about what people recalled rather than seeking specific facts, letting church members guide our conversations. For the most part, after initial surprise at my interest in the details of church life, Little Zion's members shared their memories freely, as I hope is evident in the richness of the narratives collected here.

During interviews I was often inspired by the oratorical force Little Zion's members brought to their narratives, and communicating this power in a written form became a major focus of this work. In this multimedia age, I easily could have created an Internet-based project, complete with video and audio clips. But the effort to capture the often sacred power of religious speech through the conventions of written narrative has a much longer and richer history, dating back to the poetic bards of ancient myth. I chose to work within this tradition, handling the typographical concerns of representing the spoken through the written word by looking to the efforts of other folklorists, especially examinations since the 1960s of the prejudices inherent in earlier collections of African American material by white scholars.

Many of those writing in the nineteenth and the first two-thirds of the twentieth century, for instance, attempted to capture oral black speech through the heavy use of unconventional spellings meant to indicate dialect pronunciation. The voices of the collector and other whites were rendered in unaccented "standard" English, thereby constructing a cultural superiority.[43] Later writers have abandoned dialect spellings for a simple transcription of the spoken word, allowing the sound to reverberate in the short sentences and parallel constructions that dominate speech, for instance. I've chosen this approach because it seems to capture more fully the oral power of the narratives shared with me. I've used unconventional spellings only rarely — when conventional constructions would make the flow of speech seem unnaturally stilted.[44] Of course, the potential for bias remains in the representation of sentence constructions, as the rules governing oral black English follow a different grammar than those driving "standard" written English. The trickiest area remains where the collector's written voice meets the storytellers' oral narrations. Here the conventions of good writing dictate that the collector speak concisely and precisely, while the aesthetics of oratory encourage the speaker to move along the currents of association and repetition. The very act of representing all through the written word, therefore, risks asserting superiority of the writing voice.

In the construction of this book, I have addressed these concerns by blending my voice with the others in this project as much as possible. I have adopted an informal, casual tone, more easily mixing with the conversational nature of the collected material. I have also carefully edited the transcribed interviews to capture the spirit of the story told rather than remaining stuck in an overly literal, word-for-word representation of the audiotape. As anyone who has ever read a transcript knows, speakers edit themselves as they talk, commonly starting sentences, then reversing themselves to add detail before continuing. Pauses often are filled in the flow of speech by words such as "like," "and," or even "um." Sometimes a teller begins a narrative, drifts onto another topic, and then returns to the story. These habits of speech simply do not translate to the written form, where readers expect thoughts to be organized and prioritized, ideas completed and detailed before the narrator moves to another subject. Representing oral speech literally on the page could make Little Zion's members seem less articulate, even though by auditory standards their statements carry great power. So I have balanced the need for accurate, word-for-word transcription with editorial judgment in removing backtracking statements and filler language, and in stitching together narratives told at intervals during the flow of conversation.

Elaine Lawless has called the structure of her book, *Holy Women, Wholly Women,* "an attempt to offer a polyphonic, multivoiced, multileveled analysis that recognized the position of all the participants and of the ethnographer/writer (me)."[45] I have embraced a similar structure in the hope that the reader will finish this story of life at Little Zion Baptist Church with a strong sense of the many voices and layers of memory and observation represented here. If the construction of this book does this church community and its recollections justice, it will capture something like the view through the stained-glass windows in the newly rebuilt church, where, though filtered and fragmented, the light shines on the activities of those gathered inside.

I should point out, however, that I felt the undercurrents of mistrust in all discussion of the church burning, and especially in the silences on this subject. Though the church had gone up in flames mysteriously only months earlier, many of those interviewed seemed only at most mildly interested in who might have wanted to destroy the building. As in all other areas of conversation, I let church members take the lead in response to open-ended questions such as, "What do you remember about the burning?" Silence, of course, can say many things. But to me as a white outsider it spoke mainly of a discomfort with addressing freely a highly charged subject I could not begin to understand fully.

I felt a similar discomfort when discussing the church's beginnings during or just after slavery. It seemed clear that the mere mention of this institution, outlawed only a few generations ago and with a long legacy in the sharecropping and peonage systems, remains somewhat taboo in conversations between blacks and whites in Greene County. In his videotaped family history, Rev. James Carter noted that while the people recording their story were black descendants of slaves, the cameraman was a white descendant of slave masters. "And yet there's cooperation and understanding between us," Rev. Carter said. But the sharp distinction seemed to undermine his point, as if the starkly contrasting lineages, and the very different life experiences they embody, remain at the forefront of such interactions.

Moments like these could have dampened the sharing of personal experiences during interviews. But I believe many of Little Zion's members had invested their own interest in this project, and the awkwardness was largely overcome.

ONE QUAKER'S EXPERIENCE AT LITTLE ZION

Little Zion Baptist Church and its community came to play a significant role in my personal life during the eight years of this project. I weighed my own Quaker worship style, sitting in silence, listening within for the "still small voice"[46] of God, against the much more active, praise-centered worship I respected deeply at Little Zion. Outwardly, the forms of these services seemed complete opposites. Yet, inwardly, they felt like two ways of saying the same thing or going to the same place — two ways of finding, celebrating, appreciating the sacred that lies beyond understanding.[47] Sometimes, the intersection of those two paths in this project deepened my understanding of both. And other times, the juxtaposition created confusion and comedy.

I initially came to Little Zion as one long comfortable with the unprogrammed Quaker worship style — stripped of most of the familiar elements of Christian services. I had little familiarity with Little Zion's Missionary Baptist tradition and had to reach back to the Catholic masses of my childhood for such memories. But those 1970s services — conducted in the giddy days following the sweeping litur-

A photo taken on my first fieldwork trip in October 1996, after Sunday service at St. Matthew Baptist Church — where the Little Zion community worshipped during the rebuilding effort. Standing next to Sister Courtney Porter and Rev. W. D. Lewis, I am seven months pregnant and clearly underdressed!

gical changes of Vatican II — featured folksinging and sometimes even modern dance. They bore little resemblance to the Baptist practices at Little Zion.

Taking such a broad view of Christianity — looking for understanding of Baptist traditions through Catholic practices — would have been a move unfamiliar, and probably unacceptable, to most of those who attend this church regularly. When I learned that Greene County features many Baptist churches in a comparatively small region, I asked a Little Zion congregant whether other faiths also practiced nearby. "Oh, yes," came the reply. But I was not told about non-Christian institutions, common elsewhere, or about any of the wide variety of Christian denominations that practice throughout this country. "There's the Primitive Baptists," she noted. "They wash feet." This distinction among local Baptists was pointed out to me repeatedly.

Quakers, however, commonly take broad views of Christianity, because our tradition is grounded in the belief that all outward forms of worship reflect what founder George Fox called more than 350 years ago "that of God" in everyone. The Religious Society of Friends split from the Church of England in the mid-seventeenth century because believers argued that worshippers could live simply in the Light of this obedience to the Inward Christ. Quakers dismissed the need for set doctrine and paid clergy to preach and interpret God's word, relying instead on individuals to share their insights on, and encounters with, this shared divine spark.

At the first Little Zion service I attended in 1996, the congregants engaged in call-and-response with the preacher and sang and prayed for about an hour and a half. They took a collection, made announcements, and gave testimonies to the power of God working in their lives. Afterward, I began to gather my belongings, thinking that the service had been fairly short, given the reputation for all-day worship among churches in this region. Seated next to me, Mrs. Johnnie Busby Jackson asked me what I was doing. "Getting ready to go," I replied. In late pregnancy, I was hoping to find lunch somewhere nearby in this rural community. Mrs. Busby Jackson just laughed. "You need to sit back down, now," she said. "The service hasn't started yet. That was Sunday school." Since Little Zion shared their pastor with another small church nearby, they offered a full service only on first and third Sundays. A formal Sunday school tradition provided most of the elements of the main service, however, and I easily mistook the practice for service itself. After the full two-hour worship that followed, and a special program that came after that, Mrs. Busby Jackson, my mother, and I left Little Zion in search of dinner rather than lunch.

During another service, a young boy approached me with an open Bible, appearing ready to hand it to me. Confused, I reached for the book, but he didn't let go. For a long moment he and I remained locked in a sort of tug-of-war over the sacred book. Without the presence of mind to let go, I leaned to the woman next to me and asked, "What is he doing?" Smiling, she replied, "He is *trying* to take a collection." Sheepishly, I laid my money on the Bible. Then I glanced up to see all the deacons across the room slapping their knees with silent laughter — and had to struggle to control my own giggles.

At a July 2003 service Rev. Michael Barton joked that since I was there to record the event, he would keep his preaching calm and collected. A few minutes later, he was pacing back and forth in front of the congregation, his body electric with energy. He was shouting the Word with his voice coming in short gasps. He was sweating profusely and rubbing his hands roughly through his hair. I thought he certainly had not kept the vow to stay cool. Later I learned, however, that one of the congregants had remarked to my mother during this sermon, "He's doing more teaching than preaching today. Sometimes, he walks across the backs of the pews."

These moments highlight my sense that, as an outsider at Little Zion, I could never be sure of my perceptions. Where insiders saw Sunday school, I saw the full worship service. When church members realized the Bible was serving as a collection plate, I thought the sacred book was being handed to me. What one congregant described as the preacher's restraint, I experienced as a tremendous outpouring of emotional expression. In the face of such uncertainty, I did what any folklife scholar should do: I asked questions and scrutinized my perceptions; I relied on the advice of others working in this field. But, finally, I was forced to move beyond my academic perspective and to put some measure of faith in the encounters between church members and me.

For members of the Little Zion community, academic analysis isn't enough. The cautions of today's scholars merit consideration — especially in the effort to confront a history of misrepresentation in folklife studies. But some churchgoers expressed little patience for overintellectualized self-examination. In this community, education serves the development of a deeper understanding: You must "study to show thyself approved unto God," as pointed out by the biblical passage cited several times during interviews (2 Timothy 2:15). This sense of a greater truth remains a matter of faith — immune to the doubt of its existence expressed in the poststructuralist academy. Rev. James Carter, for example, bluntly challenged the notion of education for the glory of the ego, or even for its own sake. He preached passionately at the annual Youth Day celebration on October 18, 1996:[48]

We live in a society that/
Teaches us that/
You can do this;/
You can do that./
You can do this;/
You can do that./
You can go/
From one degree to another./
You can do it./
I./
Me./
I can do it./
Me./

We can't do anything/
Except God allows it./
That's a vanity./

And then you people have to recognize that/
We live in a time/
When they tell us that/
If you get your education,/
Everything is gonna be all right./ (All right)

That's a big lie./ (All right, laughter)

People with B.S. degrees,/
Master's degrees,/ (Uh-huh)
And Ph.D. degrees,/
And all kinds of degrees/
Are down and out this morning./ (Yes, Oh yes)
Simply because/
They have missed/

The understanding that they need/ (Yeah!)
To go with that degree./ (Amen, Amen!)
People with degrees are broken today/ (Yeah!)
Because they have missed/
The understanding that/
All is vanity,/
Except/
When God is at the front/
Of all of what you do./[49] (Yeah)

Statements such as these challenged me to put "God . . . at the front" of this work. I finally came to view this project as a kind of Quaker "ministry," as observed by Rev. James Carter in an early interview. Relying on the sacred power of storytelling to make meaning for this community, for me, and potentially for outside readers, the process of collecting these memories and presenting them in this book grew into something like a Sunday morning message shared in meeting for worship — much longer, certainly, and lacking spontaneity, but drawn from the same source.

Over the years, I believe I moved a few steps toward an insider's perspective on the life of Little Zion Baptist Church. The very writing of this book has been embraced by the church's members and become part of Little Zion's history. As I prepared to defend the dissertation upon which this book is based, one church member requested that I make an audiotape of the interaction between the academic committee and me. She told me that the oral defense would be part of Little Zion's story now, and a record should be kept. So after years of tape-recording interviews with church members, I turned the recorder on myself.

Now, through the power of the words on the page, this small group of Little Zion church members invites readers beyond Greene County, Alabama, to share in their memories of this church. Regardless of your demographic background and life experiences, you remain an outsider in some or many ways to this community. But these narratives serve as a link between storytellers and audience, allowing you, in the very act of reading this book, to stretch the boundaries of

Little Zion children at church.

your perspective and participate in a small way in Little Zion's long life story.

The tale told here remains just one of many that could have been written. Notably, this account reflects only the memories shared with me by people who attended Little Zion between 1996 and 2003. The church and its traditions were changing and growing for generations before these narratives, and those changes have continued since this

A Little Zion
boy at his
grandparents'
home.

A Little Zion
boy at his
grandparents'
home.

work was completed. For Little Zion is a living institution, shaped and reshaped by each new generation. I can only hope that in the coming years one of the young people I met during this project will write a new story for Little Zion — from an insider's perspective. As Rev. James Carter preached during the Youth Day sermon cited earlier:

Sometimes we have a tendency to think that/
When our old people die out/
The church is gonna die./
But God's church/
Is gonna keep on going./
It's gonna keep on growing./
And we can see that/
In the young folks that we have,/
Plenty of boys and plenty of girls./
We count our blessings today. (10/18/1996)

John answered, saying unto them all, I indeed baptize you with water;
but one mightier than I cometh, the latchet of whose shoes I am not
worthy to unloose: he shall baptize you with the Holy Ghost and with fire.
—Luke 3:16

CHAPTER TWO

Little Zion in the Community

I went to the Mason meeting that night and got home somewhere between eight and nine o'clock. The fire chief son called
over here and said, "They called for the fire trucks." Said Zion
church on fire.

So I got in my truck and went on up there. When I turned
back northwest, I could see that light way up in the air. You
know, I don't know how I got up there. I got so shocked. I
drove up there, and I drove that truck too close, and it burned
up everything. When I backed up, I had a flat tire. I don't remember saying nothing. Put the air in the tire and come on
back here.

I ain't done nothing; there wasn't nothing I could do. That's
the awfullest sight I want to see. I hated it so bad, but there
wasn't nothing I could do. That church been built five times to
my knowing. Brush arbor. Log church. Frame church. And
two brick churches.

I said, "Lord, what'd they burned up that church for? I
don't know nobody, ain't done nothing to nobody to burn the
church up."

But during that time some white folks had come up there
and started singing and praying with us. The man that lives just

across the road from Zion got converted. He got converted, and he started coming over there, trying to get us to join up with them. Instead of him joining up with us, they trying to get us to join up with them. Him and two more fellows, one was a preacher. They come there, and we have a service on a Wednesday night, and they're trying to get in with us.

I began to think, would this burning come up by somebody that didn't like them coming to this church? But after they burned down the other churches, I said, "Well, them coming to our church didn't have nothing to do with it." Nobody didn't have nothing against us 'cause we're trying to celebrate with them, to integrate. They burned up Mt. Zoar that same night, about near that same time. They set the one on fire, come on and set the other on fire. They had burned down Mt. Zion two or three weeks ahead.

— Deacon Ed Carter, August 12, 1997[1]

Until Little Zion's destruction by fire on January 11, 1996, many church members had lived in a community within a few miles of this structure, founded generations ago on a remote hill in western Greene County, Alabama. Mrs. Johnnie Mae Busby Jackson, for instance, grew up at Little Zion and was baptized there by longtime pastor Rev. Lewis. After moving away in her early adulthood and raising seven children, she returned to her aging parents' home in the 1980s. She has remained since their deaths. On a fall afternoon in 1996 she settled into a hanging porch swing, sipped iced tea, and offered this observation as she looked out over her front yard and the neighborhood beyond:

For my parents' generation, the church was where you got your security. That was your strength. That was your rock. We were chopping cotton during the week and we needed the church on Sunday. The church was where you got your consolation. Everybody would get together and sing and pray and relieve all that pressure.

And the community meant a lot. You could go and talk to the neighbors. My mom was friends with this one lady and she would go see her, and then the neighbor would walk back part of the way home with my mom. They would stand there and talk awhile and then they would walk another piece together. Until the darkness finally came and they said good night.

If somebody in the neighborhood got sick, the oldest person would come and stay with that person until they were better. And when you cooked your dinner, you always put a little something extra in the pot, because you never knew who might come on by.

For many Little Zion members, Mrs. Busby Jackson included, the communities of church, neighborhood, and family coincide, as the church draws its congregation from homes within a few miles in this rural countryside. In fact, many of the homes within view from the porch swing above maintain ties to Little Zion, "acting in common," as Dorothy Noyes defined community,[2] "to pray and sing and relieve all that pressure," as Mrs. Busby Jackson described it.

The central role of the church in rural, southern African American communities has been widely documented. In *Community in a Black Pentecostal Church* Melvin Williams offered a succinct summary of these observations: "According to Frazier (1968), the church was the most important association next to the family in the Black rural South (see also Billings, 1934; Brunner, 1923).[3] The church and its membership often determined the limits of the rural community, which frequently bore its name. The church was the most important means of community expression, and rural southern Blacks made financial and material sacrifices to maintain it."[4] In fact, at Little Zion and most other African American churches, frequent references are made to the congregation as a "church family," with congregants addressing each other as "brothers" and "sisters" in Christ, in effect verbally elevating church relationships to the intimacy and importance of family.[5]

In the family video mentioned at the outset of Chapter 1, Deacon Ed Carter used a story from *Aesop Fables*[6] to illustrate poignantly his sense of family gaining strength by standing together in the community of church: "One time I heard my father say that there was a man, had seven sons, and he had done got old, and he was getting ready to

Mrs. Johnnie Busby Jackson is interviewed on her front porch on
October 19, 1996.

die. So he told them to go out there and bring him seven sticks, and
they went out and brought him seven sticks. He said, 'Now you take
these sticks and break them as I tell you.'" Deacon Carter then picked
up twelve sticks, one to represent each of his descendants, whom he
named one by one. He then held one stick apart, saying, "This is my
oldest son. See, you can break it." He then added two more sticks,
representing his younger sons. "Can you break three sticks? Try to
break them. Can't break them." He then added each of the other
sticks to the bundle, naming each descendant represented as he did
so. With the bundle of twelve sticks held tightly together, Deacon
Carter explained, "The Bible say, 'Together we stand. Divided we
fall.'[7] If you brothers, sons, grandsons stay together, ain't no way in
the world that nobody break you. . . . Stay together just like I give you
that ball of sticks there in your hand that won't break. Keep the Lord
as your leader and your guide, and I believe that you'll rest in peace."

Rev. James Carter sits with his son at nearby St. Matthew Baptist Church in October 1996.

Deacon Carter's grandson, Rev. James Carter, asserted that in this family, "keep[ing] the Lord as your leader" meant maintaining close ties to Little Zion. "I come up in the church," he remembered, noting that his earliest memory is of being taken outside during services, chastised for biting his mother's breast while nursing. "Sunday School was a must," he added succinctly, adding that by the time he was six or seven he understood the concept of prayer and could sing many hymns. "It's been a family experience. My family takes the spiritual side of life more important than any other."

For members of this community, Little Zion is clearly the dominant landmark in the countryside. Those interviewed almost always gave me directions around Greene County using Little Zion for orientation — even though the church site remains nestled in some trees, mostly out of view from the nearby road and surrounding houses. (As a visitor to this region, I was never quite sure I was on the road to Little Zion until I came across the small sign pointing up the

The sign for Little Zion Baptist Church.

hill!) One summer afternoon in 2003, I was surprised by the arrival of three church members at Little Zion. The women said they regularly gather at the church to exercise, walking laps up the paved hill of the driveway and around the parking lot.

But, in fact, beyond this church community, Little Zion remained remarkably invisible before the 1996 fire. A United States Geological Survey (USGS) map of the Forkland, Alabama, quadrangle seems symbolic in its oversight of the church. Though detailed enough to include individual houses, this map fails to document the presence of the church in its 1947 edition and in its 1979 photorevision only notes the presence of a building, rather than a named church as is USGS's convention.

Little Zion also seems to have been excluded from published histories of Greene County, generally written by whites. For example, *A Goodly Heritage: Memories of Greene County*, published in 1977 by the Greene County Historical Society, contains histories mainly of local white churches, even though scores of African American houses of worship dot the countryside. Similarly, the brief pamphlet *A Visitor's Guide to Historic Greene County*, given to tourists at least as late as 1996 at the Greene County Visitor Center in Eutaw, highlights mostly white churches and makes no mention of Little Zion.

The cultural and historical "invisibility" of African American spiritual life has been decried since the beginning of the twentieth century, when W. E. B. Du Bois drew his famous metaphor of the "veil," which separates the experiences of blacks from those of whites in America, rendering this entire minority culture invisible to the majority. "Leaving then, the white world, I have stepped within the Veil, raising it that you may view faintly its deeper recesses — the meaning of its religion, the passion of its human sorrow, and the struggle of its greater souls," Du Bois eloquently asserted in *Souls of Black Folk*.[8] Albert Raboteau traced the invisibility of African American religious institutions to the underdocumented worship traditions among slaves:

> We should speak of the "invisibility" of slave religion with irony; it is the neglect of slave sources by historians which has been the

main cause of this invisibility. Studies by John Blassingame, Sterling Stuckey, Lawrence Levine, Eugene Genovese, and others have demonstrated the fallacy in assuming that slaves left no articulate record of their experience. Blassingame's *The Slave Community* and *Slave Testimony*, Genovese's *Roll, Jordan, Roll*, and Levine's *Black Culture and Black Consciousness* eloquently prove that there are indeed ample sources deriving from the slaves themselves. I have tried to investigate slave narratives, black autobiographies, and black folklore in order to gather, literally out of the mouths of former slaves, the story of their religious experiences during slavery.[9]

Likewise, this book relies primarily on the voices of Little Zion's church members to construct a narrative undocumented and unavailable elsewhere.

Of course, the irony here is that in the very moment of its destruction by fire, Little Zion suddenly became visible to the world beyond the small community of worshippers it has served for generations. As the flames lit up the night sky, they alerted many in Greene County to the possibility of racially motivated arson, establishing a suspicious pattern between this fire and the one that destroyed nearby Mt. Zoar Baptist Church on the same evening. The fire also seemed eerily similar to two burnings a few weeks earlier in Greene County, one that destroyed Mt. Zion Baptist Church and another that left Jerusalem Baptist Church intact. And, of course, the burning also hearkened back to the widespread violence against black churches during the civil rights movement, including the infamous Birmingham, Alabama, church firebombing in 1963 that killed four little girls.

Almost immediately, Little Zion's destruction received national and even international attention in the mainstream media, with newspapers like the *New York Times* and the *Washington Post* picking up the story by January 20 and January 23, respectively.[10] By early February, both the Federal Bureau of Alcohol, Tobacco and Firearms (ATF) and the U.S. Justice Department had launched investigations into the Boligee fires as part of a suspicious pattern of church fires in Alabama and Tennessee. James Cavanaugh, special agent in charge of the Alabama ATF office, told the *New York Times*, "We are looking at whether there is any organized and conspiratorial ring traveling from state to state."[11] Though the investigations failed to unearth a conspiracy, they concluded that these church fires were part of a nationwide rash of violence against black churches that began as early as January 1995.[12]

Little Zion certainly was not the first rural black church to burn under suspicious circumstances in the mid-1990s. And, as will be explored later in this chapter, this small Boligee church would not be the last of this disturbing trend. Yet, perhaps because Little Zion and Mt. Zoar burned together on one night, those fires touched off national and international concern and debate about racially motivated violence against houses of worship. People a world away from the local community served by this little church in rural Greene County suddenly knew of the loss.

This chapter will explore Little Zion's place in the surrounding community, from both outsider and insider perspectives. Outsiders include federal officials, the news media and its public — and me as folklife student and Quaker activist — whose interest in this church began in the wake of the burning. Insiders include church members for whom the fire meant the loss of a sacred home with a long history in Greene County daily life, from the ending of slavery to decades of sharecropping to the civil rights movement and beyond. This chapter will also explore the interaction between outsiders and insiders during the cooperative rebuilding effort, when Little Zion's place in Greene County was literally restored with the construction of the new brick church in the summer of 1996. Though no movement toward an insider's understanding of Little Zion will be seen in such outsider interactions as media coverage, I hope to trace the beginnings of a shift in my own awareness, however limited, toward an insider's understanding of this church community. As noted in the Introduction, this attempt will be marked by the subordination of my own and all other viewpoints to those of Little Zion's members.

Since this chapter traces the path of my own experience, the collected memories will not be presented in strictly chronological order. The discussion moves from the burning as a loss of place in the community, through an exploration of that place — documenting churchgoers' memories of Little Zion in Greene County from around the Great Depression to the 1990s. Finally, the chapter ends with the 1996 rebuilding and restoration of Little Zion on its hill in western Alabama.

THE BURNING: "WHYS BACK UP TO WHYS"

As word spread that Little Zion was on fire during the evening of January 11, 1996, church members said they immediately began trying to make sense of the violence, to incorporate the tragedy into the longer narrative of the life of this church, which began at least as early as emancipation, possibly even decades earlier. Not only did they witness the burning, describing in detail in conversations for this project where they were when they got the news and what they saw when they drove to the church that evening, they also witnessed about the tragedy, testifying to its religious significance in their lives. In this context, the fire becomes symbolic, the language used by the divine to communicate with the earthly, read by church members through the tenets of Christianity. This point of view subsumes all secular explanations for the burning, especially those focused on race relations in this segregated southern county. Members often subordinated the question of whether arsonists burned the church out of racial hatred to that of why God allowed it to happen. What divine message did the event convey?

During interviews for this project, the context of the collection of church memories probably encouraged the Little Zion community to discuss the burning from a spiritual perspective. Church members might have focused more strongly on the significance of arson to a national crisis in race relations, for instance, had I framed my questions from this angle. But, as asserted earlier, I tried to do as little framing as possible, to allow this community to shape the story told for this project. Also, in conversations with a white outsider, the language of spirituality might have provided a transcendent perspective on the ugliness of racism.

This move to transform the political into the spiritual happens weekly in sermons throughout the country, and Little Zion's members have plenty of experience hearing and, in many cases, preaching, in this way. In fact, Gerald Davis called this transformation the "weighted secular factor" in African American preaching, even asserting that it is unique to the black church tradition in this country:

> Whatever the political views and sentiments of the African-American preacher, he is intimately attuned to the daily secular needs of his congregation and to the social and political environment in which black life in the United States is lived and acted out. He may use the perfection of the Christian life as example, as framework, but his focus is riveted on his congregation's need to live a fully experiencing daily, secular existence. Hence, the "weighted secular" factor in African-American sermon performance is a key concept in distinguishing the African-American sermon from sermons of other cultural groups.[13]

Even the very image of fire might have encouraged Little Zion's members to weight any secular response to the burning within a spiritual context. As suggested by Luke 3:16, quoted at the outset of this chapter, fire symbolizes the touch of the Spirit in Christian understanding. As Glenn Hinson pointed out in *Fire in My Bones*, the prophet Jeremiah described the Lord's anointing touch as "a burning fire shut up in my bones (Jeremiah 20:9)."[14] Hinson elaborated, "Rev. Bryant detailed how the anointing sometimes felt like a chill, sometimes like 'electricity,' sometimes like burning heat." In fact, Baptist deacon Edward Denkins reportedly responded to Hinson's question about the anointing, " 'Now, if you was connected into this realm as a heir of our Lord and savior Jesus, you — you, sitting right there asking the question — Amen! — you would catch on fire too!' "[15] Little Zion members often told me that in a powerful worship service, the church will "burn" or "get on fire." Descriptions of fire as God's transforming power resonate throughout the collected narratives and imbue the church burning with a sense of divine purpose.

In contrast, news media and other outsiders who came to Little Zion in the wake of the burning searched for purely secular explanations: Who might have burned this church and why? Was this burning part of a national outbreak of church arsons motivated by racial hatred? For the most part, they received secular answers from secular sources like Boligee's mayor and the local district attorney. Rev. Lewis, Little Zion's longtime pastor at the time, however, occasionally shifted the dialogue into spiritual terms. He told the *New York Times* on June 23, "All I know is that I have turned it over to God, and He is giving us a new church.... The spirit is with us, and if we go falsely accusing anybody, the spirit will leave us. I don't know who set these fires and why they were doing it. But I'll tell you one thing. They were messing with the wrong man."[16]

Outsider interest in Little Zion's destruction began just beyond the church community, with stories in both Greene County newspapers. The *Democrat*, read largely by the black population, led its January 17 weekly edition with the headline, "Arson Could Be Cause of Churches Burning," and quoted District Attorney Barrown Lankster: "Sometimes you cannot afford to overlook the obvious, and these burnings certainly are coincidental enough to raise some serious questions about arson, racism and hate crimes."[17] In the article, Lankster pointed out about Little Zion and Mt. Zoar that "the two churches were in the same general area, rural Boligee; that both were very secluded; that both burned within the same time frame; that both fit the national pattern of burnings of black churches; that two other churches had caught fire within the last month in Greene County—Jerusalem Baptist, which survived the fire; and Mt. Zion in Boligee, which burned down." Lankster also noted a suspicious coincidence between the burnings and both local newspapers' announcements the previous day that several young white men had received prison sentences on convictions of vandalizing black churches in nearby Sumter County. "I'm not saying that the same people burned churches in Greene as vandalized the churches in Sumter. But it could be retaliation for their sentencing," Lankster was quoted. The *Democrat* also quoted several unnamed sources in the community who discarded the possibility of accidental burnings, noting that at Mt. Zoar, the utilities had been cut off after the last service. Finally, the article noted a coincidence between the proximity of the burnings to the national holiday in honor of Dr. Martin Luther King Jr.[18]

The *Independent*, the newspaper serving the white community, also highlighted the likelihood of arson under such suspicious circumstances but did not focus on the possibility that the destruction was racially motivated. The January 18 front-page story led with Boligee mayor Buddy Lavender's assertion that "there's no doubt that it's arson," especially given the lack of electric and gas utilities at Mt. Zoar. Lavender continued, "These churches are 200 years old, and for all of them to burn down, and two of them in one night, something is wrong."[19] In a February 14, 1996, editorial the *Independent* stated outright, "Greene County's loss of churches to fires that, quite honestly, must have been deliberately set, is disturbing."[20] However, this newspaper did not highlight anyone's concern that the burnings followed the sentencing of the three young Sumter County men for vandalizing black churches, or that the destruction preceded the Dr. Martin Luther King Jr. holiday. Instead, the initial news story featured Lavender's opinion that local citizens could not be responsible, unless they were conducting "copy cat" church burnings of several that had been reported in Tennessee the previous year. The article concluded, "As for [local] racial tension, Lavender said he doesn't see any."[21]

As noted earlier, news of the burnings went national within a few days. The *New York Times* emphasized the ATF concern that the incidents might involve a racially motivated conspiracy. ATF Alabama office chief James Cavanaugh said, "We are looking at the possibility of a racial motive, and the key word for us is whether it's regional." Cavanaugh noted similarities between the four Boligee-area fires and four arsons at black churches in western Tennessee the previous year, with all occurring at rural black Baptist churches late at night and causing no injuries. He also cited another Tennessee fire, which occurred in Knoxville on January 8 — just three days before the burnings of Little Zion and Mt. Zoar. In this clearly racially motivated attack, an integrated church was firebombed and spray-painted with racist graffiti. Cavanaugh said investigators did not believe this burning fit the pattern of the other incidents, however.[22]

The *Washington Post* piece that ran three days later pointed out that the burning of Little Zion and Mt. Zoar on January 11 "follows a series of attacks on black churches both in adjoining Sumter County and in nearby Tennessee" and asserted that "residents here, black and white, can no longer deny that race was the motivation."[23] The surety expressed in this statement, however, clearly revealed reporter Sue Anne Pressley's outsider viewpoint. While some local residents told the *Democrat* they suspected racism, others, such as Mayor Lavender, asserted in the *Independent* that racism could not have been a factor in these burnings. And, if my interviews with Little Zion's members serve as any indicator, local residents' acceptance of race as a motivator did not break down neatly along demographic lines. As is explored later, several blacks told me they didn't believe the burning to be deliberate, or to be racially motivated, because Little Zion's members have good relationships with the local white community.

In the same article, Pressley described contemporary Boligee as a town where racial attitudes appear not to have changed much since the 1960s, where whites still refer to blacks as "colored people," and where de facto segregation is practiced in schools and other public buildings.[24] Again, she spoke with the conviction of an outsider. Local residents disagree sharply in their assessments of racial tension in Greene County. Of course, the context of comments made — whether in interviews with the press or me, or in community forums sponsored by federal Justice Department officials — must be considered when attempting to gain some understanding of local residents' attitudes.

Nevertheless, articles like this one by out-of-town journalists attempting to gain a lifetime's worth of cultural understanding in a few interviews,[25] helped to move the news of Little Zion's burning from a local story of suspicious coincidence into the national debate about widespread racial hatred and possible conspiracy to commit hate crimes against African American houses of worship.

On February 8, the Justice Department made national headlines with the announcement of a civil rights investigation into the church burnings in Alabama and Tennessee. The announcement followed the NAACP's release of a letter calling for an investigation of potential civil rights abuses, which had been sent to Attorney General Janet Reno in January. The Justice Department also hinted at a broader inquiry into black church burnings, since Civil Rights Division spokesperson Myron Marlin confirmed that the number of fires under investigation totaled more than eight, which was the number of suspicious fires reported in Alabama and Tennessee over the previous year.[26] On the same day, *USA Today* reported that at least seventeen African American churches nationwide had been damaged by arson since 1995.[27]

In June, President Bill Clinton established the National Church Arson Task Force (NCATF) in response to federal detection "in early 1996" of "a sharp rise in the number of reported attacks on our nation's houses of worship, especially African American churches in the South."[28] This task force united the efforts of state and local law enforcement officials, fire prevention personnel, the FBI, the ATF, and others. And on July 3, the president signed the Church Arson Prevention Act of 1996, giving federal authorities more power to prosecute those who commit crimes against houses of worship.

Meanwhile, the national news media, which had completely overlooked the 1995 fires, began reporting each new incident in what they now called "a rash of church fires"[29] or a "wave of church burnings."[30] As the arsons continued, the nation — and the world — tried to find a pattern, to make sense of the violence directed disproportionately against southern black churches, and Little Zion and the other Alabama churches burned in December and January remained in the public eye. By June 26, Boligee mayor Buddy Lavender told the *Independent* he had talked to seventy-three reporters on the subject: "I've been in *People Magazine*, on television in Holland, Australia, Switzerland, Japan . . . and I've talked to reporters from the *Washington Post*, *Miami Herald*, *New Orleans Times Picayune*, *Atlanta Constitution* and the *Los Angeles Times*."[31]

But almost as quickly as coverage of the story had begun in the national and international media, it fizzled. In May, Justice and Treasury Department officials told a House Judiciary Committee hearing that federal officials had not uncovered evidence of a national conspiracy to burn churches.[32] Although most of those convicted had been young white males, only a few had been linked to racist organizations. U.S. Assistant Attorney General for Civil Rights Deval Patrick suggested instead "a climate of racial division across the country" as a trigger for the violence.[33] In June, a *USA Today* article, "White churches equally subject to arson," questioned the heavy media focus on racial motivation for the burnings, noting that "white churches are burning too." In fact, the article said, of the fifty-nine fires investigated by the ATF since 1995, thirty targeted black churches and twenty-nine damaged white houses of worship. Of course, the article noted that proportionally far more African American churches had burned, since only 65,000 of the 350,000 houses of worship nationwide draw predominantly black congregations.[34] No matter, the course of the national debate had changed. Attention now centered on the role of the media in fanning the flames of racism, and on the possibility that the coverage had spurred "copy cat" crimes by arsonists craving the attention.

In October, when the well-respected *Columbia Journalism Review* printed an article by freelance writer Joe Holley, who argued that the church burnings should be covered as isolated local events, the story died. Holley asserted that the national and international newsworthiness of the story lay in the possible operation of a widespread arson conspiracy. When that conspiracy failed to materialize, the burnings no longer merited out-of-town coverage, he reasoned. In an opinion piece printed in the *Philadelphia Inquirer* in 1998, Katie Day argued that Holley's article had "put the kibosh on national coverage of the church burnings." Day said that while a clear conspiracy had not emerged, a national culture of racism had, reason enough for continued national interest. She concluded,

> The media's premature (and misinformed) dropping of the church arson story — largely because it lacked the drama of a central organized conspiracy — has had devastating consequences.
>
> Had they stuck with the story longer, they would have seen plain old racial hatred working in too many of the cases. Perhaps a cultural conspiracy — or a sense of social permission that it's okay to torch churches — is not considered newsworthy. But because the media abandoned the story, it's now harder to get much-needed resources. Faith communities already coping with the trauma of hate crimes now must add abandonment to their woes.
>
> And the national conscience, pricked by troubling images of

churches in flames, is robbed of the opportunity to wrestle with the intransigent problem of racism.[35]

But the burnings did not stop when the media lost interest in the story. Between January 1997 and August 2000, the NCATF investigated 596 suspected arsons at houses of worship: 209 in 1997, 165 in 1998, 140 in 1999, and 82 in 2000, as of August 15. Though the frequency of the fires certainly has declined, the 596 incidents of suspected arson since the media turned away from this story is greater than the number of those that received attention in 1995 and 1996: 349.[36] Even the most recent count of suspicious fires in 2000 is much higher than the fifty-two fires in 1995 that initially aroused the concern of federal officials.

By August 2000, arrests had been made in connection with 342 of the 945 church violence investigations, a rate of 36.2 percent, according to the NCATF. That arrest rate is more than double the national average of 16 percent in arson cases, the report asserted. However, the three Boligee area church remained among the 584 "pending investigations."[37]

While outsiders came to Little Zion with secular concerns about possible arson and national trends in race relations, insiders remained focused on issues at once much narrower and broader than the question of who might have burned the church and why. From their perspective in the neighborhood surrounding Little Zion, members saw the firelight in the sky as the church was destroyed. What they lost could not be summed up in statistics about violence against churches, especially black churches in the South. Rather, they described the personal loss of a spiritual home. At the same time, the Little Zion community focused far beyond the national political debate, enveloping secular questions into this search for divine answers.

On a hot afternoon in the summer of 1996, Mrs. Mary V. Smith sat in her living room and shared these memories:

> It was like a tragedy when the church burned. I was sitting almost exactly where you're sitting when Deacon Carter called me and said, "The church on fire!"
> I said, "The church on fire?!"

He talked so much, I couldn't hardly believe it. He said, "Yeah, the church on fire!"

So I got up and went outside and looked. I called Rev. Lewis and I told him that the church was on fire.

He said, "What church?"

I said, "Little Zion."

And he said, "Okay, I'll be up there." He just hung up the phone.

So I got in the car with my daughter and we went up there. We couldn't get no farther than the road because the electric wire had fell down, and they wouldn't let you go on up on the hill. It just was a tragedy to see that church going up in flames like that. It made me sad that night.

Other members of Little Zion reported learning of the burning while out of town and rushing home in the aftermath. Rev. Oscar Williams, who served as pastor from late 1999 until mid-2000, noted, "I was in Virginia when I heard about the burning. I was on the faculty at Virginia Tech for nearly seventeen years, head of the Institute for Leadership and Volunteer Development. Somebody called me about two or three o'clock in the morning to tell me the news, and I came down about a week later. I went out there, walked through the ashes, collected some of the old bricks, which I still have. I sort of felt hurt. I sort of felt it was a low-down thing for anybody to do." Longtime member Mrs. Mary Constantine echoed this experience of coming home to tragedy, calling the burning one of the saddest times in her life and describing her return from Georgia to find the church in ashes: "I was just really devastated to find out that people would want to burn the sanctuary. I don't even know how they could have a heart to even do a thing like that."

Even Little Zion's children told and retold the details of the burning, as if the tangible details could lend weight to the surreal experience. One ten-year-old boy refused to look at me as he spoke quietly of his memory:

I was nine when the church burned. My grandma told us. She told us the day after it burned. She said, "Did you know the church was burned down?" I didn't believe it.

Granddad had went to the store. Came in, said, "The church was burned down." Then I started crying.

I feel sad. I was a little mad, because I had loved that church. I loved the old church; it was the most beautiful church I ever had. It was the only one we had, and we didn't have another one.

I went to see what was left. I picked up bricks and looked at them. We took pictures.

Another little boy underscored the impact of the event throughout the community, noting that the first thing he can remember about Little Zion is that it burned down. Interviewed at age eight, he said, "I was at home. My dad just came in and said, 'Little Zion burned down.' The next week we saw it. When we drove up I saw the two doors just laying down there. We walked around and we saw the white top of the church laying down, hanging. All the bricks was burned and like somebody broke them up. There wasn't nothing but some bricks making a square around the church, everything else burned."

Certainly, these accounts embody a sense of grief at losing Little Zion. But church members also looked beyond the physical structure, expressing greater concern that the burning was a warning from God about a need for spiritual renewal. Rev. Willie C. Carter, for instance, described the fire not just as a physical crisis but also a spiritual one:

When Little Zion burned, that was a crisis time. You know the Lord speaks in many different ways. If a impact come upon our home or we come upon a tragedy, we say, "The Lord is speaking to me, telling me something." Most of the time he will warn me, and then if I don't take heed tragedy will come upon me. Little Zion burned down. God was trying to tell us something. I don't know what it was. But to me, I just feel like something was going on wrong in the church. Something wasn't right. They had a thing with the arguing every Sunday.

Reverend say, "Well the Lord gonna get tired of you all arguing so much."

I didn't know that the church was gonna get burned, but it look to me like He trying to tell them something, and they won't take heed. The church burned down to the ground. (9/7/98)

In fact Rev. W. D. Lewis, pastor of Little Zion from 1950 to 1999, said the Spirit had already warned him directly that the congregation had strayed, that trouble was in store for Little Zion:

> I told them something was gonna happen to Little Zion. I said, "Something's gonna happen." I didn't know that the church was gonna burn quick as it did.
>
> The Spirit tell me four times something gonna happen. I didn't know exactly what. But it tell me, "Something's gonna happen."
>
> The night of the burning, the Spirit tells me again something was gonna happen. That time I thought it was about how my boy was acting, didn't know it was about Little Zion.
>
> The church might well have been on fire then. It burned before I went to bed.
>
> But I knew something was gonna happen. I could see it.
>
> I think the Lord gave them a good lesson. Everybody's living high now, frustrated, don't know what to eat, don't know what to wear.
>
> Some rough days been through here and more of them coming. (9/5/98)

Deacon Henry T. Carter, instrumental in the reconstruction effort, also described his attempt to rebuild his relationship with God after the burning. He said, "This thing didn't happen just to be happening. This thing happened for us to get serious. It's happened for us to be serious about our Father's business." Deacon Carter prayed, "Lord, if there's anything that I'm not doing right, just take it straight out of me. Help me to be right. Help me to be whole." Each member of Little Zion must come to understand God's message in this tragedy, he explained, noting that "it's gonna take some time for each individual to grow into knowledge of it, to come to their sense of Christian duty."

During interviews for this project, some members of the Little Zion community did consider the explanation of racially motivated arson for the burning. But even this speculation remained wrapped in the sense that God allowed these events for a divine purpose, as part of a divine communication with Little Zion. Deacon Henry T. Carter summed up the responses of many church members: "If we were burned intentionally, God allowed Satan in for a purpose. I read somewhere in the Bible the Lord have dominion over everything. So God allowed Satan to move in. Maybe to gain our faith, help us become more stronger in the Lord, help us do His will. God wants us to love one another and do His will and bring people to Christ. He wants us to quit sugar-coating and quit shamming. He wants real people. He can't use us if we don't get real and serve Him."

People in this community also expressed considerable uncertainty about why an outsider might direct a racially motivated attack against Little Zion. Deacon Ed Carter said that several whites had been attending Little Zion before the burning and an African American man and a Caucasian woman had been married in the church community in 1991. Rev. Eddie Carter,[38] who grew up at Little Zion and now pastors two churches in the region, considered these possibilities, noting that blacks and whites worshipping together in church "could have, may have, brought on some tension."

Both Rev. Eddie Carter and Rev. Oscar Williams pointed to Little Zion's civil rights activities as a focal point for racial hatred. Rev. Williams noted:

> Little Zion was not burned out of love. They did it out of meanness, a bit of racism, as well as meanness. I am convinced of that. Little Zion was very active in the movement, and there is no doubt in my mind that that is one of the reasons it was burned. No doubt in my mind. Because of what Little Zion did and stood for in the civil rights movement.
>
> Mt. Zoar, Mt. Zion, and Little Zion: All three churches were very active in the movement. I knew all of the pastors. The fellow who had one leg, Rev. Pickens, was *very* active in the movement. When I say he was active, I mean that man with that crutch was everywhere. At every civil rights meeting he was there riding that crutch. Mt. Zoar's pastor was very active too, although he was a young fellow, probably born in the fifties. All of them were there, but none any more than Lewis and Pickens. Lewis was very much out there.

Rev. Eddie Carter cited a commitment among the current leadership at Little Zion to the Southern Christian Leadership Conference (SCLC) and the local civil rights leader Spiver Gordon: "I believe Little Zion was burned because there were some people in our church who believe in SCLC. I believe because, like my father, some others believe in a man by the name of Spiver Gordon, a leader of SCLC. They support him. And I believe — now I'm saying I don't know — I believe that because my father wouldn't turn and bow down to the enemy, because Brother Smothers and Rev. Lewis wouldn't bow down to the enemy and wouldn't talk against our people, I believe they burned our church. I believe they burned our church because these people were spokesmen."

In fact, of those who speculated on what events might have triggered the burning, only Rev. Eddie Carter openly discussed who might have committed arson. As noted earlier, this question of criminal responsibility clearly highlighted an unbridgeable gap in the cultural divide between the members of this community and me. Many people told me, "Everyone is talking about who did it," but only Rev. Carter said, "I believe Little Zion was burned by the Klan. I believe the Klan was trying to gain attention, trying to show strength. But, by what they've done, if they only had known how the churches would be rebuilt, they would never have set fire to them. I believe that because there are a few older ones in Greene County who exist; we still got to pay for this old hatred, bigotry, trying to scare, to put fear into people. The white man trying to show his supremacy."

But even Rev. Carter framed his explanation of the burning as an evil human act within divine intention. He said God allowed the fire to happen so that the races would pull together in the rebuilding effort, because "a divided house cannot stand"[39]:

> If the fire drew attention, then God's letting us know that He's drawing nearer to us. And we're drawing nearer to God. In the process, we need more black and white who believe in Christ, who believe in equality, to come on and make it reality in 1997, show that we're not gonna tolerate this evil force.

We need more whites to come down and worship with us. We

need more whites to come here to get rid of hatred. Go to Mt. Zoar and to the other churches. We need a race relation. With all the hatred, we got to come together despite that.

We're gonna bring His love in spite of how we're being treated. We're gonna set a good example of how we should live, and not get afraid. Not be fearful of our lives. Come on and worship, both male and female. It'll make a change in the society.

The nation needs prayer. The nation needs to come together. We need the people of this nation to just come on to Little Zion anyway. Come on and join in. Because we are one brotherhood. The Bible said, "Love the brotherhood." Love the brotherhood. Because we can't get to heaven — we sure ain't going to heaven — until we get together.

Two church members speculated on the possibility that the church caught on fire accidentally. Rev. Willie C. Carter suggested lightning could have struck the church, but he also noted that an eyewitness said he thought he'd heard a bomb explode.

I don't know whether the lightning hit it or arson. I don't know. You can't say. The two churches was in line, Mt. Zoar and Little Zion. When the lightning hit Little Zion, it could have hit at Mt. Zoar same time. I don't know what really happened.

Peoples say somebody burned it down, but I couldn't imagine who would have burned it down. In the county and in the town all around, we got good relationships. I mean, there hadn't been no argument and nothing going on, no protesting to cause it to come upon us like this. It's hard to think about. Hard to think about.

I said, "Lord, I wouldn't want to be the one to say somebody burned the church down when the lightning hit it." I wouldn't want to do that. On that night, it was raining, storming. I know that. I mean you wouldn't want to go out that door to get in the car, it was raining so hard.

But they say it went up in smoke. Somebody down under the hill, a young man, say it sound like a bomb was up in there. Looked like in the middle of the church, sound like a bomb. They say he heard it. He come out on his porch, say it sounded like a bomb. Boom, boom, boom. *BOOM.*

I said, "Hey, it just was a miracle to me." It was a miracle to me. I couldn't understand it. But the Lord knows. I'm gonna say that like Ezekiel said it. "Lord, thy God, you knows. You *know* what happened."[40] But I don't know what happened up there. God knows I don't know. (9/7/98)

Though National Weather Service records show rain and fog at nearby stations in Tuscaloosa, Alabama, and Meridian, Mississippi, they mention no thunderstorm activity in the area. No other church members mentioned lightning in interviews for this project, nor did local or national news reports include this observation.

Deacon Henry T. Carter, Rev. Carter's twin brother, said he just didn't believe the church could have been burned deliberately, but he did not explain his position. Deacon Carter spoke for almost everyone interviewed, adults and children alike, in summing up a sense of helplessness — and a need for faith — in the face of the unsolved mystery: "We had a loss that was tragic, and we mourned about the Little Zion Baptist Church when it was gone. We could say that it was racism, some vandal. We could say something like that. But we really don't know how Little Zion burned. None of us were there. Could have been a malfunction. Whys back up to whys. I don't know what happened, because nobody came up with no type of clues to tell us that this was arson. We just don't know."

THE COMMUNITY'S LOSS:
"WE NEEDED THE CHURCH ON SUNDAY"

For Little Zion's outsiders, the burning meant the loss of a place of worship in this small community. It took many extended conversations with insiders for me to gain any understanding of the significance of that loss, to get a sense of Little Zion's place in the everyday lives of church members. As those interviewed described the difficulties of getting an education, making a living, and providing for their families in twentieth-century Greene County, I came to see Little Zion as a place of refuge and source of strength. Church members reiterated this point countless times, describing their secular struggles within the context of their spiritual connection to the church.

The argument for the black church as a refuge in an oppressive world, however, risks biasing analysis toward white culture — as if the church gains its stature from its reaction to external pressures instead of from its inherent worth in its own cultural context. The intent here, though, is to present Little Zion as the center of the larger community to which its members necessarily belong — that of the arguably segregated Greene County. Even so, the difficulties of interaction between black and white cultures surrounding Little Zion probably receive undue attention in this analysis; my outsider's ignorance prompted church members to explain their experiences to me. As described previously, this story will move progressively inward from this wider perspective, toward ever more focused examinations of the church and its power in people's individual lives.

Before the 1996 burning, Little Zion was at the center of the nearby African American community, reportedly, for generations. However, public records maintained by outsiders, such as the Greene County government, offer little information about the church. The deed granting full ownership for the property was transferred from R. I. Smaw to the trustees of the church in September 1924 in exchange for $300. The trustees included John Bragg, Isikiah Hubbard, Dick Knott, West Murphy, Boz Hubbard, Forris Watson, Charley Hubbard, Ike Paul, Ennis Davis, and John Hubbard, the first trustees listed on the brick marker installed in 1996 outside of the rebuilt church.[41] Some names could be missing from this compilation, though, as the original ten trustees comprise two-thirds of the fifteen trustees documented for Little Zion's entire history. Even if the church originated in 1924, the addition of only five trustees in more than seventy-five years seems improbable.

Even the church's own cemetery provides limited insight into Little Zion's early history, as the oldest grave appears to date only as far back as November 23, 1918, honoring the passing of Mr. William Washington. Some tombstones have fallen into disrepair, however, with engravings difficult to decipher. Also, several members mentioned an older church cemetery outside of the property boundaries, although none could clearly recall its location and efforts to locate the site proved futile.

While details about Little Zion's early history are scarce in the public record, members agree the church dates back to at least the mid-nineteenth century, possibly earlier. Rev. Oscar Williams explained:

> I'm almost certain Little Zion got started around the 1850s. Dick [Richard] Small [Smaw] was a large plantation owner. I know the plantation well. His family still had plenty of land in Greene County when I was a youth. They were among the last of the large landholders. In many cases, the white who owned the property would allow the blacks to have a church there, as long as there was a congregation to meet there. But when the church stopped meeting, the land was to go back to the family that had owned it. That happened all over the South. I dare say that is what happened with Little Zion because the deed was not granted until very much later: 1924. Blacks were granted land enough to have a cemetery and a church meeting place. Very rarely would the landholders outright sell the land or give you a permanent deed. If the old white man made the agreement, his son would honor it, his grandson would honor it, and churches got built and used forever.

Was Richard Smaw the son or grandson of the original landowner who had informally granted use of the property to Little Zion? Smaw's birth certificate indicates he was born in "about 1875," to William Smaw and Sarah Johnson Toulmin. William Smaw's father, Isaiah Buxton Smaw, was born "about 1819," according to public records. *A Goodly Heritage* lists "Isaiah B. Smaw" as one of the county's large planters of 1856.[42] A map published by Snedecor of Greene County in the same year, however, showed I. B. Smaw's holdings slightly to the north of Section 28, Township 20, the church's location. In 1856, Snedecor documented the following landholders in Section 28: David Bragg, Bryant Goatley, Thomas Baltzell, and R. W. Garrett. Quite probably, the Smaw family expanded its holdings through the purchase of property from one of these landowners sometime after 1856. But the record of that exchange has not been found.

Sister Courtney Porter said, "I think Little Zion started when my grandmom was a kid. That was her church, and my mother's church, and now my church too." Sister Porter, the oldest living member of Little Zion when I began this project,[43] said her mother was born in 1889. So her grandmother conceivably could have been born mid-century. Sister Porter also said her mother remembered Rev. Steve Burnett, the church's first pastor: "My mother said Steve Burnett used to pastor that church. The way they tell it, that church was in better shape then, because when that pastor start preaching, them mules and horses would nicker and holler right away. They used to go to church in the wagon, and they'd tie the horse up to the tree outside. They'd be in church singing and praying, with that man preaching in there, and they say those horses start nickering on up. He was a powerful guy. Of course, that was before my day, but I heard a lot of people saying that." It is unclear, however, whether Sister Porter's mother and grandmother personally knew Rev. Burnett or simply knew the folklore surrounding his tenure. This anecdote fits a common theme in animal tales, where the beasts of the field possess greater wisdom and spiritual understanding than the humans who have dominion over them. (In Christian lore, for example, farm animals are said to fall to their knees at midnight on Christmas eve, in remembrance of the birth of Jesus.)

Deacon Ed Carter's widely repeated description of Little Zion's origins in a "brush arbor" certainly suggests the church has roots in plantation slave culture, where slaves' use of these temporary structures for religious meetings, often conducted in secret, has been widely documented. Interestingly, Deacon Carter's account remained ambivalent on whether Little Zion's members originally worshipped with the planter's knowledge and consent or in secret. According to his grandmother, the slaves "couldn't afford to pray around the slave masters, because they didn't believe too much in that."[44] In the next sentence, however, Deacon Carter reversed the implication of secret worship, indicating that "the white folks didn't bother with them [the worshippers] as long as they stayed together." In fact, this narrative ambivalence could embody the planter's shifting attitudes toward religion as practiced by his slaves. In *First Freedom: The Responses of*

Alabama's Blacks to Emancipation and Reconstruction, for example, Peter Kolchin summarized planters' reactions to slave religion:

> Throughout the antebellum period, Southern whites held ambivalent attitudes toward slave religion. On the one hand, some feared that an immersion in Christian doctrine was likely to impress slaves with the equality of all souls before God and make them less subservient. The 1831 insurrection led by slave preacher Nat Turner appeared to confirm the worst fears of slave owners that education, even religious education, tended to make slaves less content in their servitude. On the other hand, many Southerners saw religious indoctrination as a useful method of social control. The biblical injunction of obedience to one's master seemed clear, and the promise of reward in the life after death could be useful in keeping an oppressed class docile.
>
> Despite an 1833 state law forbidding blacks to preach except in the presence of five slaveowners, the latter viewpoint generally came to predominate among slaveowners in Alabama.[45]

The very presence of the brush arbor suggests slave worship away from the prying eyes of the planters, who commonly brought slaves with them to church or sent itinerant preachers to spread Christianity among the slaves. Certainly, Deacon Carter's description of the brush arbor meetings suggests independently run religious services, perhaps not yet indoctrinated into the white nineteenth-century conventions of the Baptist faith. He said, "They [the worshippers] went up there and my grandma say they would rock back and forth, groan and moan and rock. They had the zeal, but they didn't know what should be done. . . . They had a lot of emotion with them, and they would get happy and shout."[46] But these narratives include no mention of efforts to maintain secrecy, such as the frequently cited use of a vessel of water or overturned pot to catch sound, or the hanging of quilts and rugs, wetted down to mute voices.

While the exact age of Little Zion remains uncertain, church members described the church's role as the center of this community as far back as living memory serves — from around the Great Depression. The recollections move from the difficulties of sharecropping and farming, to getting an education and even making moonshine, in the attempt to make ends meet in the first half of the twentieth century. When the civil rights movement came to Greene County in the 1960s, Little Zion organized voter registration drives and supported African American candidates for public office. Even after the 1996 burning, Little Zion's members kept the church at the center of their experience. They initiated a rebuilding effort that embraced volunteers from around the world, restoring the church both physically and spiritually to its place on a hill in the woods and fields of Greene County.

Deacon Ed Carter remembered vividly his family's experience as tenant farmers during the Depression. The Carters farmed on the Haggan plantation, approximately 1,300 acres reportedly owned by a wealthy family from Massachusetts. Deacon Carter asserted, "[My] parents weren't sharecropping; they paid rent. They paid a bale of cotton for approximately twenty acres of land."[47] During the Depression, the young Carter made twenty-five or thirty cents a day, hired out as a farm hand after the family harvest was complete.

> Depression hit peoples in '32. We had plenty of food, but we didn't have no money. We couldn't buy clothes; everyone you see had patches on top of patches, old shoes run down. But we always raised our food. We had cows for meat, plenty of milk, butter, eggs. We had grit meal, grind our own for our bread. We had to buy a little flour, rice, sugar, coffee. We would make our own syrup, and sometime that syrup would go to sugar, and settle at the bottom of the container. Then we'd get that syrup off there, get that sugar and beat it up and wash it off. Then we have sugar for in the coffee.
>
> My grandma would sell eggs and chickens and things to the slave master on the place, Mr. Lynn Davis.

It is interesting that Deacon Carter referred to the white landowner of the 1930s as "the slave master on the place."

Even as a young child, Deacon Carter said he realized the dependency of tenant farming. He asked his grandfather why he couldn't buy his farmland and was told, "No, I don't need to buy it. The owner give it to me."[48] Deacon Carter explained, "See, the white man would tell them, 'You got a home here,' until you disappoint him, don't do what he want, and then you ain't got no more home. So I told my granddaddy, 'When I become a man, I'm gonna buy me some land. I'm gonna pay taxes.' I ain't gonna be looking for somebody to give me something. I feel like every man ought to be able to live on his own integrity and pull up by his own bootstraps. I just feel you ain't free during all that time."[49]

In fact, as Deacon Carter's grandson, Rev. James Carter, recalled, the landowner later threw the family off of the plantation and burned their farm:

> In the early 1940s, the USDA had set up this agricultural assistance program for farmers. The overseer on this plantation signed up every farmer on his place, with the intention to defraud them out of the money. So my great grandfather, Henry Carter, was one of the first ones he went to, telling him to sign over his check. He could read and write, though most folks couldn't.
>
> Henry told him, "This check is made out to me. As far as I'm concerned, it's my check. If it's your check, you sign it and cash it." Because he refused to sign, none of the other farmers signed the check either.
>
> The last thing my great grandfather was told was, "If you're here when we get back this afternoon, we're gonna burn up the place and you too."
>
> And they did burn the place up, burned the house and the barn and all the facilities. It all went up in smoke.

As in many other narratives by church members, Rev. Carter described this crisis as a spiritual challenge. While the Carters found themselves materially "the poorest of the poor in the community," they survived and later prospered because they were "not poor spiritually." Rev. Carter explained, "I think we've always had that spiritual pull from generation to generation. That has been the nucleus of our family, to always stay with God, always stay in the church." He deemed himself very fortunate to grow up in an environment where "the church is more sacred than self," noting, "It's like being protected. In the world my family lives in, the good overpowers evil. That's the best way that I can say it."

Land, however, was not easily acquired by African Americans in Greene County throughout much, if not all, of the twentieth century. During one interview, Rev. James Carter asserted, "Land is still not easily purchased here," and Sister Gladys O. Smothers, formerly a teacher at Little Zion School, added, "You can buy most anything except a spot of land." According to many Little Zion members, whites have avoided selling land to blacks. Likewise, "you come up to the banking institution, you can get financing for a car or anything else. But when it comes to land, that's a different thing altogether," Rev. Carter said.

The Carter family bought approximately eighty acres in 1944, when prices were low after the Depression. Deacon Ed Carter still recalled the opportunity with puzzlement decades later, attributing it to impending civil rights legislation: "I heard this. I don't know whether it's true. The white folks knowed that this civil rights bill's gonna come down. Us Negroes didn't know it. So they said the government was gonna protest them if they didn't do something, said there wasn't enough Negroes owning land in this county. They made agreement that they would sell some land to some Negroes."

Rev. Oscar Williams spoke with some pride about his family's ownership of their land, which made it possible to avoid sharecropping. But the family had paid a price for this economic freedom. "My mother's husband was killed in the coal mines. With whatever money they paid, my mother bought forty-some acres of land. We did not have to be sharecroppers. We owned our own land and we had a mule."

Mrs. Busby Jackson described in detail growing up under the sharecropping system as late as the 1950s, from which her family "needed the church on Sunday . . . where you got your consolation." She remembered clearly the physically demanding work and her outrage at a system that kept her family poor:

> You almost stayed up all night picking cotton. My dad would walk out in the morning and say, "We're gonna get seven bales this year." But it was just the four of us. My dad was doing most of the picking. He could do more than anybody else.
>
> One day my brother and I tried all day long to pick 100 pounds. I

think we had 75 pounds. We had water and bricks and cotton balls and all in there and still only 75 pounds.

When the cotton first opens and it's heavy and all, you get pretty good weight for it. But as the sun gets on it, it gets lighter and lighter because it dries out. And the more the sun stays on out, the lighter and lighter the cotton gets. So you almost have to send in three bales to make one by the time you're all done picking it.

That was our life. We had to go to the fields and work to make the money. We planted and we picked and we took it in town for weighing and selling.

And every year the people would say, "Joe. You just made it. You broke even." They'd say, "You broke even."

Which means they take all three bales and there is nothing left for us. And we got to go right back and borrow from them to start all over again. So we can break even another year. Yeah, so we can break even another year. My dad never said anything. It was whatever the white person said, that's what you did. You had no choice.

We didn't talk about these things. We would break even year after year and my dad never said anything on the way home. My grandfather sharecropped and my father and my oldest brother. Three generations of this. And it went on until well into the fifties. And it was always the same. We never got ahead.

Little Zion's families recognized that education provided a key to escape from Greene County's limited economy, and, until desegregation, the church ran an elementary school in an adjacent building. Although heavily subsidized and administered by the church, Little Zion School operated as part of the public school system throughout the first half of the twentieth century. Graduates of Little Zion then attended Greene County Training School, now Paramount High School, in Boligee. The oldest members of Little Zion recalled that in the early 1900s the school operated only during the winter months before finally adopting a nine-month schedule, because families needed their children's help in the fields.

Rev. Williams recalled the conflict between fulfilling his farming responsibilities and staying in school:

I was the oldest son, so in the afternoons when we got off our school bus (truck really), I did not play around in the house with toys. Within fifteen minutes I was in the fields. I knew to go get my school clothes off and get that mule and start plowing. . . .

In the mornings I was in the field at daybreak, until that truck came around 7:00 or 7:15. That way I could continually stay in school. The driver would blow his horn while he was going up to the end of the route; that gave us about 15 or 20 minutes to come in from the field, throw some water under our arms, grab a biscuit, and then catch the bus and go to school.

So I missed very few days because of farming, very few. I worked hard in the evenings and on the weekends. On Saturdays, instead of going to town, I'd be in the field. At night if the moon was shining, we'd do what we called "running the middle" using another plow. We'd do that even by moonlight. Because of that, I could stay in school.

Federal census figures reveal lack of education as a major challenge faced by African Americans in Greene County throughout the twentieth century. Oral narratives underscored this difficulty. Rev. Williams was one of the few blacks of his generation in this community to earn a doctorate degree.

His mother, Sister Courtney Porter, sat in her living room one summer afternoon in 1996 looking at pictures of her seven children hanging on the walls around her and reflecting on her struggle to educate them. She attributed her ability to finance their education to the lessons learned during countless Sundays at Little Zion, about faith and the power of prayer over all obstacles:

You know I had to pray a lot to raise seven kids. I had to pray. And He answered. He was good to me. When my kids were all going to school, the oldest one called, said he needs $125.

I went downtown, told the white guy, "I need $150."

"What you want it for?"

"To send to my son in college."

"Okay." Just like that.

I said, "I'm gonna give you a note on a cow, a red cow with a white face and tail."

The next month my son need the same thing, so I walked over next door to that place. Told that guy I need $150.

"Okay."

Gave him a note on the same cow, and they didn't know it! So that's what prayer'll do. God let me make enough money to pay every bill I ever had, and still have some left. If you put God in front, He'll help you.

With a quiet laugh, Sister Porter gave God the credit for the ingenuity to negotiate informal loans in Eutaw at a time when the community was served by only one white-controlled bank: Merchants and Farmers Bank of Greene County. In a 1983 report by the U.S. Commission on Civil Rights, several African American community leaders asserted that the bank discriminated against blacks in both its hiring and lending policies. For example, Mr. Spiver Gordon, the local president of the SCLC, stated, "There have been complaints with the bank, and its impact on blacks has been devastating. The bank had to be forced to hire blacks. It finally hired a black after SCLC marched on the bank a few years ago. The bank now employs 2 black tellers out of 35 employees. The bank is selective when it comes to loaning money. Blacks are forced to apply for high-risk, high-interest loans."[50] Today two banks operate in Eutaw, and, while most whites reportedly continue to patronize Merchants and Farmers, most blacks now bank at Citizens Federal Savings Bank.

Other members of Little Zion's community did not fare so well in obtaining an education, and thus had to settle for local unskilled, low-paying jobs. Sister Rosie Lee Hendricks, cousin to Mrs. Johnnie Busby Jackson, returned to visit the church of her childhood in August of 1997. She took time out to participate in this project one afternoon and sat cooling herself with a cardboard funeral home fan in Mrs. Busby Jackson's shade-drawn living room. "My granddaddy never bought me a book," she commented. "I had a uncle to buy me some books one time, and I went to the fourth grade. I never had the opportunity. When I married, I had to work. Cleaning people's houses. Whatever needed to be done, I had to do it." Other members of the church recalled jobs such as mining, logging, construction, working at the paper mill, and digging ditches. Deacon Ed Carter said, "I feel like education is the rolling wheel for success. You just can't make it without education. As long as you're not educated, you're just a tool for the man to work with. You're just a man out there digging a ditch, ain't got sense enough to do nothing but throw some dirt out of a ditch. And that's the lesser pay. They call it common labor."[51]

While Little Zion helped local families educate their children during the first half of the twentieth century, the church leadership frowned on another major tactic for getting ahead in Greene County: The illegal making and selling of moonshine. Deacon Ed Carter said that he "made the whiskey for a living and sold it," because, as he succinctly put it, "People not in moonshine, they're picking cotton, making about a dollar a hundred pounds. I'm making much better money. I own a farm; I bought a farm in 1944" (October 20, 1996). While other members of Little Zion did not admit making moonshine, Deacon Carter asserted, "Most folks what was in the church, them that wasn't selling it was drinking it. Everybody knew" (ibid.). Mrs. Johnnie Jackson agreed, saying, "At the gatherings here at the church, in those days, they would be all out under the hills, selling it. The Reverend [Lewis] now, he didn't abide by it. But there were so many of them right around these hills, right here."

In fact, both Mrs. Busby Jackson and Deacon Carter asserted that most of the local community, including law enforcement, knew who was running whiskey, but they looked the other way for economic reasons. She said, "There was certain ones; everybody knew who was running because they had to get the sugar. You'd back the truck up to the back door of the grocery store and put about five or six hundred pounds of sugar on there." Deacon Carter described the financial interdependency between local merchants and bootleggers in greater detail: "Depending on how much you was running, you had to buy a whole lot of sugar. I had four or five barrels. Running maybe thirty, forty gallons off at a time, maybe twice a week. It sold for six or seven dollars back in 1940, '41, '42. But I need about two or three hundred pounds of sugar a week. The merchant man, he know what's going on. No family eats that much sugar! He let me have it. When the war time came, you couldn't get that much sugar. He would let me have it. Go out the back door with it. I pay high, twenty, twenty-five dollars a hundred [per hundred pounds] for it. I'm paying a higher price; he's making a good sale."

Both Deacon Carter and Mrs. Busby Jackson described police efforts to stop bootlegging as somewhat lackadaisical. According to Mrs. Busby Jackson, "They would let them run it for about six months, and then they would send the revenuer down to blow it up. And then they [the bootleggers] would stay out of business for about three months. They would take the dynamite and blow the whole thing up. Now some people, they knew when it was time to get caught. And they'd move on. Sometimes you'd hear something go 'boom' at three o'clock in the morning. That'd be the still. And after that everything would be cool for a little while." Deacon Carter called the relationship between bootleggers and authorities a game of "cat and mouse": "The man, he probe the woods, and if he find a trail he go there and bust it up. If they catch you, they put you in jail. If they don't they tear up that thing. It be down there in the woods; you got to have a trail to it, a road. Then I go get me some more barrels and move somewhere else" (ibid.). If they escaped detection, Mrs. Busby Jackson remembered, bootleggers would pack their wares to sell in Sumter County, Greensboro, and other places. She said, "They'd come in with cars, packed down in there so you couldn't hear a jug say nothing. They had it packed down just that well. It didn't make a sound."

As Mrs. Busby Jackson said, Little Zion's former pastor, Rev. W. D. Lewis, did not approve of making, selling, or drinking moonshine. He said he knew about Deacon Carter's bootlegging, adding that he "wasn't a good member" because of it (8/7/97). Yet Rev. Lewis did not attempt to force Deacon Carter to stop. Rather, he tried to reason with him: "Every time he put it up in [his store], I seen it. I'd tell about it. He thought I didn't know nothing about it, but I saw it. I asked him about it" (ibid.). When Deacon Carter finally got caught bootlegging, Little Zion and Rev. Lewis responded, paradoxically, by appointing him to the Deacon Board: "In 1955, I got caught with the whiskey in my pocket, bootlegging, and they put me in jail. My wife told them up at the church to put me on the Deacon Board, on trial for Deacon. So they put me on trial for Deacon; they ordained me some time ago, around 1960. To straighten me out. And I been around here with the church, faithful, ever since" (10/20/96).

When the civil rights movement began, many black churches nationwide faced criticism for their adherence to the status quo and refusal to participate in the struggle. Milton Lee Boykin noted in his dissertation on the civil rights movement in the region,

> Traditionally, it [the black Protestant church] was a place to withdraw. In many cases, religion offered an escapist cultism promising future glories in Heaven and an emotional catharsis for present difficulties. The clergy in these churches have been called "Uncle Toms," "cornbread preachers," and "fried chicken preachers" by civil rights activists, implying that they are subservient to the white power structure and more concerned with their own welfare than that of their parishioners. The "other worldliness" of these black churches complemented the separatist policies of their parent white denominations and provided a justification for accepting current conditions passively while awaiting Judgment Day.[52]

But in Greene County, the African American churches served as the local organizers for the movement, leading voter registration drives, marches, and rallies: "It was believed that organizational involvement in Greene County was deeply rooted in the county's eighty-two Negro churches. These institutions provide a vehicle for self-expression and a training ground for developing organizational skills. A church building was the site for the organizational meeting of the NAACP. The mass-political meetings preceding the 1969 special election were held in Negro churches. In answer to a question regarding the most important types of leaders in the county, ministers received a majority of the positive responses."[53]

During a 1999 interview in his office at Tuskegee University, Rev. Oscar Williams remembered how this unity among the county's African American churches was accomplished: "I do remember having to organize some opinion campaigns right in Greene County for black preachers who didn't want this civil rights mess in their churches. In fact, I know one situation where the deacons were in favor of civil rights and the pastor was not. They gave him thirty days to look over his mind to see if the Lord was still leading him against the movement. Within about twenty days, you know, the Lord changed his mind."

Rev. Williams asserted that Little Zion "was one of the first churches in the area to step out into the movement." As a senior in high school, around 1959 or 1960, he said he helped organize voter registration drives at Little Zion, following the lead of local activist O. B. Harris [phonetic spelling]. Rev. Williams added, "Little Zion was very much at the forefront of getting folks registered to vote. Many, many civil rights meetings were held at the church. Former pastor W. D. Lewis was one of the main organizers of those meetings. Hosea Williams was there. Ralph David Abernathy was there. All of these folks came to Greene County."

Rev. Lewis received tremendous leadership support for voter registration efforts at Little Zion from Deacon Ed Carter and Deacon Jonas Smothers, according to many church members. "When you couldn't meet nowhere else, you could always meet at Little Zion," Rev. Williams remembered. "Reverend Lewis made sure of that, and Lewis himself was at virtually 90 percent of the mass meetings. Reverend Lewis was very vocal. He carried people up to marches in his truck." Deacon Smothers also transported people to meetings and marches in Eutaw, his wife, Sister Gladys Smothers, remembered. Deacon Carter braved a boycott against the freedom riders who came from outside Greene County to help in voter registration efforts, supplying them with gasoline and provisions, according to his youngest son, Rev. Eddie Carter. In the Carter family video mentioned earlier, Rev. James Carter shows a picture of Rev. Lewis, Deacon Carter, and Deacon Smothers, noting: "These three men walk with great big sticks. They are the kings of this community. They set the example. They make the rules. If you break them, you're gonna have to answer to these three."

But the church did not rely on the efforts of these men alone. "A lot of our members were active," Rev. Williams explained, singling out the efforts of Mr. Joe Braggs, Mr. C. H. Develle, and Sister Courtney

Porter. Sister Gladys Smothers remembered how Little Zion conducted fund-raising events and food drives for the freedom riders. Rev. Williams said that as a young army recruit at the time, he "wore out two cars in the movement, just carrying folks to the polls all day, registering people, going to meetings, speaking here and there. When they had marches in Greene County, I was there." In the special election of 1969, Rev. Williams said he managed the campaigns of all of the black candidates. But he added, "Of course, almost everybody in the church helped in some way. I dare say you would be hard-pressed to find anybody of voting age not registered to vote at Little Zion. As fast as they got to be of voting age, we insisted that they vote."

Rev. Williams recalled how difficult it was to prepare voters to overcome the registration barriers that faced them:

> During that time the voter registration form was a legal-sized paper with questions on both sides. You had to answer all of those questions, including giving an interpretation of the U.S. Constitution. We organized workshops at Little Zion and brought community folks in, taught people how to fill out the form. You had to answer all questions correctly. For example, if you were black and mistakenly put "Mrs." in front of your name, that automatically disqualified you. If you did not dot your i, that meant it was an e; if you did not cross your t, that meant it was an l: Misspelled. So we taught folks how to answer every question on that form.

Little Zion's members faced the constant threat of violence in their efforts to register voters and gain political power for African Americans. Rev. Williams remembered one local civil rights march in which "a fellow who owned a small engine company waded out into the crowd with his chain saw blazing." He continued,

> Everybody knew it was dangerous. Everybody knew. I was a campaign chairman, for example, for the candidate for sheriff. I can remember driving him home down in Forkland, maybe twenty miles away, and walking with him all around his house to make sure it was safe to go in. Then he'd come back part of the way with me. We'd do each other like that. I remember the time in Greene County when black families didn't ride in the same car together.

Your daughter might ride with me. My son might ride with you. So if somebody blew up the car, the whole family would not be destroyed. I remember those days in Greene County. We all knew there was danger involved.

Anyone who has ever driven Greene County's back roads at night knows how lonely, how potentially frightening they can be. Rev. Williams described the terror of "state troopers driving down the country roads, just stopping any blacks driving and beating them. I've seen beatings. If we were driving along at night, and we saw a car approaching us in our rearview mirror, we would try to speed up and get out of the way, outrun it. Why? It may be the police. It may be the police. No black during those days, and few now, looked at police officers as friends." Rev. Williams asserted that the white sheriffs in Greene County before the 1970s wielded so much power that when they wanted to arrest an African American, they simply sent for him. "Why would he show up? Because to not show up, and have that sheriff come get you, meant almost certain death."

But the reverend also credited one white sheriff during the movement for refusing to tolerate Ku Klux Klan meetings in Greene County. "We did know Klan members, sure. The Klan operated outside of Greene County and there were local members. But the KKK tried to have one meeting in Greene County, and that sheriff told me he walked into that meeting with his big cattle stick, just rapped on the table as hard as he could. He said, 'When it come down again, it'll come across asses.' He broke up the meeting. That's one decent thing I can say about him. He simply did not tolerate the Klan."

Churches in the region provided more than just spiritual and physical nourishment and support for civil rights activists in the face of constant danger. They literally served as safe havens. Consider Anne Moody's autobiographical account of her voter registration efforts in nearby Mississippi:

> Now every Negro church in the county was opened for [voter registration] workshops. The nine of us split into groups of three. Almost every night we had workshops in different churches, sometimes sixteen to thirty miles out of town.

One or two of our protective guys had cars. They were usually sent along with the girls out in the country. It was dark and dangerous driving down those long country rock roads, but now that we always had two or three of the guys riding with us, it wasn't so bad. In fact, once we got to the churches, everything was fine. Listening to those old Negroes sing freedom songs was like listening to music from heaven. They sang them as though they were singing away the chains of slavery. Sometimes I just looked at the expressions on their faces as they sang and cold chills would run down my back.[54]

Efforts to secure political power for the majority African American voters in Greene County ultimately proved successful. Before 1965, the U.S. Commission on Civil Rights estimated only about 5.5 percent of the eligible black population of Greene County were registered to vote, comprising about 275 of 5,000 people. In contrast, more than 100 percent of the white population were on the rolls, with 2,305 registered voters out of 1,649 eligible citizens.[55] The Greene County NAACP, the Greene County Civic Organization, and the SCLC worked through the churches to change those numbers, so that by 1967 the 3,953 registered black voters represented about 79 percent of the eligible African American population.[56]

Rev. James Carter attributed this victory to the black population's determination to secure a better way of life. "When the civil rights movement came, I believe that we were probably the poorest of the poor, linked to the southern plantation. But when we got the vote, blacks just rose up, physically, and took charge.

"It started in 1966," he remembered. That year, Little Zion's pastor, Rev. Lewis, became one of the county's first African American elected officials, winning a seat on the Greene County Democratic Executive Committee. Of the four other black candidates in the Democratic primary, only Rev. Peter Kirksey was elected, attaining a seat on the school board. Though two of the losing candidates filed suit to contest the election, the courts ruled against them.

In 1968, six African American candidates ran in the Democratic primary, but all were defeated. This time candidates concentrated their efforts on getting on the general election ballot as representatives of the newly formed National Democratic Party of Alabama (NDPA). When local and state officials refused to certify NDPA candidates, a class action suit was filed by Sallie M. Hadnott of Augusta County. *Hadnott v. Amos* went to the U.S. Supreme Court, which ruled on October 19, 1968, that a temporary restraining order be continued until further action on the case, guaranteeing NDPA candidates a place on the November 5 ballot. However, Greene County's judge of probate, Dennis Herndon, defied federal authority and withheld the NDPA names from the ballot.[57] When the Supreme Court finally ruled on the case on March 25, 1969, it reversed lower court decisions and specifically called for a new election in Greene County, in which the NDPA candidates' names would appear on the ballot.

In the special election of 1969, to the credit of the voter registration campaign, voters elected all six of the NDPA candidates. "In one election, blacks won probate judge, sheriff, county commissioner, school board, tax collector, everything with the exception of tax assessor. They took political control of Greene County and they've kept it ever since," Rev. James Carter explained. "That didn't happen in any of the surrounding counties. But Greene County had to have been one of the most oppressed places." Rev. Carter gave the glory to God, saying that when people are most oppressed, God puts the drive in them to fight for their rights.

Two years later, Judge Dennis Herndon was fined $5,452 in damages for civil and criminal contempt in defying the Supreme Court order. "It took two Supreme Court orders to get the names on the ballot," Rev. Carter reiterated in a tone still reflecting amazement decades later. He added that to his knowledge "that's the only time in the history of this country where a local government defied the Supreme Court of this land and overrode the national government. It had never happened—except that time."

Greene County's special election was a "first" in many ways, and it made a significant contribution to the national civil rights movement. Civil rights leader Ralph Abernathy "proclaimed the results of this election more significant than the moon landing which had taken place just nine days earlier," according to Milton Lee Boykin. In fact,

Boykin concluded, "The election, having been ordered by the United States Supreme Court, was no ordinary one. By many of the civil rights activists in Greene County it was viewed as the first substantial fruits of the Selma march and as an important juncture in the long struggle by Negroes to obtain the vote. It was also the first time that a special election was ordered to vindicate the election rights of Negroes and also the first time since 1954 that a public official has been convicted of negligence in complying with civil rights legislation."[58]

Certainly, the local African American community's ability to achieve almost unimaginable success in the special election can be attributed to a familiar sense of religious mission that allowed activists to expect miracles and to summon the commitment and courage to make them happen. As in many other places in America, the civil rights movement in Greene County tapped into the strength of black church traditions. Boykin noted that "the election campaign was conducted in the mode of a religious revival in which participants crusaded against the evils of white racism. At the mass meetings, most speakers adopted a preacher-of-the-Gospel style," always careful to remind audiences not to wait for the glories of heaven but to work for their attainment now.[59]

However, the political power gained by the African American community in the early 1970s did not eliminate the legacy of racial tension and economic deprivation in Greene County. Rev. Eddie Carter said, "Even today, I know things are not right. I support the civil rights movement up to now, the righteousness, doing the right thing. I believe that if America would come to its senses and realize that all men are created equal, everything would be better. Greene County would be a better place."

At a community forum held by the U.S. Commission on Civil Rights following the burnings of Little Zion, Mt. Zoar, and Mt. Zion, chairperson Mary Frances Berry cited commission studies done in 1968 and 1983, which examined "the racial climate here and the social and economic problems, and found that little change had taken place." She added, "In looking at 1996, we again come back, we look and note the lack of progress."[60]

While blacks and whites alike called for communication and understanding between the races, they starkly disagreed on whether, or to what extent, racism afflicted their community. Interestingly, in the context of a public forum to inform federal justice officials, local opinions clearly reflected racial demographics, with black citizens describing Greene County as a place of racial tension while whites denied the assertion. As described earlier in this chapter, Little Zion members shared many conflicting opinions about racial tension as a possible motivating factor in the church burning during interviews with me. Perhaps churchgoers found racism more difficult to consider as motivating, not just general ill will, but the specific destruction of their church home. Or perhaps members of the African American community found it both easier and more important to speak openly of such issues in the context of a public debate, rather than in the one-on-one exchange of a personal interview with a white outsider. Of course, the community's citizens most willing to talk about race dynamics self-selected themselves by requesting time to speak in this forum, while I asked everyone I interviewed about the church burning. Also, as alluded to elsewhere, the context of this project as a vehicle for preserving church memories surely influenced the way in which the dynamics of race were discussed. Though many in the Little Zion community might feel strongly about local racial tension, they might not feel it appropriate or necessary to include such comments in their collection of church memories.

While no representatives of Little Zion spoke at the forum, Rev. Levi Pickens, pastor of Mt. Zion Baptist Church, called Greene County a place of racial discrimination. He said, "From what I been hearing, that we don't have a problem here in Greene County—I've been living here around 71 years, and it hasn't just now started. I wish we could do something about it. Somebody said that we don't have a racial problem. I don't go along with that, because I know we do. . . . I'm supposed to have all of the rights as anybody else has, but we don't have it."[61]

Garric Spencer, the black chairman of the Greene County Board of Commissioners, echoed the pastor's assertion, describing a segregated society: "Is there a problem with race relations in Greene County? We're not fighting in the streets or slapping each other every day, but one only has to ride up through Eutaw . . . and there's Warrior Academy. Right down the street . . . there's Paramount High School, the building that we sit in. It is my understanding that 99.5 percent of the children in this school are black children. One hundred percent of the children in Warrior Academy are white. Well, there's something wrong: There's clearly something wrong with race relations in this county."[62]

In contrast, H. O. Kirksey, a white writer for the *Independent* and cofounder of Citizens for a Better Greene County, said, "Our positions in this organization [Citizens for a Better Greene County], and most people that I deal with, and I deal with most of the people here in Greene County, our problems is not interracial, it's intraracial. Now, what do I mean by that? Our problems are black against black, basically."[63]

When asked if the local pools were segregated, Mr. Kirksey replied, "They can swim in either pool they want. There's no restriction." When asked if the Greene County school system was segregated, he said, "It is segregated, but by choice."[64]

Jan Lavender, also white and wife of Boligee's mayor at the time, Buddy Lavender, ascribed racial tension to outsiders who work to stir up animosity among locals:

> I would say that our number one problem [in Greene County] is paid agitators. Those of us in Greene County know who those paid agitators are.
>
> Our number two problem is our so-called public school system. What white mother or father would be expected to send their children to a school system in which there are no white principals, no white supervisors, and no one working in the central office that is white? . . .
>
> Two swimming pools in Eutaw? Yes. There are two swimming pools. I visit one of those swimming pools and frequently do I see black children, and no, they are not mistreated. They are not mistreated. I've seen it myself.[65]

Spiver Gordon, a local Southern Christian Leadership Conference representative and Eutaw City Council member, suggested a problem of racial intolerance among both federal and local officials in response to the burnings. He called FBI/ATF efforts to investigate the fires "lackadaisical" at best, racially biased at worst, criticizing the FBI's decision to combine the investigation of the church fires with an inquiry into voter fraud among African Americans in Greene County. Thus, those victimized by the church fires faced potentially intimidating questions about vote fraud during the same interview with federal officials. "The wrong people are being investigated," Mr. Gordon asserted. "The victims are being investigated as opposed to the people who are the actual people burning these churches."[66]

Robert Langford, the FBI's special agent in charge in Birmingham, responded that the voter fraud interviews had been planned before the burning investigations began, so the agencies simply expanded the subjects covered in the inquiry to include questions about church burnings.[67]

Mr. Gordon also aired concerns about the management by local government and civic organizations of donations made by people worldwide toward the rebuilding effort.[68] In fact, one fund managed by the white Mayor of Boligee at the time, Buddy Lavender, required the ministers to submit receipts before obtaining funds to purchase rebuilding supplies.

According to Mr. Lavender, the funds required "full accountability."[69] Mr. Lavender also asserted that there are economic and political problems in Greene County but not a race problem. "We are here to discuss racial relations. We do not have a problem as black and white or have it as black [sic] and whites. We do not have a problem — I feel we get along well, but as far as job opportunities in Greene County, if you're not correctly politically aligned, you cannot get a job." Mr. Lavender also argued that a discussion of the burning of black churches fails to tackle the "real issue" — that quite a number of white churches were burning too.[70]

Dr. Berry countered that proportionately far more black churches had burned in 1995 and 1996, and that racial motivation had not been alleged, to her knowledge, in any of the white church burnings during that time. She also called on the governor of Alabama, who did not attend a meeting on the church burnings called by President Bill Clinton, to "fit into his busy schedule some concern for this matter."[71]

Mt. Zion pastor Levi Pickens offered religion as a solution to racial tension in Greene County: "We have a problem and we just have to admit that we have a problem, and we ought to have enough love in our hearts to solve our problem where we come down to living together. God created all of us equally. God intended for all of us to live in this great big world."[72]

Mr. Gordon concurred, saying Greene County's churches offer hope for healing a racial divide: "I think it's going to have to come through churches. We're going to have to recognize that we're all God's children, that we're all the same blood, and that we're all human beings and that's my hope, that we will come forward and work toward resolving those problems."[73]

Many members of Little Zion echoed this call for doing God's will in eliminating racism in Greene County. Deacon Ed Carter seemed to sum up the feelings of the entire congregation when he said, "It is the will of the Lord for people to be able to work together. That's the will of the Lord. When Jesus came, He say, 'I come not to destroy the law. I come to fulfill the law. You children, love one another as I love you.' So Jesus, God the Father, He intend for us to love one another. He don't advocate for no hatred. He expect for white and black to love one another until we die. We are his children, and he expect for us to be kind to one another. You can't go around hating folks and look to make it to the eternal home."[74] His grandson Rev. James Carter elaborated further: "We're only a few hundred years away from slavery that involved physical chains. I think we're still enslaved mentally. We have to be moved by God to find a way to reach out to those who hate, to reach out to those who destroy, whether they destroy the church, whether they destroy their lives with drugs and alcohol. You say, 'Well, how can that happen? Will it ever happen in our lifetime?' It does not matter how long it takes for it to happen. This is God's will. And all my appointed time, I will wait upon the Lord. I will be moved even more by God."

This, according to the members of the church, is the role that the religious practices and traditions developed in the long history of Little Zion Baptist Church play in the larger community of Greene County. Even with the church structure lying in ashes, those activities help people to "be moved even more by God."

THE REBUILDING: "IT WAS GOD'S SUBMISSIVE WILL"

Media attention to the burnings in early to mid-1996 prompted outside support for rebuilding efforts — from financial and in-kind donations to volunteer skilled and unskilled labor. Little Zion received direct help from people all over the world, enabling its complete rebuilding within a year and the dedication of the new brick building on January 19, 1997. The project cost approximately $282,000, according to Rev. Willie C. Carter, pastor of Little Zion since 2004 and president of the construction company that served as general contractor to the rebuilding effort. An insurance policy covered approximately $116,000, "but we never ran out of money," Rev. Carter noted (9/7/98). As Rev. Lewis and many other members of the church have pointed out, donations allowed the rebuilding to be paid for completely, without a mortgage. Other burned churches have not received this level of support; however, permanent federal funding established under the Church Arson Prevention Act of 1996 has coordinated grants awarded by the National Council of Churches and the Congress of National Black Churches, as well as low-interest loans through the Department of Housing and Urban Development. By August 15, 2000, the NCATF had recorded $8.6 million in grants and $6.2 million in loan guarantee commitments to burned churches.[75]

While outsiders told the story of Little Zion's rebuilding through publicity and financial support, church members described a spiritual journey, from desperation and sorrow to faith and renewal, a church literally reborn out of the ashes of its destruction. Their narratives reveal a worldview where natural events are imbued with supernatural significance.

These stories open with a sense of hopelessness, such as Rev. Oscar Williams's observation that "I guess we sort of felt that all was over, for we had probably $100,000 in insurance. There was a question about whether even to try to rebuild." Rev. W. D. Lewis noted, "With Little Zion, it didn't look like we could hardly make it, but we made it" (9/5/98). In fact, his despair — and that of other church members — seems to have succumbed to the practice of his faith, and to the transcendent experience of God's intention to renew Little Zion. Rev. Lewis's prayers, direct conversations with God, prophesied the success of the rebuilding effort: "One thing about the Lord, He'll show you what you gonna do and what you ain't gonna do. Here you go. If He tell me I make it, then I make it. I ask him all the time. He told me Little Zion would be rebuilt" (9/5/98). Rev. Willie C. Carter described receiving a similar reassuring sign from God:

> About two weeks after Little Zion got burned, I had a vision that the church was up. I had a vision. I went up there and looked around, praying about the church. I come on back and was praying so hard that night. I had a dream and I saw it built back. I was standing up in the road by the big tree over on the right. In my sleep, I said, "Oh! Little Zion is built back!"
>
> I called Reverend. Told him I had a vision. I said, "Little Zion looked like a cross in my sleep. It looked like cross to me." The shape of the church was a cross.[76]
>
> He said, "Well sit down and draw it out."
>
> I went on to the office, sit down and start drawing it out. My vision come back to me. It was the cross. Yes. The cross just like Jesus be on it. You notice the shape of the church now; it's made just like a cross. That's the way the Lord let me see it in my vision.
>
> I holler out, "Oh, the church is built back!" (9/7/98)

The vision assured Rev. Carter of the church's renewal and motivated him to put God's plan into action. He used the cross, the Christian symbol of death and resurrection, as a model for the shape of the new church because God had shown it to him. Thus, Rev. Carter became the instrument of God's creation.

Other church members described the rebuilding as a human effort through which God completed His work. For Deacon Henry Carter, the rebuilding started with human beings picking themselves up and going to work in the face of what seemed like insurmountable destruction: "When we first started, we said, 'Well, everybody's decided to do a little clean up.' People start to say, 'Well, I'll bring my truck.' Somebody say, 'Well I'll bring a shovel.' Somebody say, 'I'll bring one, too.'" These small gestures, seemingly mundane, became infused with the energy of divine purpose for church members who live by biblical injunction. Deacon Carter said: "It's in the book of James about working and faith. You got to have those two to work together. Without work, faith is dead; without faith, work is dead.[77] All we got to do is serve Him. Somewhere down the line, if we just serve Him and trust Him, God will bless us. We can get our blessings. They already prepared for us. It's up to us to apply ourselves, and once we apply ourselves, it may not come when you want it to come, but it always be on time."[78] For Deacon Carter, the blessing of the rebuilding was already in God's plan. But faith in that outcome wasn't enough. In fact, church members had to apply themselves to the task of rebuilding to realize what many later called a miracle.

As Little Zion's members set to work, many expressed surprise at how light the Lord had made their burden, how quickly the rebuilding progressed. Rev. Willie Carter took his sketch of the cross-shaped church, with the added fellowship hall, to Birmingham for blueprints. Meanwhile, the burning's publicity had begun to generate tremendous financial support, as outsiders sent donations to three different rebuilding funds maintained by the churches, the SCLC, and Boligee's Mayor Lavender. Rev. Lewis recalled, "A few of us got together, organized ourselves to raise money. We went out everywhere. The Lord just blessed us with money. I said, 'Well, it'll take about two years,' a year to raise money and a year to build. But the Lord blessed us. He gives us money by the thousands, ten thousands. One year to the day we were back inside. The Lord willing, we come out of debt too. We don't have too much money, but we don't owe nobody. There's no debt. I tell people they ought to be glad of it, because the Lord worked a miracle. I say, 'God worked a miracle'" (9/5/98). Rev. Willie C. Carter said, "It got burned in January. We start building in June and it went back so quickly! Oooh! The fastest one I ever seen in my life. Yes, Lord. It went fast. Then we got back in it, and it look like it never been burned" (9/7/98).

Little Zion in midsummer, 1996, when my family participated
in the rebuilding effort.

At the outset of the construction in June, church members and contractors at Little Zion were joined by volunteers, mostly teenagers, organized by Washington Quaker Workcamps (WQW) to help
the Boligee churches rebuild.[79] Working one- to three-week shifts
throughout the summer, hundreds of WQW volunteers helped speed
the construction. A June 30 *Washington Post* article reported that contractors at Little Zion estimated that the extra help was "shaving as
much as 20 percent off of the time it will take to complete the [struc-
ture]."[80] Deacon Henry Carter said, "Everybody applied themselves
like an education program. We looked around, and everybody started
helping, and the ceiling started showing up. And look around, the
walls start showing up, and the windows start falling into place. And

we all got jumping. All these people, they had it in their heart to work. It was not a burden to them. They sanctified themselves to do this. It was a great joy, everybody working. Everybody looking forward to tomorrow."

While teenagers told *Post* reporter Ruben Castaneda they'd come to Little Zion to right the wrongs of racism,[81] church members took a broader view, telling me the volunteers had been sent by God. Mrs. Mary Constantine explained, "I feel like God sent those people to us. That was part of His doing. Up until now, I don't know why the burning happened, but it was for some reason, and one of the reasons was to bring us closer together. There's a togetherness here real strong now. Everybody just seems close and depending on each other. The church burning brought unity among us and people far away, because people came with love. They just showed so much love, showed how much they cared about us by helping to rebuild the church." In this cultural context, God worked through the volunteers to heal the racial divide, and they did not even need to be conscious of their role in this spiritual drama.

Deacon Henry Carter described the outpouring of help as the fulfillment of "God's submissive will":

When we start our church, those people started coming in from everywhere. I guess out of each of the fifty states there was somebody come in and help. If they didn't come, they sent financial aid. The Lord had people coming together to rebuild, and they had brotherly love. I know we couldn't have put this building back ourselves with the insurance money alone. We needed brotherly love, people coming from north, south, west, east, all over the place, feeling our need. People just were real serious about whatever they thought they could do; they committed themselves. Folks in the mail send money to us by the thousands of dollars. God had opened up their hearts, not only for Little Zion, but the other churches too.

The Lord built all the three churches back in the same year, and nobody was left without. People are still coming. People are saying they have it in their heart to come here and help us. It was one of those things that God willed. It was God's submissive will. God allowed things to happen, but He built Little Zion back better than it was before. He always makes the church membership stronger in faith. After all of these things our faith is a little bit more deep, a little stronger in the Lord. I believe God allowed it. He arranged that some of these things happen to Little Zion members, to make us stronger in Him, to believe that He is Jesus and there is no other greater than Him.

During construction, I think everybody had a smile on their face. Everybody worked just like one body. I never saw things happen like this. I have said it was God's submissive will. God caused things to happen for a time, for a season. This was God's submissive will to bring his people together and apply with brotherly love.

When the volunteers arrived, Little Zion's members embraced them as fellow children of God, arranging opportunities not only to work side by side but also to sing, pray, and fellowship together. The church's women began providing a daily potluck lunch, and the event quickly grew into a small worship service. Deacon Henry Carter recalled:

We decided to have a free lunch for the volunteers every day. Sometimes we almost have a service, joint activities during the hour. Sometimes somebody sing; sometimes they have prayer; usually had a preacher among us; he would say a few words of encouragement. Then everybody'd sing together, harmonizing together. People were feeling good; it was something that I know I hadn't never experienced. Yeah! I had never had that type of fellowship. We had cornbread, peas, collard greens, string beans, cake, and chicken and all the kinds of meats.

It looked like they were so faithful. Nobody wasn't saying nothing, just bringing the food on every day. That was an amazing thing. The food was so good. Everybody enjoyed their food, and when we got through, everybody went back to work, until three or four o'clock in the afternoon. Then they'll go home, get ready for tomorrow and come right back again.

In this fulfillment of God's plan through the unity of African American church members and mostly white outsiders, Little Zion was

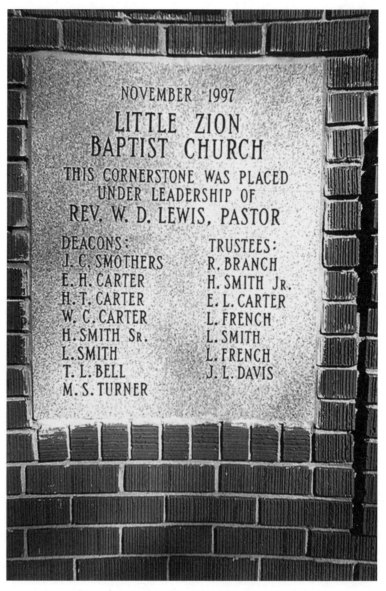

The cornerstone of Little Zion Baptist Church.

rebuilt better than ever before, and faith was renewed. Rev. Oscar Williams recalled speaking at Little Zion's dedication "about how the church represented a place where everybody can come together, black and white, Quaker and Mennonite. They can come together and lift up from the dust and ashes a new monument to unity and togetherness." Mrs. Constantine described a powerful spiritual transformation: "I can't altogether explain what it felt like when the church was finally rebuilt, but it was a glorious feeling, like when you first become in Christ. You feel like you're cleansed, and you feel so happy and overjoyed."

Almost a year after the completion of the rebuilding effort at Little Zion, members added a cornerstone to the new building. Deacon Ed Carter, who said he had wanted such a monument for many years, saw the cornerstone placed just to the right of the front stairs, at eye level to those entering the church, just days before his own unexpected death on December 2, 1997.

This cornerstone joins a brick-and-concrete monument standing to the right of the church entrance that summarizes Little Zion's history on one side, and recognizes past church leaders on the other. (See Appendix for the list of names.) Written by Rev. Oscar Williams, the monument's short narrative provides one of the few public documentations of Little Zion's history by church members. Thus, with the rebuilding effort completed, the church itself declared the restoration of its place in this community:

Little Zion Baptist Church
Founded (circa 1850) on this spot as a "brush arbor" under
the leadership of the Reverend Steve Burnett.[82]
After many years as a large wood frame structure,
the church was rebuilt and bricked in 1970.
Active in the Civil Rights Movement (1950–90s)
this church was burned to the ground January 11, 1996.
With grace, love and labor of scores of
Mennonites, Quakers, members and volunteers,
this church was rebuilt and rededicated to justice and God.
Rededicated November 17, 1996[83]

Tablet donated by Montgomery and Pulaski County, VA. NAACP
in recognition of dedicated work of Dr. Oscar M. Williams
to the peoples of New River Valley and Virginia.
Nannie B. Hairston, area chair —
George Penn, president, Pulaski Branch
Col. William Brown, chief of police, Blacksburg, VA.

Looking back, church members gave thanks to God for the restoration of Little Zion in this community, perhaps none more eloquently than Deacon Henry Carter:

> God was just so good to us and God is still good to us. We just don't have words to express ourselves what God has done for us and that community of our church. We don't have words to express ourselves. If we had ten thousand tongues we wouldn't even be able to keep on saying, "Thank you! Thank you, Lord. Thank you for what you have done for us, all these things." We don't have enough money to repay, saying, "Lord, I give you this for what you done." All we have is grace and mercy. And that's what I am leaning on now, His grace. The scripture says, "Grace was sufficient."[84] But I'm gonna hold onto His grace. Because I believe He'll make a way for me not one time but *all* the time. He has made a way for our church. He has put this church back, and He has made it a little bit more lookable. All this God's work. I give all the praise and honor to Him to how He did it. I wasn't praying such a prayer, but when He did this I'm still praying for God to do His will. Because I knew that if He could build this whole earth in six days, He could just stand these three little churches up overnight. That's what He did.

Looking forward, the people of Little Zion said the church has been revitalized in faith and begun to grow. At the summer revival following the dedication of the new building, seventeen children were baptized, many more than the usual four or five, members reported. Mrs. Constantine said, "A lot of people that wasn't coming to church before is coming now, and more young people are coming back to church." Their attendance was encouraged, too, by the new wing of Sunday school classrooms built in 1998 with a grant from the National Council of Churches.

When Rev. Lewis retired in 1999 after serving as pastor for nearly fifty years, the church entered a time of transition. Initially, Rev. Oscar Williams was appointed pastor, but his declining health in battling Amyotrophic lateral sclerosis (ALS, or Lou Gehrig's Disease) forced him to step down the following year. The church then appointed Rev. Michael Barton, a young pastor who continued to revitalize Little Zion. In the summer of 2003, Rev. Barton noted that since his installation in July 2000, church membership had grown from around 90 people to more than 200, with about 75 percent of the members under age twenty-five. He also noted that the Sunday collection, formerly yielding between $200 and $300 per week, now averaged $1,800 to $2,000 each Sunday. The church had purchased a van to bring shut-ins to Sunday services, to give members a convenient way to visit nearby churches for special events, and to provide field trips such as bowling and restaurant excursions for young people. Rev. Barton said, "The Lord has truly blessed us. . . . The gentleman that preached at my installation service gave as his subject 'Going places you've never been, and doing things you've never done.' And he prophesized over the church. Ever since then, we've been going places — and doing things — that we've never been or never done before."

But by early 2004, Rev. Barton had left Little Zion after trying unsuccessfully to introduce new practices such as foot washing. The church sought a new pastor to help it continue to grow while remaining rooted firmly in the traditions that have kept it strong for generations. By fall, Rev. Willie C. Carter, life member and longtime deacon of Little Zion, had been appointed pastor.

*But ye shall receive power, after that the Holy Ghost is come upon you:
and ye shall be witnesses unto me both in Jerusalem, and in all Judaea,
and in Samaria, and unto the uttermost part of the earth.*
—Acts 1:8

CHAPTER THREE

Recollections by Sister Rosie Lee Hendricks

I interviewed Sister Rosie Lee Hendricks in the home of her cousin, Mrs. Johnnie Busby Jackson, on August 9, 1997. Sister Hendricks had been visiting from Birmingham, and when she heard about this project she asked to participate.

As the conversation began, we were all sweltering in the August Alabama heat. My infant daughter fussed and refused to nurse, and we were distracted by a fly that buzzed around us. Within moments, however, Sister Hendricks had transported all of us beyond these mundane everyday discomforts as she spoke forcefully of her memories of Little Zion.

The interview yielded plenty of details about Little Zion's changing traditions and practices. For example, Sister Hendricks described the old prayer style, which required that the worshipper respond to the Spirit: "pat their hands, pat their feet, move something about. When I was converted (I can't do it now like I used to), I could go down there [leans down] and get it, bring it up: 'I got Jesus all in my soul and I'm so glad!' We used to talk about it." But her narrative is not included here for those observations. Rather, Sister Rosie Lee Hendricks's tale reveals the heart of this project: She told her own life story — with Little Zion Baptist Church at the center. That approach

Sister Rosie Lee Hendricks in the home of her cousin, Mrs. Johnnie Busby Jackson. Sister Hendricks is recalling her conversion experience here.

was shared by the other adults and children interviewed, and by me as I drew the narratives together for this book.

Jeff Todd Titon advocated this way of handling personal narrative as early as 1980. He defined life story as "any purportedly true personal experience story, sacred or secular, that has significance in the storyteller's repertoire."[1] Using language that at first glance might be off-putting to collectors, storytellers, and readers alike, he advocated looking at the life story as a kind of fiction, not necessarily untrue but created out of the play of language: "The language of story is charged with power: it creates. The language of history is charged with knowledge: it discovers."[2] Rather than mining the life story for factual data, which might or might not be provided given the tricks of memory and the impossibility of objective reporting, Titon said the folklorist should look at the life story as a narrative that "tells who one thinks one is and how one thinks one came to be that way."[3] The tale offers to readers its own pleasure, because "we are curious and the life story is intrinsically interesting," as Titon noted.[4]

In this life story, Rosie Lee Hendricks framed all her life experiences, everything she has learned, within the context of her spiritual journey, an "extended sacred personal narrative," in Titon's terms.[5] In reviewing her life of almost eighty years, Sister Hendricks relied on religion — as Patrick Mullen observed about a believer in *Listening to Old Voices* — "now, in [her] old age, to order [her] past and to secure [her] present place in the world."[6] She began, "Little Zion was the only church I knew for many years," and she described childhood milestones such as learning to pray and finding Jesus. She spoke of her marriage as "a blessing," with God providing for the couple to build a house, get a car, pay the bills. She said she recovered from her husband's death when God spoke to her, saying "that John's time was up and he had to go. And that I should continue to live." Finally, she looked forward to her own death as a reunion with Jesus, who would "come on and ease me away from this world."

But it is not the events Sister Hendricks narrated — childhood, marriage, death — that make this the sacred narrative of a religious journey. As Titon asserted, "Instead, it is the teller's interpretation of the events, based on shared, traditional beliefs and attitudes . . . that makes the personal narrative sacred."[7] Thus, Sister Hendricks punctuated her narrative throughout with explanations like this: "I have my ups and downs, / but that's all right! / I know I got JESUS! / Able to do anything but fail! / Jesus looks at me, / He takes care of me, / He feeds me, / He rocks me to sleep! / God is all I got!"

One of the most interesting parts of Sister Hendricks's tale is her conversion experience. I can only hope that this written narrative captures something of the power of her oratory, which should be familiar to readers acquainted with African American religious speech traditions. Sister Hendricks relied on poetic language to reach beyond everyday awareness and embody the contact with the Spirit in her life. This communication is set apart from ordinary speech by markings such as the chant, which "calls forth special attention to and heightened awareness of both the act of expression and the performer."[8]

Within the first five minutes of storytelling, Sister Hendricks noted, "Little Zion, that's where I found Jesus." When I followed up, "Can you tell me a little bit about that?" the conversation quickly shifted gears. As she described the revival that triggered her conversion experience, Sister Hendricks's speech moved into an elevated preaching style, punctuated by short, rhythmically driven sentences with parallel constructions: "My grandmother done prayed over me. The Reverend done prayed over me. Now Dick Knott prayed over me. But I had to pray for myself. I was a hard believer." Moments later the prose fell away, replaced by a driving chant: "She said, 'Keep on praying!' / I said, / 'I can't stop now; / I'm too close! / I'm too close to turn around!'" Returning to a conversational tone a few minutes later, Sister Hendricks declared, "Little Zion look over me. It taught me a lot of things about the word of prayer. And that's what I live on. Girl, I love to talk about Jesus!" When we both laughed appreciatively, and I followed up, "Well, tell me!" Sister Hendricks testified again, providing further details of the conversion experience first in a conversational tone, then quickly returning to a chant.[9] Though physically exhausted and sweating, she gazed heavenward seemingly oblivious to the discomfort, while my questions dissolved into expressions of amazement.

Glenn Hinson documented a similar moment with Elder W. Lawrence Richardson in *Fire in My Bones*. Here, the believer attempted to describe for the folklorist the moment of "anointing" when he feels the Lord's touch:

> "I wish I could just expose this so greatly to you that your heart and mind would set on fire. But if you know not this. . . ." Elder W. Lawrence Richardson pauses, momentarily grasping for words. . . .
>
> Suddenly a cry of "Hallelujah!" explodes from Elder Richardson's lips, transforming his countenance from earnestness to undeniable joy. "Something hit me right then! Sure enough! I ain't kidding you!"

. . . There's no need to ask what that "something" was. If the preceding words hadn't made it clear, the overall conversation certainly had. In those few fleeting moments, Elder Richardson had experienced the emotional transport of transcendence.[10]

In this way, the storytelling event becomes folded into the religious journey itself, as the words of the tale become vehicle for the living Word of God they are attempting to describe. Mullen asserted that these moments of transcendence can be seen as "a rite of passage," pushing the believer "into closer contact with nature and the spirit, and further remov[ing] him from the secular world."[11] As Sister Rosie Lee Hendricks surrenders to the Spirit, her individual life story melts into a larger life story of the human relationship with the divine, told in many different places and many different ways.

Little Zion was the only church I knew for many years. My grandmother and my grandfather raised me. My mother and my father, they say they died on the same day when I was three weeks and three days old. On the eighth of January, 1919. In three weeks and three days, my mama was already gone. Dead from the flu.

My grandmother say my mother took the baby and give it to her. She say, "Mama, ain't nobody got no business with this baby but you."

My father came in, and he wanted to know why that sheet was hanging up there over that door. He say, "Mary? Is she gone?"

They say, "Yeah, Mary gone."

He say, "I don't have anything else to live for."

Then he went on and died. Died before day. Heart attack, that's the word they use now. But mainly he died of a broken heart.

So my grandmother and my grandfather raised me in Little Zion. That's where I found Jesus. My grandmother taught me to pray. She said if I pray, God will bless me. My grandmother sit me up in the chair, I remember, and she told me, "Our Father, which art in heaven." She said, "Say, 'Our Father, which art in heaven.'"

I repeat that.

Today, that's still in me. I have to pray. If I don't pray, things'll go messed up. But if I talk to Jesus every day, if I talk to Him every day, through the night and through the day, things go right. I don't have no certain time to look up and say, "Lord, have mercy." He's a wonderful God; He's worthy to be praised. He's a good God.

And He has blessed me. He's brought me a mighty long ways. I been hungry. I been where I didn't have shoes, where I didn't have clothes to put on my back. But God has blessed me. Whatever I want, He may not give it to me right then, but He always on time. I'm so thankful.

My granddaddy, he was a deacon in that church. And they had a amen corner, where the old ladies sit and moan to the preaching. But they don't have all that now. They done changed it. It's a city church now!

Back then, it was a frame church, with them old seats. They wasn't nailed together; they left a crack in there what you sat down on. Benches. Old benches. They didn't have nothing like they do here. Zion has grown. It really has.

Back in that time, it was more spiritual. Them old folks get in that church; they'd moan, and when they'd get to moaning you could feel something. Preachers now just preaching through the talk. But back then, you better say something!

My grandmother told me, she said she just wanted me to be sure. She said, "I want you to be sure." She told me she'd knock the devil out of me if I come up there and didn't have nothing to say.

I told the Lord to give me something to say, and He did. Child, I had to be sure. When I converted, peoples used to pat their hands, pat their feet, move something about. When I was converted, (I can't do it now like I used to), I could go down there [leans down] and get it, bring it up: "I got Jesus all in my soul and I'm so glad!" We used to talk about it.

You don't talk about Christ now like you used to. You don't *feel* it like you used to. Reason why, the devil got in. The devil just about done took over everything. Easing in, easing up on us.

We don't pray like we used to. I know I don't pray much as I used to. I used to wouldn't iron on a Sunday. I had the thought that everything had to be exact to live.

My grandmother used to tell me, say, "Can't nobody hurt you but your best friend."

So I said, "Lord, you be my friend, Jesus."

I try to treat peoples right. What's the use of living if I don't make nobody happy? If I don't make somebody happy, my living will be in vain.

Little Zion is where I found Him. And I'm gonna hold on long as I'm able. Oh, girl, I can talk about Jesus. Rev. Jennings [phonetic spelling] was preaching that night, the last night of the revival meeting. And all my friends had left me. Already had their conversions. Gonna be baptized and I'm not. I didn't have nowhere to turn to. That revival was gonna close out on me.

I told the Lord, I said, "Now, I still ain't got nothing." I'm the only one left on the mourner's bench. I told the Lord that Friday night that I didn't have nobody.

And the preacher said, "Whose child is this?"

My grandmother got up and say, "It's my grandchild."

He say, "Well, come on round and pray for her."

She went to praying; she fell out. When she went out, I thought the best thing for me to do is to ease out the church! I had to go.

I went on; I left the church. And I told the Lord to send somebody, tell somebody to come for me.

There was a place with white dirt between my house and the church. And I went there down in that white place, down in the ditches. Stayed out all night. "Lord, send somebody! Send somebody!" That's all I can say.

That morning before day, a deacon named Knott, Brother Knott, he come. I heard him that morning before day. I had already asked the Lord to send somebody. I heard him coming, singing, "A charge to keep and a God to glorify!"

He ask Mama where I was. She say, "She out there somewhere."

My grandmother done prayed over me. The Reverend done prayed over me. Now Dick Knott prayed over me.

But I had to pray for myself. I was a hard believer.

When Dick Knott got through talking to me, I said, "Lord, here I come again." I said, "I done prayed every prayer I know to pray. I done everything the folks done told me to do." They told me get on my knees. I did it. When people begin to talk to me, whatever they say I repeat it down in my heart. If you say, "Rosie Lee," I say, "Rosie Lee." You say, "You do such and such a thing." I say, "You do such and such a thing." I was praying down in here [points to heart]. I repeat whatever people said to me. That's the way I was. Girl, I sent up some prayers. Uh-huh.

I stayed up there, till Jesus fixed me. When He got me fixed up, I tell you, I'm all right with Him.

My grandmother went to town; she told me, she say, "Continue in prayer."

When she came back, she say, "Nook?" [phonetic spelling of nickname]

I say, "Ma'am?"

She say, "I thought you was gonna have something to tell me."

I say,

"I got something to tell you

but I can't tell you now!"

She say,

"What you gonna tell me?"

I say,

"I can't tell you now!"

The day I confessed Christ was on a Saturday. A girl was washing. Her name was Beth; she wash every Saturday morning.

She say, "Hey, Nook!"

I say, "Hey!"

She say, "I got something to tell you! You got something to tell me?!"

I said, [shaking head negatively] "Uhnt uh. But I can tell you one thing: God working with me!"

She said, "Keep on praying!"
I said,
"I can't stop now;
I'm too close!
I'm too close to turn around!"
Then Mama told me, say,
"Go out there and get the cow,
and carry on down the bottom;
we got to pick them peas."
I went out there and untied the cow,
and when I looked at my hands,
my hands looked new!
I looked down at my feet,
and my feet looked new!
I said, "I know!"
I looked around
and it looked like the sparkling clouds
was trimmed with gold!
I said, "I know!"
I said, "I know
there's a God *somewhere*!
I *know*
There's a God somewhere!"
About that time, Mama say,
"You going?"
I say,
"I'm on my way."
As I picked them peas,
looked like them peas was hopping!
Lord in me
and I could hear a voice,
say,
"Go and tell Uncle Freed [phonetic spelling].
I done died one time
and I ain't gonna die no more!"
I said, "Mama!"
I said,

Recollections by Sister Rosie Lee Hendricks 97

"Don't you hear that man talking to me?"
She say,
"Ain't nobody talking to you.
That's the devil!"
I say,
"Well, it's still telling me,
don't you hear him say,
'Go and tell Uncle Freed,
I done died one time,
and I ain't gonna die no more!' "
(Uncle Freed was a old man,
about ninety some years old.)
And when I got to the end of the row,
I begun to pull the sack off my shoulder!
She say,
"Girl, where you going?"
I say,
"I got to go and tell Uncle Freed,
'I done died one time,
and I ain't gonna die no more!' "
She say,
"Girl, sit down!"
I say,
"I can't sit down!
I can't be still!
I got to go!"
And I began to pull that sack off,
and I began to run!
And as I run,
I had to go through some woods.
And when I got in those woods,
I was just a cold.
I didn't feel nothing.
I said,
"Lord, if I done told a lie,
I done told a lie in your name!"

I heard a voice say,
"Go, and tell Uncle Freed
I died one time. . . ."
[shouts] And I been *going* ever since!
Every day, every night!
I have my ups and downs,
but that's all right!
I know I got JESUS!
Able to do anything but fail!
Jesus looks at me,
He takes care of me,
He feeds me,
He rocks me to sleep!
God is all I got!
You know you can't mistreat me!
You can't hurt me!
JESUS!
I got Him in here! [Points to breast.]
And I'm gonna keep Him here.

God got me, and He gonna keep me till my time comes. He took my husband; that's all right. He still look over me. I tell Him every day. Shelter me under His wing. "Keep me. Keep me, Jesus. Shelter me." I know I got Jesus! I know it.

I appreciate Little Zion, because I wouldn't have been what I am today. Little Zion look over me. It taught me a lot of things about the word of prayer. And that's what I live on. I'm not educated, but I thank God, whatever anybody else got in this world, He give it to me too. Sure did.

Girl, I love to talk about Jesus. [Laughs.] I love to talk about Jesus.

My grandmother and my grandfather raised me. I stayed with them till I was about fifteen. Then I had to marry. I wasn't expecting no baby or nothing like that. But my grandfather was sort of, well, mean. So rather than get in a lot of trouble, I just eased out and got me a husband. I had to pray for one though, and the Lord sent me a good husband. Yeah, we lived together for fifty-five years. Fifty-five years, six months and twenty-one days. That's my husband. So we had our ups and downs, but we loved one another.

My grandmother paid fifty cents for some material and she made me a little white dress. She paid two dollars for some white shoes, and she cooked me a cake. The eighth of December.

The door to the house wasn't on good. The steps, you had to be careful how you walk up on them. If you don't, you fall through! And it was raining. It rain hard.

They said, "John ain't got here yet; it's raining out there."

I said, "Lord, have mercy on me."

When he did come, he brought a truck with some folks from down at his church. We married right on the porch, right on the steps. You had to hold something to get down those steps. That's where we married. The eighth day of December, 1935.

I thank God for whatever He done for me. Because it's been a blessing. You know I been hungry. My husband and I build a house. He nail a nail and I nail one. Put the top on the house. He got up there; I got up there too. We had some money, we put it on the house. We didn't have no money, he lay his hand on the wall and pray to God.

When I married, I had to work. Cleaning people's houses. Whatever needed to be done, I had to do it. My granddaddy never bought me a book. I had a uncle to buy me some books one time, and I went to the fourth grade. I never had the opportunity. It's been rough, but looking back on my life, it's been joy.

I remember one time, I didn't have no way to go to work. A man brought me home, brought me over the hill and put me out and charged me four dollars. I didn't have but two dollars, and I gave them to him.

I come across the hill, going over to my house. I say, "Lord, all these cars in this world belong to you. I ain't even got a dime. Show me a way to get a car for me, Jesus."

And my husband came on home that Friday evening. He said, "Let's go look for a car."

I said, "Baby, we ain't got no money."

He said, "I know we ain't, but I'm gonna sell some cows and hogs."

He carried them cows and hogs up there and sold them. And he had twelve hundred dollars. And we went and looked for a car.

And the Lord fixed it so every now and then we could pay double, and no kind of problem. I ask Him for it. It's His car. Whatever I want, I say, "Lord, you know what I need." God is a good God, sure enough is. He's a good God.

My husband, I found him dead in the bed. I went to Chattanooga. He fix me my lunch and he give me extra clothes.

He say, "Because you might get sick up there."

I already been sick; they was talking about putting me in the hospital.

When I came back, he was in the bed, dead.

We left at 8 o'clock, and we got back here around 4:30. He supposed to pick me up, and he never did pick me up. And so I called my brother-in-law, told him come on and take me home.

When I got home, he was in the bed.

I said, "John? Is you dead? Is you dead, John?"

Shaking him. He was in a sweat all over.

I said, "John, is you dead?"

And I kissed him and tried to shake him and tried to bring him back. He was already gone.

(He had so many different complaints. He had sugar [diabetes]; he had been hurt in the mine.)

Girl, I want to follow him. What was there to live for? He's gone. All I had was gone. I have no sisters, no brothers, who I'm gonna lean on?

But God always got somebody. I know He been good to me, honey. Yes, Lord. He been good to me. You hear what I say? Every day. You don't own your self. God lent it to you. He don't give us anything. What you gonna carry out with you?

I got a dining room, got a breakfront over there in the corner. And I love pretty dishes, pretty china. I go out of my way to get it.

Recollections by Sister Rosie Lee Hendricks 101

But when my husband died, I walked in that dining room one day. I put all that stuff, piled it in the middle of the floor. It meant nothing.

That's the day the Lord spoke to me, told me He was too holy and too righteous to make a mistake.

I start back to living.

He say, "I'm too holy and too righteous to make a mistake." He let me know that John's time was up and he had to go. And that I should continue to live.

My life been beautiful to me so far, and I so happy to say I know Jesus, and I know Him for myself, because I got to see Him. You can't see Him for me, and I can't see Him for you. I got to see Him for myself. And I know, when my time roll around, I'll be ready. I'm praying for to be ready. Because you never know.

Some of those older members, they go to heaven every night. Cousin Tilly [phonetic spelling] go to heaven every night, and when she and mama get together shelling peas, they'd sit out there and talk about it.

Cousin Tilly used to talk about what she seed. She says heaven is a beautiful place. She says everything up there is white.

She'd say, "I went there last night. Sure did." And she'd talk about it.

Mama walk her home a little piece with her. They'd turn around, walk a little piece this way, turn around, walk a little piece back.

Keep talking about heaven. She'd tell mama it was beautiful up there. Everything is white. I don't know if she was sleeping or what. I imagine she was dreaming.

She'd tell you about angels, watch over you all night while you sleep. Sometimes, that be in my prayers.

I got one time where I couldn't walk. You could point at that foot and it wouldn't move. I couldn't move it myself.

I said, "Lord, is you gonna let your child live in the world, won't be able to walk no more?"

I said, "If I be able to walk, Jesus," I said, "show me a sign. Show me so plain that a fool can understand."

And when I saw myself (in my mind's eye), I saw myself running.

And I began to run. And it come to me, it said, "Is this me running?"

I looked at my foot and said, "Lord, have mercy. This is me running." I been running ever since.

And Little Zion, I love it. I always will love it. We had a program here for the older members.

That's the day I told them, I said, "This is where I found Jesus."

Yes. This is where I found Him. It's been a long time, a long time. 1932, and I still haven't turned Him loose. And I'm getting closer now than ever to the grave, I know. But I know I got JESUS. He ain't gonna let me lay and suffer. When He get ready for me, He gonna come on and ease me away from this world. And I'm ready. Whenever He gets ready, I'm ready.

Whosoever cometh to me, and heareth my sayings, and doeth them,
I will show you to whom he is like:
He is like a man which built an house, and digged deep, and laid the
foundation on a rock: and when the flood arose, the stream beat
vehemently upon that house, and could not shake it: for it
was founded upon a rock.
But he that heareth, and doeth not, is like a man that without a
foundation built an house upon the earth; against which the
stream did beat vehemently, and immediately it fell; and
the ruin of that house was great.
—Luke 6:47–49

CHAPTER FOUR

Little Zion in Church

When I was growing up, the church was just a old wood frame building, painted white. But on the outside the paint begin to blister and to break, break up into small pieces. And you could see that old paint chipping off the walls, chipping away. The church structure was embarrassing when we'd have people come visit us, because the frame building was sort of like leaning, leaning to one side. It was built upon some old cement pillars, handmade by our ancestors a long time ago. And the doors of the church, one door when you opened it, most of the time it dragged against the floor. You had to be very careful that it didn't fall off the hinges. So we had a problem in trying to even pry open the door at times to get inside.

The building was all sanctuary, basically. There were just two back rooms in the church, and no such thing as a pastor's study. It didn't exist. Little Zion was just a overhung shell, where you'd just come in and go out.

People'd come in, and have a hallelujah good time before they went out.

We didn't have any carpeting on the church floor. There was never a hole in that floor. But you could see the weight actually making it sag down. It was made of all pine, but it wasn't painted or anything, just pine wood, natural color. There was no carpeting anywhere, not even in the pulpit. Just all pine. The pews wasn't made of any kind of shellacked wood either; they were made of just pine too. Splinters sometimes would be in the bench, but we still served God.

Sunday mornings at Little Zion. Although it was a church that was leaning to the right, that's where we would go.

— Rev. Eddie Carter

This chapter explores Little Zion's traditions, from the care of the building to the order of services, from the practices marking special occasions like weddings and funerals to the education of children. The concept of tradition is broadly defined here to include both the outward church activities and the interior attitudes and beliefs that give rise to and shape them. Ann Hawthorne summed up this inter-relationship between thought and action in faith communities in her concept of religious gesture, noting,

> Members live their religion by doing it, acting its rites, restating its memories, speaking its hopes, obeying its commands, thus gaining an identity and a world to live in. In these actions members carry on by carrying out the calls and promises of their religion. Their gestures of singing and remaining silent, of praying and preaching, of listening and meditating, of weeping and smiling are not secondary means to other, primary ends. Gestures are not instruments that translate into a language understood elsewhere. These gestures, on the contrary, are the thoughts of the religion they express, the forms of the religion held by its members. Gesturing is a way of holding one's religion, gesturing is a way of being held by one's religion. By attending to gestures, the serious observer working in the field to learn a religion seeks to avoid a reductive formalization that smoothes out its singular features, the eccentric edges that render distinctive the identity of the religion.[1]

Undated photo of Little Zion when it was a frame church,
from Rev. Oscar Williams's collection.

Here we look at the traditions at Little Zion as meaningful gestures that express a cultural perspective — and serve as the foundation for the religious life of this community. It might seem oxymoronic to consider something so apparently ephemeral as gesture to be the solid rock upon which this church is built. But when the physical structure of Little Zion was destroyed, the activities of the church continued. Though fire consumed the building, it could not reduce to ashes the daily religious experience at Little Zion, the gestures passed down through generations. Perhaps the very intangibility of tradition gives it the strength to weather many kinds of storms.

As considered earlier, many members of Little Zion viewed the burning of the church building as a warning from God that they had somehow strayed from the fundamental beliefs and practices of the Baptist faith. They spoke of the literal fire as a sign that they had lost their spiritual fire, and they spoke of a need to revive "the old ways," traditions that allowed their parents, grandparents, and ancestors to maintain a closer, more personal relationship with God.

Mrs. Johnnie Busby Jackson even attributed a loss of spiritual energy to a change in the church architecture — to the loss of the "amen corner" when the brick church was built in 1970. During the 1996 rebuilding effort she unsuccessfully urged the deacon board to restore this area near the pulpit where the older women used to sit and informally lead the congregation's emotional response to the service. She said, "The people of that church, they used to serve God every day. We do it now when there's a need and on Sunday, some of us. In the old church, the older ladies, the mothers of the church, would sit in that amen corner. And during services you could see them praying. That meant a lot to me. Now I'm just looking at their backs in the pews. I'm just looking at the backs of those older ladies." Mrs. Busby Jackson recalled a legendary church mother, Sister Julia, "who could strike a moan here and you could hear it way on that other street down there."

This space was not restored in the rebuilt church, but Mrs. Busby Jackson noted that she has nicknamed one of Sister Julia's grandchildren, "Sister Julia," in recognition of her ability to get the church fired up, suggesting perhaps that the role assumed by the women in the amen corner continues without the traditional designation of seating space.

Rev. W. D. Lewis also spoke nostalgically of this lost space, saying, "The amen corner was a hot corner. Oh, I'm telling you when they sat there that church would burn, would get on fire. You'd get the moan there going from the benches on either side of the front, where the older women of the church, the mothers of the church, would sit" (8/7/97).

But if the burning of Little Zion warned of a loss of tradition among church members, its rebuilding confirmed a revival of spirit. In fact, the church traditions of this community proved cohesive enough to hold the congregation together in the confrontation of a possible hate crime, in the glare of international media coverage, and in the confusion of welcoming and incorporating the rebuilding efforts brought by hundreds of volunteers from many different religious and secular backgrounds throughout the United States and abroad.

This chapter considers church members' sense of how traditions at Little Zion have changed in the past century, influenced by the community's growing prosperity — and perhaps by the nostalgia of memory. Many noted how the style of worship has changed from highly emotional to more cerebral, for example. Sister Rosie Lee Hendricks observed, "Back in my time, the service was more spiritual. Them old folks get in that church; they'd moan, and when they'd get to moaning you could feel something. Preachers now just preaching through the talk. But back then, you better say something! You better pray!" The young Rev. James Carter even suggested that as this community has become better educated, intellectual analysis has been privileged over emotional experience: "Through education, there's a better intellectual understanding now. It's not as hard as it was back then to understand who God is, the purpose of God in your life."[2]

Rev. Lewis, longtime pastor of Little Zion, summed up this community's mixed feelings toward material progress with a folktale frequently recounted in his sermons:

I've attended church in many brush arbors, but not at Little Zion. I've been inside of many churches built of grass; all the churches around here came from brush arbors. But Little Zion was already built of wood when I first came here.

Oh, we've come a long way. Children don't remember the floors having more cracks than the windows and doors. The Lord has kept us. It's like the frogs in the milk jar. We used to milk the cows, and at night they put it in the jar, put it to the fire with a rag tied over it. The heat from the fire would make the milk sour, make the cream come to the top. Later you'd churn the cream to make butter.

Two frogs got on top of the jar and fell in it. Down and up, they'll kick all night long. Next morning, they're sitting on top of butter. We ought to be thankful. (8/7/97)

Rev. Lewis implied that living by tradition, relying on wisdom passed down for generations, has kept Little Zion's members in tune with nature and in accord with God's plan. In the face of scarcity, churchgoers have made the most of physical and spiritual resources, setting the milk by the fire to sour with the faith that cream will be provided. In the mornings, they've awakened to find the butter already churned by the two frogs, unwitting animal helpers conveniently placed in the jar by a higher power. By their hard work and effort, the frogs have saved their own lives and participated in the creation of a miracle. For this, "we ought to be thankful," Rev. Lewis reminded his congregants each time he told this tale. Even if the product initially seems unappetizing, people must recognize and appreciate the miracle of its provision. This is how "the Lord has kept us," Rev. Lewis pointed out, urging that this relationship continue with a balance between faith and hard work, through the gestures of received wisdom.

A SACRED SPACE: "ALTHOUGH IT WAS A CHURCH THAT WAS LEANING TO THE RIGHT"

Little Zion has stood at the center of this community for well over a century, and possibly much longer. The building itself, which has grown from a brush arbor to the contemporary brick structure with a separate wing of Sunday school classrooms, encompasses the religious traditions of this community, which have sheltered and protected it in ways the church architecture sometimes could not. As Rev. Eddie Carter noted in the narrative at the outset of this chapter, even when the people could not afford to adorn Little Zion with material comforts, they "still served God." Those practices symbolically filled the literal cracks in the structure of the church, keeping the congregation warm against the cold, for example. Rev. Carter continued:

> People would come from everywhere in the community to be there on Sunday morning. During the winter months, we hardly ever missed church. If we had snow, snow about ankle deep, normally it would snow during the week, but when Sunday morning comes around, the Lord would send us sunshine to dry the snow up so we could still go to church. It would still be briskly cold but we would go on, regardless of how the wind may blow outside. You could hear the wind blowing against the wall. You could hear the sound of the wind beating against the old windows. You could hear it like it was making music. The wind was coming through the windows and coming through the back door and coming through the front door. The way it would come in, those two doors on each side had a big crack hole on the bottom and on the top. And even though you closed the door, the cold air would still come in. But we still prayed to God.

Many church members expressed a reverence for the church as a tangible reflection of the sacred worship space inside it. In fact, when asked about their earliest memories of Little Zion, almost all members began with detailed descriptions of the church structure, with community recollection in this older congregation centered nostalgically on the wood frame church, built early in the century and torn down in 1970. Certainly, the occasion of the burning as the impetus for this project encourages a focus on the architecture of the church. But these narratives, especially Rev. Eddie Carter's, also show considerable attention to a sense of place at Little Zion, a space juxtaposed with material need and spiritual abundance.

Rev. Carter used the style of the performed African American sermon to point out these juxtapositions throughout his description of the wood frame church. Gerald Davis, drawing on previous work by Milman Parry, Albert Lord, and Bruce Rosenberg, has defined the performed African American sermon as "a verbal mold readily recognized as such by African-Americans in performance; it usually has three or more units structured formulaically, is organized serially in performance, and is given cohesion through the use of thematic and formulaic phrases."[3] In the narrative at the outset of this chapter, for instance, Rev. Carter proceeded by accretion of detail, describing the building's peeling paint, rough benches, sagging floor, and leaning structure. Yet he transformed these observations with the theme of overcoming adversity through faith and religious practice, conveyed by the formulaic phrase "We still served God" (which occurs repeatedly in Rev. Carter's narrative) and through balancing observations about the respected ancestors who built the cement pillars on which the church stood and who made the plain pine benches.

Other church members described Little Zion's old pews with the same respect for workmanship, even though the handmade product did not provide nearly the comfort of today's highly polished benches. These wistful memories even perhaps imply an attitude that a little bodily discomfort kept members more spiritually focused. Sister Hendricks noted, "Back then it was a frame church with them old seats. They wasn't nailed together; they left a crack in there what you sat down on. Old benches. They didn't have nothing like they do here now. Zion has grown. It really has." After a pause, Sister Hendricks added slightly disdainfully, "It's a city church now!" Rev. Oscar Williams concurred, remembering when "Little Zion had old wooden pews, handmade — and not in any carpentry shop. They made these pews with cross-cut saws and hand tools, plain benches, no pillows on them."

But though members remained nostalgic about some material discomfort, Rev. Eddie Carter asserted that the building's overall disrepair had endangered occupants. He attributed the congregation's escape from harm to God's protection. For instance, he said of the church bell, "We had a old bell in the church, up in the loft. The bell would ring at the time when people were gathering to come up to worship. You could hear that bell ring. You could hear it for miles and miles, that bell ringing at Little Zion Baptist Church. And that bell was way up high, sitting on pine beams. Sometimes I had a fear; I thought that bell might break and fall and come down through the roof and ceiling and hurt somebody. But it remained there till they built a new church. It stayed there for a long time. God kept it up there." Little Zion's members showed spiritual strength by continuing to worship in uncomfortable, even dangerous, surroundings, and for this God rewarded them with His protection.

Rev. Carter repeated the theme in describing the church's well:

We didn't have any running water, just a old well with a pump. We didn't have indoor toilets; we had to go outside. If you wanted a drink of water, we had two white buckets in the church, sitting on top of the table with a white cloth, with a dipper on one side of each bucket. You dip your water and drink. Everybody drink from that dipper. You weren't thinking of a germ or disease that would attack the body. Everybody drink from that dipper. I remember the dipper was white with a red handle. And the buckets, you could see where the galvanize had broken, with little chips in the white part. Somebody had evidently dropped them.

The water would come from that well; it was not fresh water. It was salt water, too salty to drink, really. Evidently it wasn't good, because the old pump, the pipes were turning rusty-like, a brownish color. It wasn't anything we should be drinking. It come out of a rock and was salty. So it wasn't good for us. But we had no choice but to drink it. Around that area, we didn't have any city water at that time.

The church well had a old electrical pump. It had two wires that ran from the church, up high in the air. Sometimes those wires was worn out where the rats or something had cut. As young boys, I remember we couldn't go out there unless an adult would go with us and cut the pump on, because it would spark fire, and we could have got electrocuted. It was an unsafe environment that we were in. And some way or other the Lord just kept us, just kept His loving arms all around us.

The white hills near the church.

The link between the church building and the traditions of those who worship inside it reveals itself most clearly in Rev. Williams's memories of the whitewashing of the old frame church. As others alluded to in their descriptions of the handmade pews and the home-made building foundation, the act of caring for the church structure itself helps to bind the community together, with workers passing on centuries-old maintenance methods from one generation to the next, relying primarily on labor and skill and available natural resources rather than expensive hardware supplies. Rev. Williams recalled:

> I remember as far back as the 1940s when Little Zion was simply an old wooden structure, whitewashed. That was before the days when we had paint. The deacons and men of the church would come out and whitewash the church. This was nothing that you would buy out of a store. They went out to the clay hills where you will notice a lot of white clay dirt. That whole area is white clay. They probably went just right under the hill where the church sits,

less than a quarter of a mile away. They would dig down and get some good white clay dirt, mix it with water, sometimes boil it. Just right under the hill, they just dug it out of the ground and whitewashed.

Normally, whitewashing would be done every one or two years, because the rain would wash it off. Often it would be done before revivals or big days like that. Of course, women would come out as well and help, but mostly the men would whitewash the outside while the women cleaned the inside of the church.

Clearly, the gesture of whitewashing renewed not just the church's appearance but also the spirits of the congregation as they worked together to improve the building that was "leaning to the right."

SUNDAY SERVICE: "WE WERE NEVER LATE"

Church members explored the same relationship between material need and spiritual fulfillment in their memories of going to church at Little Zion. For many, lack of transportation made arriving on time for services an additional challenge. Rev. Eddie Carter remembered:

We had to get up to church the best way we could. We didn't have a van that will pick us up and carry us there. We either went by wagon or mule. My grandfather had two mules. And I remember one Sunday we went to church on the back of his wagon. The bottom of the wagon need some more boards in it. All the boards would be shimmying and shaking as the wagon would carry us up the hill. The only joy we got out of that, we would stay on the back with our feet hanging down to the ground. The road was not paved at that time. It was a dirt road and we dragged our feet. We could of fell out of the wagon and gotten hurt.

And when we'd get up there to church with the mule, they'd be all tired, and we'd tie the mule and wagon out by the tree near the church. And I do remember that some people used to ride horses to the church. They didn't have cars and things. That was in the 1960s. All the way up to '63, '64, '65, same way.

Mrs. Busby Jackson recalled walking to church as a young child, hurrying to be on time for Sunday school at 9:30: "We had to walk from way, way away, but we were never late. It was about a mile, a long way when you're four or five years old. We'd walk a piece, and we'd stop and rest. And every house we'd pass, I'd stop and get a drink of water. If it was summertime, you walked barefoot until you got about twenty good steps from the church, and then mom wiped your feet off and you put your socks and shoes on — that is, if you had shoes — and you went on. When you finished, you left the church with your shoes on, and when you got twenty steps away, the shoes came off again." Rev. Lewis commented wryly on the custom of carrying the shoes, saying, "Everybody will be stylin' on the way to church; they will be toting the shoes to church in their hands so they don't get dirty. Then everybody get happy during the service and throw the shoes all away!"

Also, the observation that though getting to church was difficult, "we were never late," was echoed by many other members of the church, who noted with pride how services always started on time. Mrs. Bessie Smith, for example, said, "I like the way they run the service at Little Zion. I like the way they come to Sunday school on time. Nine-thirty was their time year-round, winter and summer. It never go up; it never go down. We always would meet there, and if it wasn't but two people, when 9:30 come we'll start on time. We'll start on time, and we'll come out on time. That's the way we did." Mrs. Mary Constantine recalled, "We had to walk about a mile from home to Little Zion. We used the old path through the pasture and the woods, and we would look down at our watches all the time. Close to 10 o'clock we would take off running, because we wanted to be there on time. We were never late."

Rev. Lewis often admonished the congregation during his sermons for their lack of religious commitment, pointing out how those who drive to church can't seem to get there on time, whereas their ancestors who walked or rode in wagons arrived promptly. For Rev. Lewis and others, this generation's tardiness reflects the lessening of faith in a community grown too comfortable.

Little Zion's Sunday school, held from 9:30 to 11 A.M. weekly, with separate classes for adults and children, helps to preserve and transmit the traditions of the church—from the Baptist belief system to the customs and practices on which the worship services depend. As in many area churches, Little Zion holds full worship services only every other Sunday and shares its pastor with another church. (For several years under Rev. Barton's leadership, the church changed to a weekly worship service. But after the installation of Pastor Willie C. Carter in 2004, the biweekly services resumed.) The Sunday school program offers all of the elements of an abbreviated service. It also serves as a training ground for children and laypeople in conducting many aspects of the service. A child often serves as church secretary, for example, reading the Sunday school minutes and making announcements —and receiving constant encouragement and advice from members of the congregation ("Speak up now! Stand up tall when you're talking to us!"). Young preachers or laypeople who have not yet heard or heeded God's call to preach sometimes give the abbreviated sermon that follows small-group discussion of the day's Bible readings. Members of the congregation, rather than the choir, lead the hymns a cappella in Sunday school, lining out the verses as everyone keeps the beat on the wooden floor. This format not only develops musical talent but also preserves the practice of a cappella singing that was common at Little Zion before the burning and rebuilding. Though the old church contained a piano, members said it was rarely used. Since the rebuilding and the donation of a new piano, however, Little Zion has appointed a pianist who accompanies the choir during worship services.

Many adult members emphasized the lifelong value of Sunday school in transmitting the beliefs and values of the Baptist faith. Mrs. Patricia Edmonds noted succinctly, "And going to Sunday school, I love that. In Sunday school I have gained that you can live your life day to day off of some of the scripture in the lesson. It's in Timothy: 'Study to show yourself approved.'" During the several Sunday school classes I attended, church members relied on a written outline of the lesson provided in *Baptist Teacher*, a publication of the National Baptist Convention, U.S.A., for scripture selections and an outline of discussion topics. The pamphlet includes daily Bible readings and prayer suggestions for practice at home during the upcoming week. The Sunday school lesson quickly moves off of the printed page, however, relying on the oral call-and-response tradition practiced in Little Zion's services and in African American churches throughout the United States. After the opening hymn and prayer, the preacher begins to read the Bible verses indicated for study. Though the text does not assign the congregation any responsibility for this reading, members of Little Zion assume control of every other verse, reading in unison.

This sharing of responsibility for the teaching of the Word is carried forth as the congregation breaks into separate classes for discussion led by laypeople. In one women's Sunday school class, for example, the young leader opened with a confession that she had never led an adult class before, and the older women responded both by advising her to follow the printed outline and by assuming informal control of the conversation. While the leader announced the topic for study and asked for comments, the older women directed the discussion with a pouring forth of increasingly preacherly testimonials punctuated by the group's responses, such as, "Amen, all right, that's all right." Thus, the older women moved the topic beyond the printed page, teaching the teacher as they shared their spiritual insights and demonstrated how to lead the call-and-response.

Of course, the children's Sunday school classes, perhaps more than all others, demonstrate the transmission of the church's beliefs and practices from one generation to another. Sister Porter remembered vividly the books of catechism used during her childhood to instill the Baptist faith in the youngest members of the community:

> When we went to Sunday school, we had these little books of catechism. Now we had to study the lesson like we study our books, because when we got to Sunday school, those peoples were gonna ask those questions, and we had to answer them. We had to *study*. We was gonna know the answer, don't worry. [Laughs.] They didn't have to get the switch out.
>
> I remember the first question in my little book. The lady said, "Who is God?"
>
> I said, "God is our heavenly Father, maker of all things."

She said, "Well, how did He make all things?"

I said, "By His power, He was created and made all things."

The church furnished the little books. I had one here about ten years ago, but it got away from me. They were for little beginners, from five years old on up.

Though Sister Porter alluded to a loss of tradition in the replacement of the catechism with the outlined discussion format in children's classes, adults still take the Sunday school lessons very seriously, as evidenced by the strict discipline maintained in classes. Even young children who fail to sit quietly, pay attention, and participate in the classes are threatened with corporal punishment by teachers, choir directors, and parents who wield switches in church. In my observation, the gesture of reaching for the switch restored immediate order to lessons.[4]

Many adults also pointed to Sunday school as a springboard for promoting religion in family life, as parents are expected to follow up with daily instruction and prayer. Mrs. Edmonds said:

> You have to be taught. Once you get into church, your parents or whoever have you, they need to keep you in church. That way you will grow. It's just like in school; if your parents don't help you with your schoolwork, what do you know? Nothing. I was in Sunday school, and I was taught all the time.
>
> When Timothy mother and grandmother was teaching him, I can relate that to my grandfather and my grandmother who raised me. They used to teach me things when I was growing up; it stick within me now. The way they taught me, in morning time when we get ready for to have breakfast, we have to thank God for the blessing that He have given us, and we thank Him for the night that we lay down, get up and continue on through life. We would gather round the table. Most time my grandmother or my grandfather would ask the blessing. At night we say our prayers, thanking Him too. They would teach us when we first start saying our prayers, "I lay me down to sleep. I prays the Lord, if I should die before I wake. . . ." When we got a little older, they began to teach us the Lord's Prayer. I began to remember a little bit when I was five or six years old.

Mrs. Patricia Edmonds is interviewed while she holds her
granddaughter on September 4, 1998.

The formal instruction of Sunday school continued informally at home throughout childhood. Rev. James Carter remembered the words of his grandmother. "Right in that kitchen," he recalled, "the day I got ready to go to college in Tuskegee in 1979. I'll never forget it as long as I live and God gives me a sound mind. She said, 'Now you're getting ready to leave home, and go on and get your education so that you can get a good job, so that you can better yourself and everything.' She said, 'And all you're getting, in everything you get, don't you forget to put God first.' Now somewhere along the way, somebody taught her that. She had to pick that up in her childhood; it was part of the family structure."

Many adult members decried a lack of informal religious instruction in today's families. Sister Porter said, for example,

Back then, older people taught us church. You was taught to pray. Older people would get on their knees and say the Our Father prayer with you until you learned it. They taught us. They told us, "Anything you want, just ask God for it, and He'll open the way." You know, that's true. That's true. Kids wasn't hard like they are now. If I done anything before other grown people, it was worse than doing it before my mother. Because they was gonna spank you, and then you was gonna beg them not to tell your mother. Because if she hear of it, then she gonna whip you. But now kids talk big, curse, do anything they want to, ain't nobody say anything. We didn't do that.

Rev. Lewis expressed similar regrets with his sense of the change in the culture surrounding Sunday school instruction:

We went to church every Sunday. We had to go to Sunday school. We'd be in church every Sunday morning, all of us. Old folks kept me in a harness. They'd get down and pray.

When folks be in there praying, I'd go out the door!

Old lady'd come out of the amen corner and catch me. I'd tell a lie why I was out of the church.

She'd say, "You go back in that church." She'd round me up.

They told you to go back in the church, and if you didn't go, they would go and tell Mama. If they say, "I tell that boy to go in the church and he didn't do it," oh Lord! You'd better not say that they didn't tell you, because you'd get it sure enough then! She'd whip you, and she'd stop, and you would think she was through with you, and she'd start all over again.

They kept me in a harness. I grew up in church. But now the old folks don't pray and the children neither.

I tell them, say the Lord's Prayer. If you don't know nothing else, say the Lord's Prayer. You pray in the home when you wake up; you got to talk to the Lord. Go in your closet and pray for your family. (8/7/97)

Though it certainly seems likely that in the past few decades expectations have eased for children's behavior at Little Zion — as throughout America — many members' statements suggest that Sunday school lessons have continued to be reinforced by regular prayer and instruction at home. Rev. James Carter, the youngest of the Carter family of preachers, described religion as central to his daily life as a child, and to the daily lives of his children:

I come up in the church. I spent about six years under my great grandmother. I lived with her, slept in the bed next to her. She was just full of the Holy Spirit. Not only her, but my grandmother and granddaddy, and my own parents too. My education in the Bible came from following my granddaddy and my great grandmother. I was just blessed, being around my grandparents and my great grandparents, and all that spiritual experience started for me. I see it now starting for my son. When I was six, seven, eight years old I understood what prayer was; I could sing a hymn: "Must Jesus bear the cross alone and all the world go free. There's a cross for everyone; there's a cross for me." "A charge to keep I have, a God to glorify."

Several children at Little Zion echoed Rev. Carter's memories, singing snatches of hymns for me and reciting prayers. One child said, for example, "They taught me the Lord's Prayer, and they taught me, 'If I die before I wake, I pray the Lord my soul to take.' I pray that every night. In the morning, I say, 'Thank you God for waking my whole family up for another day.' I say that when I wake up every day. Before meals, I say, 'God is gracious, God is good, and we thank Him for our food, all well, Amen, thank you Lord, our daily bread.'" Also, many women described raising their children in the church as central to their adult religious experience. Sister Leola Carter noted, "I got all of my seven children in the church; that's the most important thing that's happened to me since I've been at Little Zion. We took them to church ever since they were born."

After Sunday school class discussions, the congregation reassembles in the sanctuary for a short sermon on the lesson, often conducted by a layperson or novice preacher. On November 14, 1999, for example, lifelong member Frederick Dale Porter offered the sermon, having just accepted God's call to preach the previous day after ten years of consideration.[5] He told the congregation, "For those of you who don't know, the Lord moved my heart in a wondrous way yesterday morning — so much so that I had to proclaim that the Lord has called me to preach the Word. You know the Lord, He's calling people every day, but it's up to us when we will answer Him." As the congregation responded with encouragement like, "Yeah, that's right," Rev. Porter's preaching moved from a conversational style into the chanted rhythm of the performed sermon described by Gerald Davis. In the quote below, church members' spontaneous responses are included in parentheses. They fill the pauses in Rev. Porter's rhythm and help to drive the sermon onward both musically and thematically:

> You know we should pray, and pray without ceasing, /
>   (That's right)
> 'Cause the devil he don't want us to come forward, /
>   (That's right / that's true)
> 'Cause when another man makes it to the battlefield, /
> That's another soul he gonna have to fight. / (That's right)
> The Lord said He's called, He said He's chosen me. /
> Then He said these things: / (All right)
> He said be faithful unto me. / (Yeah, all right)
> You know this is not anything that I take lightly. / (All right)
> If it had been I would of accept this 10 years ago. / (Laughter)
> But you know there's some equipping that the Lord has to do with
>   you. / (That's true)

And there's some things you need to get straight. / (Yeah)
Before you go in the firing line, / (Amen)
Take me down to the potter house, / (Yes sir)
So He can shape me, mold me, the way I should be, / (That's right)
Because He says the battle is not of mine. /
   (That's right/that's right)
It's of the Lord. / (That's right)
So He had to get rid of self, / (Uh-huh)
Take me through some trials and tribulations. / (Uh-huh)

The congregation's responses not only support the performance of the sermon rhythmically, they also affirm Rev. Porter's acceptance of the call to preach and encourage his continued efforts.

As he preached, Rev. Porter wove together his personal experience in response to the call to preach with an explication of biblical verses assigned to Sunday school for this date: The story of Joshua leading the Israelites over the Jordan River and into the promised land. He equated his struggle to heed God's will with the trials and tribulations faced by the Israelites in getting to Canaan. Then he brought the entire congregation into the struggle, saying:

How many times have you come close to the promised land — /
   (All right)
And didn't make it in? / (That's right)
How many times has God knocked at the door of your heart, /
And nobody was home? / (All right)
How many times has He sent his prophets, /
Getting up EARLY, / (Yeah)
Seeking those who're lost? / (Uh-huh)
This is what He did in this lesson. /

In this way, Rev. Porter maintained and transmitted the traditional beliefs of the Baptist faith, narrating the biblical stories and applying them to the everyday lives of the people at Little Zion. He also established himself in an unbroken line of prophets who heed God's call to lead others, following the customs and practices to bring the congregation toward the promised land.

As a novice preacher, Rev. Porter both teaches and is taught by the congregation. Toward the end of the lesson, Rev. Willie C. Carter (at the time pastor of two other churches and deacon at Little Zion), affirmed that Rev. Porter had God working in him. But the older preacher corrected the statement that after going down to the potter house, where God molds you and shapes you, you can do something right. "You can do some good," he said, "but you can only do it through His will." The exchange was good-natured and genial, punctuated by laughter as Rev. Carter said, "I don't want to mess with you, but, wait a minute!" And Rev. Porter invited the critique, answering, "Go ahead!" Rev. Carter reigned in the young preacher's enthusiastic ego, maintaining the long-standing role of the Baptist preacher as one called by God to be a humble vessel for divine work.

Little Zion's worship service, held from 11 A.M. to approximately 1 P.M. on first and third Sundays,[6] is the most sacred time of the week for church members, as they offer their beliefs and practices to, and hope to receive spiritual guidance and nourishment from, their very personal God. In reflecting on countless Sunday services, many in this community detailed again the position that Little Zion has lost some of its religious zeal as the congregation has become materially richer. They looked back nostalgically to services from childhood, when the difficult physical conditions seemed to correlate with deep spiritual commitment. Rev. Eddie Carter, for instance, ordered a preacherly narrative around a serial description of the practical challenges posed to worshippers by the seasons of the year. He said of winter:

> They had one stove to warm the inside congregation in the wintertime. And we had to go outside to get firewood to keep it going. And of course, we would all have to sit around the stove. I went in some days with my feet getting cold. Went in some days with gloves to keep my hands from getting cold. Went in some days with a overcoat, sitting by the fire trying to have worship service. There was no such thing as central heat. You just be in there around that fire stove in the cold. But within our hearts it was warm, because we were serving God. We never did give up on serving God.

Underneath, the church was not sitting on anything. It was sitting way up high off the ground. And the air could just shoot up from under there. The floor was cold, but the heater would keep us warm. We would all get around that heater. Sometime we would get too hot, had to get up and go back to the second seat. And when you get too cold, you'd have to go back to the hot seat. You couldn't never get comfortable. You just keep moving from one seat to the other. Too hot, too cold, just kept going back and forth. But we never stopped serving God in church.

Reverend Lewis would preach. He'd tell you go ahead and warm up and let's have service. And one of the old people would normally strike a hymn. And the services would go on.

Many others remembered vividly the winter cold and the uneven heat from the wood stove. Mrs. Constantine said, for example, "In the wintertime, we had this old, big, potbelly heater. When they fire that thing up, you had to sit way back. You couldn't sit around close to that heater." But none summed up more poignantly than Rev. Carter the persistence of the congregation that, as he repeated formulaically, "never did give up on serving God."

Rev. Carter continued to preach on the challenges of spring at Little Zion: "When the spring of the year would come, and it was raining most of the time, we had to go around the other side of the church, around through the woods and come up the hill. The church didn't have a proper road. There'd be water, slop, mud, all alongside the way. More than once my father's truck got stuck in the mud and we had to get out in our Sunday suits, roll our pants legs up, and push that truck on up the hill. Because we were going to church." Here, the phrase "because we were going to church" takes the place of the formulaic statement about faith, leaving the listener to make the connection: "We were going to church . . . because we never did give up on serving God." Rev. Carter punctuated this narrative by placing these formulaic statements at the end of the description of each season, emphasizing the transcendence of faith and practice over each season's obstacles.

Rev. Carter depicted summer with a vivid image of the congregation using their fans to beat away the insects that attacked during worship:

During the summertime, we had a problem with a lot of wasps. We didn't have air-conditioning; we didn't have ceiling fans. We didn't have screen windows. And the church was wood. We'd have to raise all the windows up, six long windows with a high, probably sixteen-foot-high, ceiling. A lot of insects, gnats, wasps, came on the inside. And when we were serving God, worshipping God, you'd see all the dirt daubers, they would fly in around the ceiling. And they'd be in large numbers, and we had to fight them off. Sometimes they would fly down and come get you close nearby. We would take the fan and beat them, bat them down. But that didn't stop us from serving God. We served Him right on.

Though he did not specifically identify his description of fall at the close of this narrative on the seasons, Rev. Carter was clearly referring to the time of late harvest when the persimmons ripen. He said, "Not too very far away from the church there used to be a old tree, stood there until the 1960s. There used to be all kinds of fruits on it, all kind of good sweet fruits around the church. We used to go out there and pick the simmons from the tree and eat those things after service. Everything was nice back then to us as kids." Interestingly, Rev. Carter departed from the depiction of physical challenges in this final season. The narrative seems to imply both that the struggle has been won by those who never gave up throughout the year and that the battle has not yet been entered by the children still innocent in their understanding of worldly and religious hardships. The performance of this narrative, which advances through the accretion of detail and repetition, follows a complete life cycle, through the seasons and adult understanding and back again to childhood beginnings. At that time, Rev. Carter said, "[Little Zion] was the most happiest place we would go."

In the rebuilt church, members gather for the worship service on polished benches, under the color-suffused light from the stained-glass windows that line both sides of the church. The flip of a switch triggers central heat in the winter, air-conditioning in the summer. Yet, perhaps due to budgetary concerns, much seems unchanged. On winter mornings in the late 1990s, the heat was not turned on until the service began and the congregation crowded around a kerosene space heater while the church warmed up. On many stifling August evenings the air-conditioning remained off and church members cooled themselves with paper fans. Likewise, worship practices seem to express something of this culture's past.

As congregants took their places for worship throughout the 1990s, strict gender roles became physically clear. Facing the pulpit, women and small children sat to the right, men to the left — with the deacons on the front bench. If children became restless during the service mothers sometimes handed them off to fathers, but they had to traipse across the church to do so. Rev. Williams observed, "In our church and in all the churches nearby, the men sat on the left side, women on the right. It's still almost a tradition. It's not rigidly held to, but invariably the older men will go to the left side of the church, and their spouses and others will sit on the right. Of course, the middle will be there for guests. Kids: It depends on how big they are. The older kids usually sit together somewhere in the middle or the back." This seating arrangement reflected the overt male control of the church; there were no female deacons in front, no female preachers in the pulpit. In fact, with the loss of the amen corner, where the older women sat until 1970, women literally were relegated off to the side in service activities. Of course, outside of Little Zion many of these same women held down full-time jobs and raised families single-handedly.

Rev. Williams, however, vowed in 1999 to change traditional gender role expectations for women at Little Zion. He said, "I will be controversial as a pastor, for I will say whoever is called — male or female — can preach from the pulpit in Little Zion as long as I am pastor. I will not practice discrimination according to gender. We will have females on our deacon board and on our trustee board. When female ministers come to our church, they will be welcomed to the pulpit. I find it interesting in the black church that religious discrimination is practiced by people who ought to be painfully aware of how painful discrimination is. Yet they practice it." Rev. Williams predicted that resistance to this change in tradition would come from both men and women at Little Zion. But he believed that the congregation would accept his moral leadership:

The congregation will follow the lead of the pastor. The men will not like the idea, and I dare say, most of the women will probably still say, "Well, I don't think no woman's got no business preaching." I think most of the women at Little Zion will say that. They will not fight for a woman to be in the pulpit preaching.

But they probably will not leave the church, and that's probably because they respect me. They are just waiting for someone who they know, love, and respect to come and say these things, to take a real stand.

I fully expect that other preachers will have something to say about it. But they can take their opinions and go to Florida or any other hot place. That's somebody else's problem; it ain't gonna be mine at the pearly gates.

Interestingly, Rev. Williams attempted to overcome ingrained attitudes about women's roles by invoking long-held community beliefs about God's wrath toward injustice. He added, "When I warned Little Zion that God is gonna pour out His spirit — and already has — on our flesh, because we discriminate against women preachers, they said, 'Well, we understand, Pastor.'"

By the following year, Rev. Williams's illness had incapacitated him. The church, busy searching for a new pastor, had not appointed any women to the deacon or trustee boards — or admitted female preachers into the pulpit.

When Rev. Michael Barton was installed as pastor in mid-2000, he continued Rev. Williams's efforts to change rigid gender roles. He combined previously separate men's and women's Sunday school classes, and he asked families to sit together during service. He also said he would welcome women to preach at Little Zion. By 2004, however, Rev. Barton had departed, and the church had turned to Rev. Willie Carter for leadership. In mid-2005, church members reported that women had not been appointed to traditionally male leadership positions, and previous seating customs during services had been largely reassumed.

From the late 1990s through early 2000, Little Zion's worship services featured sermons by numerous preachers, both because members worshipped at nearby St. Matthew Baptist Church during the rebuilding and because Rev. Lewis stepped down after almost fifty years as pastor and Rev. Williams succumbed to health problems shortly thereafter. During my fieldwork, I heard at least eight local ministers preach at Little Zion. All worked in the tradition of the performed African American sermon, speaking without written notes, relying on the chanted rhythms of call-and-response. In general, the younger preachers had received more formal theological training, although Rev. Lewis, who was born in 1903, graduated from Selma University.

The clear contrast between Rev. Lewis's preaching style and those of the younger ministers at first seems to confirm the notion that there has been a shift from heart to mind in Little Zion's service — away from more emotional ways of understanding and expressing religious impulses toward more cerebral analysis. Many members of the church found Rev. Lewis's speech difficult to understand. When he preached, his oratory quickly moved beyond prosaic, explanatory language into a poetic chant where words drew their meaning not from expository definition but from musical inflection and association. It is as if Rev. Lewis's language itself became a gesture reaching from the physical realm we can measure and dissect, into the mystery beyond it. He said about his preaching, "All services ain't the same. You're not the same all the time either. Sometimes you can't hardly control yourself. You get in a certain place and you can't hold it. . . . It's too much for words. When you get in the Spirit, you don't know how you act. Afterwards, you know what happened, but you can't describe it" (8/7/97).

In fact, many said they believe Rev. Lewis to be a prophet, implying perhaps that his inspired language transcends ordinary speech, as a conduit for the voice of God. Mrs. Busby Jackson explained, "Reverend has a direct line to God. He doesn't have to wait for a sign. Whatever the problem is, he goes directly to God. When he comes back he has the answer and he's satisfied. . . . This is how God talked to the prophets in the Old Testament. . . . When Reverend really gets into the preaching he says, 'MY God!' That's HIS God, nobody else's but his right then. And bless his heart, he'll just cry; tears will just come down his face. He'll just cry." Mrs. Edmonds pointed out that if

Longtime pastor Rev. Lewis preaches in October 1996, with the
young Rev. James Carter behind him.

you read your Bible you could understand much of what Rev. Lewis
said, because he was "basing his life today on the Bible what happened
yesterday." Thus the very struggle to understand the words of his
sermon becomes a spiritual exercise. The fact that Rev. Lewis still
preached at Little Zion with such fervor in his late nineties deeply
impressed Mrs. Edmonds and others, who heard strength and wisdom in his language. Mrs. Edmonds added, "I tells him all the time
that he is a walking Jesus. Doesn't matter what happen to him, he
come right back real strong. If he gets sick or has to go to the hospital,
the next Sunday he's with us again, up strong, talking strong."

Little Zion in Church 131

Rev. Lewis described the human being as two spirits: "The flesh is a sinful spirit, but you got a Holy Spirit. And that Holy Spirit, it makes the sinful spirit behave. You have to go forth on Christ." In contrast, Rev. James Carter sometimes called on God to rule the whole being, the combination of mind, body, and spirit. In one sermon, for instance, Rev. Carter talked of materially successful people who are empty:

Because they have failed to get /
That what they need the most. /
And that is God, / (Amen!)
Allowing Him to regulate the whole being: / (Yeah, right)
Our minds, our bodies, our spirit, /
The whole being. / (Oh yeah)

In the sermon, Rev. Carter and other preachers use the call-and-response more directly to appeal to both mind and heart, sometimes inviting intellectual understanding, other times working the emotional connection. For instance, later in the sermon quoted above, Rev. Carter made a pointed argument for gender equality between married couples. In fact, he even directly addressed one church member (Leroy), whom the community knew had been struggling with this issue.

But the problem is /
We still live in a day when /
We got male chauvinism, Leroy. /
"I'm the man!" / (You're right)
"What I say goes!"
And sometimes it's just the opposite. / (Laughter)
My granddaddy always said /
There's a weak man /
When there's a woman running the house. / (Yeah, that's right)
Well, in order to have /
A house that is ran right /
Both man and woman /
Must be filled /
With the love of God, / (All right!, yeah!)

Must be controlled /
By the spirit of God, / (Yeah)
'Cause he didn't make /
Male and female /
For one to walk /
Behind the other. /
He made us /
That we would complement each other, / (All right, all right)
That we would walk together, / (All right)
And that we would be a good example /
For our children. /

Rev. Carter used the call to elicit the status quo reaction, that the man should be in control ("There's a weak man / When there's a woman running the house. / (Yeah, that's right)"). Then he attempted to transform this belief by setting it in opposition to another traditional attitude, that man must allow God to be in control. As he worked the congregation into responses of "yeah" and "all right," he used the sermon's form to push for acceptance of an argument about the need to change cultural attitudes in this community.

Yet upon further reflection, the contrast in Rev. Carter's and Rev. Lewis's preaching styles becomes less stark. Many members of the Little Zion congregation noted that Rev. Lewis's preaching became difficult to understand only in the last decade of his life. Rev. Willie Carter noted, for example, "He [Rev. Lewis] got a good heart and a desire to deliver the sermon. There's still power there. But he got old. Most people can't understand what he's saying anymore" (9/7/98). In this light, the acceptance of Rev. Lewis's style of preaching seems not so much to affirm a form of worship as to express respect and reverence for the preacher who, as Rev. Willie Carter put it, "is one of God anointed" (9/6/98).

Also, Rev. Carter and other younger preachers at Little Zion have not turned completely, or even predominantly, toward a more cerebral use of call-and-response. In fact, Rev. Carter followed this argument for social change with the sermon's highly emotional epiphany, where his words become punctuated by the quick intake of breath and language almost falls away. He concluded with the altar call, inviting congregants to experience a conversion to faith or renew their Christian commitment, and people clapped and shouted, "Preach! Preach!" Rev. Carter's voice boomed out:

We got to serve today, huh /
Oh yes, huh /
If we, huh /
Want to walk, huh /
In the newness, huh /
Of life, huh /
. . . In Tishabee, huh /
In the state, huh /
Of Alabama, huh /
In the United States, huh /
Of America, huh. /

In this latter part of the service, emotions run high as people stand to offer short testimonials of faith, or turn and kneel before their seats to pray silently or out loud.

In fact, Rev. Porter, the young minister who accepted the call to preach in November 1999, described his consciousness not in the currently popular terms of mind, body, and spirit embraced by Rev. James Carter but in language that echoed Rev. Lewis's description of the "sinful spirit" and the "Holy Spirit." He said when God originally called him to preach ten years earlier, "I knew, but my natural man didn't want to know. And I was more of a natural man then than a spiritual man. So the natural man won out. It's really like any everyday situation where I sort of know what I should be doing, but yet, I don't *really* know! And I know that it's time for me to make a change in my life, but I'm not *really* ready! And then, it's not so much that I'm not ready. It's more, 'I can't.'"

Finally, Little Zion's recent pastor, Rev. Michael Barton, attended seminary and had formal theological training, but his preaching style was highly emotional. From the moment he inadvertently dropped the pages of his first sermon on the floor, Rev. Barton said he has preached "more from what the Lord puts within me. . . . As the Lord speaks to me, I share. I love listening to the Spirit." During the sermon I attended on July 20, 2003, Rev. Barton shouted, whispered, shed tears, and danced up and down the center aisle as he exhorted listeners not to just "go to church" but rather "*be* the church!" After hearing the title of this project, Rev. Barton interrupted his sermon to note, "Shelly, you done blessed me so much this morning!" Then his voice rang through the church:

> I understand now why so many people /
> Can *greet* you in such a respectful way /
> On Sunday morning and *treat* you /
> In such a bad way on Sunday night! / (Laughter, Amen!)
> I can fully understand why! /
> It's because maybe they have only just been *baptized* /
>   (All right, yeah)
> With water, and have not been *baptized* (By fire!) /
> WITH THE HOLY GHOST FIRE! (Yeah! All right!)

As an outsider without a long history of experience at Little Zion, it is very difficult to see subtle changes in worship styles. I rely on what church members share with me — and often events seem to confirm those descriptions. Yet sometimes explanations are more complicated than they would initially seem. Certainly, many church members described a lessening of emotional emphasis at Little Zion over the past generation. But it is impossible to be sure how or why that change has played out in the hearts and minds of those who pray in this church on Sunday mornings.

That change also would be difficult for an outsider to perceive in Little Zion's music program, which creates an emotionally charged religious experience, both in the performing and in the witnessing of the song. Sometimes, as in Sunday school, the songs begin spontaneously as the preacher or another church member prays out loud, for instance, and one of the deacons or older women begins to line out a hymn. Most of the time, music punctuates the service with selections by the pianist and choir. As C. Eric Lincoln and Lawrence H. Mamiya asserted in *The Black Church in the African American Experience*, "In most black churches, music, or more precisely singing, is second only to preaching as a magnet of attraction and the primary vehicle of spiritual transport for the worshiping congregation."[7]

Deacon Ed Carter described beautifully how the hymns intertwine with the preaching at Little Zion to move him spiritually:

> I always liked to sing. Before I got religion, I had a dream; I saw myself singing, "This little light I got, I'm gonna let it shine. Oh, this little light I got, I'm gonna let it shine." Now I was a sinner then, but I saw myself in my dream in the church, singing that.
>
> When the preacher's preaching good and folks get to singing, I get so tickled. When I feel the Holy Spirit I get tickled, go to laughing. Big Mae and them say they can tell when I get fired up. I go to patting my head and tapping my foot and laughing. I be just laughing in the church.
>
> Big Mae and them, they watch me. When I reach up and pat my head, they say, "Oh, the preacher's gonna get him now." They say when I don't do that, well, that preacher ain't preaching good. They watch me just like a hawk watch a chicken!
>
> "Brother Carter, we didn't see you patting your hands and you didn't laugh none. You didn't feel nothing today?"
>
> "Well, not enough to tell nobody!" (8/7/97)

Glenn Hinson touches on the relationship between song and preaching in *Fire in My Bones*, referring to a comment by a member of a small African American church: "Song . . . is one of the three 'walking sticks' of faith, standing alongside prayer and preaching as a basic support on the heavenbound journey. . . . So in every service — be it Sunday morning worship, midweek prayer meeting or even afternoon funeral — the saints raise their voices in jubilant praise."[8]

Like many black churches, Little Zion has a long-standing tradition in which hymns are handed down through generations as young people feel called by God to sing. As Joyce Marie Jackson pointed out in "Music of the Black Churches," "Religious music often enters the lives of church members during childhood. Most Black religious music, especially as sung at this age, is passed on aurally. It is very rare for a Black traditional church not to have a children's or 'cherubim' choir, as they are so often called."[9]

One ten-year-old Little Zion boy recalled his early experience singing solo during worship: "The first time I start singing, that was Easter Day. God told me that Saturday in my mind, He said, 'You should sing a song, and this song should be "If I had Wings I'd Fly Away."' That's what He told me. I went to my grandma during the service. I say, 'Can I sing "I Know I Been Changed" and "If I had Wings I'd Fly Away?"' She said, 'Yes.' So I sang those on that Easter Sunday. Some people cried and some people shouted. That's when I start singing. I was nine years old. I'm ten now." Though only ten years old, this child already understood musical performance at Little Zion to be a communication by and with God, moving both singer and audience in response. He described the experience: "I just feel it in my heart to sing. It just feels great, because my mind, everything will go blank while I sing what God has given me to be able to sing on out. When I sang 'I Know I Been Saved,' Mrs. Busby, she had started crying because I had sing that song so good. My whole body was just comfortable. It feel like God was just coming in my body and taking over, singing, singing. I practice that song that night, and then I pray and I ask the Lord for to help me sing it in the morning time. And then when I sing it, some people be crying and stuff."

Hinson used similar language to suggest this sense of transcendence through song in African American churches: "Obeying the Word,[10] the saints lift their voices in exaltation, accompanying passionate words with clapping hands, patting feet, swaying bodies. The singing stretches up, reaches out, and touches within; it simultaneously magnifies the Lord's name, heartens hearers here on earth, and welcomes the indwelling Spirit."[11]

Of course, as parents attempt to teach their children the power of music at Little Zion as a religious experience, sometimes the tradition is not passed on quite so gracefully. Sister Porter, who served on the choir for more than forty years, remembered how her mother forced her and her brother to join the choir:

> My mother was a good singer on the choir, one of the best there. My brother and I were supposed to start on the choir. My mother say, "Come on the choir."

My brother says he didn't want to sing. He was older than me, getting to be a little man. He just told her he wasn't gonna sing.

So she went out the back door of Little Zion and broke down a switch. Then she put it on him, gave him a good whipping.

When she came back to see where I was, she found me sitting on the choir stand with my book open! I'm ready for singing, because I didn't want what he had. I was sitting on the choir with my book open. Not gonna be hitting on me in church! And I've been on the choir ever since, all my life.

In 1997 Sister Porter said she was considering stepping down from the choir because she wanted to make room for young people to grow into the church in this way. "I can't help the young people by holding my position," she reflected. "I should get down and let the young people to do it."

As in other areas of church life, a few members pointed to a loss of tradition in the changing role of music at Little Zion during the past several decades. Like many other African American churches, spirituals passed down through generations have given way in recent years to the more formalized arrangements of gospel music. The older songs could be sung without instrumental accompaniment; they were developed through complex harmonizing and inserted into the service as a somewhat spontaneous expression of the worship experience. Because of this informality, these hymns could be led by those in the church who did not have the overt power to control the dynamics of the service, namely the older women considered the church mothers. But with the growing popularity of gospel music, Little Zion has moved toward a more structured music program, culminating with the recently hired pianist who accompanies many of the hymns.[12] An eight-year-old boy summed up, "In '98, everything started changes. We got a new piano player, and we got new songs and a new church." In the face of all of this newness, however, longtime member Sister Rosie Lee Hendricks said:

> They don't sing them old hymns that they used to sing now. They say you're ignorant when you don't do that stuff you used to do. There's all that stuff gone away. But I'm gonna hold onto mine.

I am. The young people now trying to sing hymns, but the old folks done forgot about them old hymns they used to sing. Johnnie's mother and I used to love to sing, "This time another year, I may be dead and gone. But before I go, I want you to know." Oooh, her mama could sing that hymn. Her mama could sing. "What a Friend We Have in Jesus." "I Shall Not Be Moved." "Come and Go to That Land." My favorite song is "They said I wouldn't make it, but I'm still here." I love that song. They said I wouldn't make it but I'm still here. Johnnie's mama know she could sing that song. And another: "I'm So Glad Trouble Don't Last Always."

Alan Lomax noticed this shift in the kind of music sung in African American churches as early as 1942 in a recording session at First African Baptist Church in Clarksdale, Mississippi. He was told by research team member Lewis Jones, "What is going on . . . is a big power struggle in the church. The preachers are taking charge. It used to be that the sisters and the old deacons ran the service. They raised the songs, they kept them going, and those songs brought the mourners through. But they've lost most of that power now. The preacher controls the choir and the pianist and the music director. And so now he runs the service. His bunch holds the floor with the new gospel songs that the old sisters and deacons don't like and can't sing. The church is pushing those songs right across the country."[13] In contrast, Lomax described the popularity of "Dr. Watts' style" hymns, classic Protestant hymns recorded by Dr. Watts in the 1707 *Hymns and Spiritual Songs* but lined out in African American churches with an oral complexity unrecordable on the page:

They so prolonged and quavered the texts of the hymns that only a recording angel could make out what was being sung. Instead of performing in an individualized sort of unison or heterophony, however, they blended their voices in great unified streams of tone. There emerged a remarkable kind of harmony, in which every singer was performing variations on the melody at his or her pitch, yet all these ornaments contributed to a harmony of many ever-changing strands — the voices surging together like seaweed swinging with the waves or a leafy tree responding to a strong wind.

Experts have tried and failed to transcribe this riverlike style of collective improvisation."[14]

Little Zion's members remain nostalgic for Dr. Watts'–style hymns, making comments like, "Give me a good, old Dr. Watts."

SPECIAL EVENTS: "THERE'S A TIME FOR EVERYTHING"

Of course, Sunday school and worship services only begin to describe the regular activities at Little Zion. About once a month the church sponsors an afternoon program, which usually begins around 2 P.M., following a short break at the conclusion of the service, and which sometimes lasts several hours. Church auxiliaries such as the choir, the usher board, and the women's mission conduct these services to raise money for Little Zion, recommending hefty admission donations (such as $20 per person) and inviting members of nearby churches to attend. Sometimes, a potluck church supper follows in Little Zion's kitchen. (When Rev. Barton assumed leadership of the church, however, some of these fund-raising functions were discontinued in favor of fellowship activities such as bowling and eating out. The fund-raisers were restored under his successor, Rev. Willie Carter.)

During my fieldwork, I attended an annual Choir Day celebration, featuring performances by many local church choirs; an annual Youth Day program, including preaching and testimonials to inspire young folks and performances by local children's choirs; and the yearly state march, with song and sermon concentrated on welcoming Little Zion's church family home from the far reaches of the United States. All of these programs offered church members the formal opportunity to share their worship traditions with nearby congregations, as each included most of the regular features of the Sunday service, from scripture readings to hymn singing to the passing of the collection baskets. They also promoted a sense of church community beyond Little Zion, as people from the area churches gathered afterward to share a meal or just chat before heading home.

I attended only one church supper at Little Zion, the one marking the very special occasion of the dedication of the new church building. Remarks by several women suggested that perhaps the custom of providing dinner following special programs had waned as the population of the church had grown older at the close of the twentieth century. Mrs. James (Jane) E. Anthony said, "I used to do things like take food for events. I used to like to cook and bake. I'd make macaroni and cheese, corn muffins, greens cooked in a big boiler. I usually take about two pies or cakes, plain cakes like pound cake. I don't like cooking now. There's a time for everything. But if we gonna have a dinner at Little Zion, I'm still busy fixing it. There's just a few who fix now. Prior to, all of the women would cook, for Women's Day, Men's Day, or whatever."[15] Mrs. Busby Jackson also remembered food being served more often at Little Zion when she was growing up during the mid-twentieth century. Before the kitchen was built in the 1970s, church dinners were served outdoors, picnic style. Mrs. Busby Jackson said, "Just about once a month, you'd cook for the church, because one Sunday out of every month there'd be something. Each auxiliary in the church would have a special day set aside to raise money for the church. Everybody just cook and help on that day. Before they built the kitchen, people just cook and bring their food in a basket, and served it from right there, from either the car or the wagon. Then maybe next month it would be Choir Day. It would be the same thing all over again." In fact, several members recalled that when plans for the kitchen were under way, Rev. Lewis initially objected based on a taboo against serving food in a house of God.

Regularly scheduled special events at Little Zion also include the week-long summer revival that culminates in baptism ceremonies, which is explored in Chapter 5, and a Christmas play performed by the children, which I did not have the fortune to attend.

Weddings and funerals also mark other important occasions for the church community. Little Zion's members provided much more insight into funeral practices than wedding customs, perhaps because customs do not dictate a church wedding in this community. Many people report getting married at home or at the preacher's home, or even in secret. In this way, Little Zion extends beyond its physical structure, serving as the foundation for the practiced gestures of the wedding ceremony among church members in any setting.

The wedding of Mr. Derek French and Ms. Felicia Smith at
Little Zion on September 5, 1998.

I attended one church wedding, that of Derek French and Felicia
Smith on September 5, 1998, reportedly the second marriage to be
consecrated in the new building since its January 1997 dedication.
The ceremony, which lasted less than an hour, packed the church to
standing-room-only capacity and featured a large wedding party of
bridesmaids, hostesses,[16] and ushers. The best man used a flambeau to
light dozens of candles on large stands in the front of the church, and
a white carpet was rolled down the center aisle before the bride entered the sanctuary. Pews were decorated with white bows and green-
ery and draped with beads.

The bride and groom enjoyed apparent freedom in decorating the
church, in choosing a guest minister, and in making musical selections ranging from traditional hymns to gospel hits to pop tunes, sung
by a male/female duet, a cappella and with piano accompaniment. In
fact, Mrs. Constantine noted that "weddings can be done however
you want, but if it's something that did not agree with Rev. Lewis, he

Decorations at Little Zion for the Smith-French wedding.

wouldn't let you bring it in there. He would be outspoken about it." During one church wedding, for instance, "they moved the sacrificial table out of the sanctuary, and that's never supposed to happen. Rev. Lewis was walking around, standing tall. He said, 'Where is it? Don't take it out of here anymore. If you've got to move it, move it. But always put it right back. Never take it out of the sanctuary.'" The gestures of the church ceremony can be personalized as long as they remain respectful of the occasion and the space.

The weddings of those married in other settings rely completely on the ceremony to transform a secular space into a sacred one. In describing her 1935 home wedding, Sister Hendricks strongly emphasized the material lack in her surroundings, from the rickety steps to even the uncooperative weather. Yet the ceremony seems to transform those details, infusing them with God's grace. For though conducted in externally meager circumstances, the union was blessed. Sister Hendricks noted that God had sent her a good husband, and

Smith-French wedding attendees.

He kept the couple in a loving relationship for fifty-five years. "Fifty-five years, six months, and twenty-one days," she added. Wherever Sister Hendricks stood to receive the marriage blessing became a sacred space, especially as she looked back on it from her perspective of a long and happy marriage.

My grandmother paid two dollars and fifty cents for some material and she made me a little white dress. She paid two dollars for some white shoes, and she cooked me a cake. It was the eighth of December.

The door to the house wasn't on good. The steps, you had to be careful how you walk up on them. If you don't, you fall through! And it was raining. It rain hard.

They said, "John ain't got here yet; it's raining out there."

I said, "Lord, have mercy on me."

When he did come, he brought a truck with some folks from down at his church. We married right on the porch, right on the steps. You had to hold something to get down those steps. That's where we married, the eighth day of December, 1935.

Sister Hendricks's juxtaposition between material need and spiritual nourishment recalls the narratives discussed at the outset of this chapter, in which Little Zion's structure is held together by the practice of those worshipping inside.

Sister Porter asserted that a church wedding "ain't no big thing" in recalling how she and her husband eloped many decades ago: "I got married in secret. I didn't tell anybody. My mother told the story like this: 'When she got married, I was sitting right here in this house feeding the baby, and I didn't know till it came out in the papers.' I didn't want no big church wedding. If you don't, you don't. Ain't no big thing." Thus, the sacred power of the ceremony to join a couple in marriage resides beyond the boundaries of the church.

While church members feel free to marry in secular settings, they stay close to Little Zion for funerals, where rites are performed in the sanctuary and burials take place in the adjacent cemetery. Though I did not witness any funeral services during my fieldwork — and church members did not detail these rituals — I collected extensive narrative on the practices surrounding the service, from the preparation of the body to the burial.

For much of the twentieth century, limited health care resources meant many in this community died at home rather than in hospitals, without access to a conveniently located funeral home serving African Americans. Instead, church members handled the burial preparations. Sister Hendricks, whose parents died on the same day in 1919, described the custom of hanging a sheet over the doorway after a death to separate the dead from the living — and to allow for privacy in tending the body. She explained, "The curtain hanging down meant, the dead person over here, the live person over there. That sheet hanging up there, it kept people from just coming in and looking on my mother when she was dead." Sister Hendricks, just three weeks and three days old at the time, was told that as soon as her father saw the sheet hanging in the doorway, he knew the flu had killed his wife. She said, "My father came in and he wanted to know why that sheet was hanging up there over that door. He say, 'Mary? Is she gone?' They say, 'Yeah, Mary gone.' He say, 'I don't have anything else to live for.' Then he went on and died. Died before day.

Heart attack, that's the word they use now. But mainly he died of a broken heart." The sheet in the doorway triggers the widower's grief, which, according to family lore, proves to be so powerful that it kills him before the sun rises again.

Before telephones became commonplace in Greene County, the church sexton,[17] always male, would toll Little Zion's bell to alert the community that someone had died, Rev. Williams recalled:

> He'd ring that bell for a different length of time depending on who had died. If he rang it only thirty minutes, that was somebody in the community who had died. But if he rang that bell for about an hour, that was one of Little Zion's old soldiers had gone on in. They called it "tolling the bell."
>
> Those boys could pull that bell in a special way so that the striker would hit and seem to say, "Goin' home. Goin' home." Not everybody can ring an old church bell. But them boys knew how to pull it. It would say, "Goin' home. Goin' home," and you could hear it for *miles* around. Miles away.
>
> Folks would be in the cotton field and hear it. They'd say, "Well, I guess that's Sarah. She's passed." We didn't have telephones out there. But you'd know what had happened. Sometimes, we'd be in school and they'd ring that bell. We knew that somebody had died, somebody who had been *low* sick.

The striking of the bell had a language of its own, communicating specific information recognizable only to those raised in this church tradition. Rev. Williams also noted that each of the ringers pulled with his own style, distinguishable to those who had heard the bell tolled countless times. "You could tell who was ringing the bell by the sound of it. People would say, 'That's George Croxton ringing that bell,' because he'd pull it so much. Not everybody could toll the bell."

After the community learned someone had died, funeral preparations began. Until the mid-twentieth century, when a store in Boligee began selling caskets, many families built their own. Sister Gladys O. Smothers recalled that her husband, Deacon Jonas Smothers, often would be asked to pick up the lumber in his truck. "They would make the casket and line it with fabric. They took some white fabric and went down the sides inside and tacked that in there. Then they laid the body in there." At least until midcentury a few caskets also were kept in storage under the church, Rev. Williams explained, "so that if someone in the community died and the family could not afford a funeral, we had a casket ready." Deacon Smothers and Rev. James Carter both recalled the tale of Henry Carter, Rev. Carter's great-grandfather, who once was sent to Boligee to pick up a casket in his wagon. "He went up there, got in a domino game, and stayed all day and all night," Deacon Smothers said. "He didn't come back home. He stayed so long that they finally sent someone else to get the casket. They said the horses had done pulled the wagon and they was eating grass. They sent him to get the casket, and the man got into a domino game and didn't come back." Rev. Carter added, laughing, "He was a big domino lover."

Several of the church's women would bathe and dress the body, "maybe put turpentine on it and stuff of that sort to prepare for the funeral in a couple of days," Rev. Williams said. The body would be laid out at home "on a cooling board," Deacon Smothers noted, and members of the community would keep a vigil before the funeral, "just sitting up all night with the body," his wife added.

Invariably, the community relied on Deacon Smothers to move the body — at first only from the home to the church for the funeral, in later years to the professional undertaker in Eutaw or Demopolis. Everyone agreed that this responsibility fell to Deacon Smothers because he owned one of the few trucks in the neighborhood. In fact, his wife recalled that one time someone died in a mental hospital in Mobile and Deacon Smothers "had to go out there and get the body and bring it back here. Mobile is around nearly 200 miles."

Deacon Smothers said he never felt uncomfortable around the dead, asserting, "I could go get the body, and the body could lay out there in the back of the truck and I could go to sleep. It wouldn't bother me as far back as I can remember." Sister Smothers added, "That's true. I remember he told me once he went to get someone and he got sleepy. He pulled on the side of the road with the dead person in the back of the truck and him in the cab. He just took a nap." She laughed, "The dead people couldn't outrun him! The living couldn't outrun him, so you know the dead couldn't!"

Deacon Smothers would bring the body to the church before service, "and again, they would pull that church bell. They don't do that now,[18] but they used to do it back then. After bringing the body in, just toll that bell way up there. It's a great big bell. They'd have that big bell just rocking the church," Rev. Williams said. He added, "The body would be there sitting in the back in the casket while we were having Sunday school, regular service, and on until the funeral."

Rev. Williams also remembered in great detail how until very recently graves were always dug by hand at Little Zion:

> The men of the church would meet on the day of the funeral and dig the grave. I've dug plenty of them. Normally, the funeral would start around eleven or twelve o'clock. Somewhere around five or six o'clock in the morning, the men would gather out there. Sometimes we would just finish digging the grave about the time the funeral would start.
>
> We always kept measuring sticks under the church so that we knew how long, how wide to dig the grave. We had spades and shovels under there. We probably still have some shovels somewhere around the church from those days, and I dare say there probably are some churches still digging graves that way. Normally, we dug six feet. Very few graves are now dug six feet; most are just dug deep enough to put a vault in. But that was the formula: Six feet and they put that pine box in there. Normally, you'd sit two pieces of wood in to rest the coffin on. Then you nail it shut, put the dirt on it and mound it up. The dirt gets mounded up. I have dug plenty of them, out on that hill many a day. It was just something that the men of the church expected themselves to do. It's that simple. Somebody would call you and ask you to come out and give them a hand.

Rev. Williams noted that construction equipment was used in Little Zion's grave digging for the first time in 1999. "We didn't plan to change the way the digging was done. We were digging a grave and hit that white rock. When you're down there with that pick, and it's jumping back at you each time you swing it, you look for help. We told the Carter boy, 'Go get your backhoe.'"

Though the prevalent use of undertakers in recent years has meant that many of Little Zion's burial practices have been abandoned, church members expressed few regrets at the loss. While in other areas of church life, church members have greeted traditions changed by prosperity with mixed feelings, here they showed some relief at no longer bearing the full responsibility for building the casket, bathing and preparing the body, and keeping the all-night vigil in the home. Even the bell-ringing tradition, an art lost to the convenience of the telephone, seems to have passed without comment.

Only the digging of graves by machines appears to trouble the congregation. Rev. Williams noted, "When we started digging graves using backhoes and equipment, I can remember one family saying to me, 'Boy, that's mighty disrespectful, y'all bringing out that stuff to dig. That's mighty disrespectful. You all ought to take the time to dig with your hands.' People complained, but the complainers weren't the diggers!" The objection to the digging of graves by machines underscores the meaning this community attributes to the burial ritual. The men of the community gather to dig the grave — not simply because it needs to be done — but as a last gesture of concern and caretaking for the one who has died. For many, the use of construction equipment seems like a shortcut, an effortless — and therefore poor — tribute. They respect the practice of digging the grave by hand for the same reason they miss the rough-hewn church benches made by hand by their ancestors, now replaced by comfortable, ready-made pews.

Little Zion's members expressed tremendous gratitude that the burning did not force the church to relocate — and to abandon its ancestors. After the burning of nearby Mt. Zion Baptist Church, site problems prevented the congregation from obtaining the necessary building permits — which meant the rebuilding had to take place more than a mile from the church cemetery. Little Zion's burial ground, which reportedly has been used since the church began, contains marked graves from as early as 1918. Church members believe,

Grave with wreath in Little Zion's cemetery, July 2003.

however, that earlier burials took place, but the graves are unmarked. Rev. Williams observed that the church has kept few written records of burial site locations, relying instead on the grave markers and the memories of the grave diggers: "I have been down there when we started digging one grave and run into another. You've got to close that up and move over. We have poor markings, poor cemetery records as to who is buried there. It started off, 'Well, we gonna have the Hubbard line coming across here. Beneath them will be the Smith family, running side by side.' But after a while folks die, and folks who have not participated in the grave digging do not know. Some of the headstones wash away. We even have fifteen or twenty graves outside of the property we own. We have not surveyed, and we've lost track of the boundaries."

Interestingly, though, I have never seen anyone visit Little Zion's cemetery, and several church members expressed discomfort with the graveyard. Mrs. Busby Jackson refused to give me a tour, saying she hates cemeteries so much she had watched the burial of her father from her car nearby. Sister Porter noted, "I have my mother and two brothers, and God knows who all else, over there at Little Zion. I hardly ever go out to the cemetery, and I only go out there by myself. I don't like to talk about it either. But sometimes I can hardly stay here in the house, thinking about my mother, my brother, my husband, all over at Little Zion."[19] The markers, including large cement slabs, flat marble nameplates, and headstones adorned with plastic flowers and wreaths, remain somewhat overgrown for most of the year, until the community tends the graves and removes debris on periodic clean-up days.

LITTLE ZION PREPRIMER SCHOOL: "YOUR FOUNDATION IS REALLY LAID ON"

The space next to the cemetery, where the paved parking lot meets grass, remains empty now. But many in this community still point out the former location of Little Zion's three-room elementary school, which operated until 1957 and was torn down in the 1970s. The church school provided not only a basic elementary curriculum but

Undated photo of Little Zion's school, from
Rev. Oscar Williams's collection.

also instruction in the beliefs and customs of this religious community, and former students speak nostalgically of their experiences there. Mrs. Busby Jackson, for example, noted, "Your foundation is really laid on growing up in that church school. If you're anything like me, and it meant anything to you, you preserve every bit of that." As previously mentioned, some of the wood from the school was used to build Mrs. Busby Jackson's current home.

Though written records and oral recollections of the exact year in which the elementary school began have been lost, the oldest members of the community reported attending Little Zion's school as early as the 1920s, when education was offered for only three months of the year. Under Alabama's segregated school system, Little Zion operated as a public school, church members reported. In fact, throughout Greene County, black churches operated schools for children who were excluded from local secular schools. "Each church had a community school, because for a long time all we had around here were horses and wagons. Parents couldn't take their children far to school," recalled former Little Zion teacher Sister Gladys Smothers. Church members agreed, however, that schools operated by local Baptist churches such as Little Zion, Christian Valley, and Spring Hill received very little governmental support. Rev. Oscar Williams noted, "Little Zion was officially a public school, but it was supported very heavily by the church. For example, the teacher may have been paid for about three months. But the community folks chipped in and paid the teachers with corn, chicken, meal, molasses. Every year when school let out, folks would bring stuff to give to the teacher. My mother went to school when there was anywhere from three to four months a year of teaching."

Sister Smothers, who taught on a nine-month schedule at the school from 1944 to 1957, said when she first came to Little Zion the county provided no resources other than a few textbooks. "They had to share the books, with you carrying it home to study one night, and another child the next." Three teachers,[20] one of whom doubled as principal, taught all subjects, including art and music, Sister Smothers remembered, noting that each was responsible for one two-grade class of about thirty students. Teachers and parents provided all classroom supplies, from paper to crayons, to arts and crafts materials, she said. Students studied on pews carried from the church on Monday morning and returned on Friday afternoons for services. Sister Smothers noted, "In later years another school somewhere near Eutaw received some new desks, and they gave our school their old desks. So that cut out moving church pews from one place to another."

As with other aspects of church life, Little Zion members recalled somewhat nostalgically the practical hard work with which the school community overcame material hardship. Sister Smothers's father built the teachers each a desk, she recalled, and fashioned blackboards out of wood painted with dull black paint. Rev. Oscar Williams noted that all of the furniture in the school was "homemade, wooden benches and tables. Nothing store-bought until later years, when the white school gave us their hand-me-down desks and chairs." Rev. Williams also recalled that the school relied on kerosene lamps until electricity finally arrived midcentury, "and then we had one bulb on a string, hanging down." Every few months, the students would oil the wood floors with used motor oil, he added, saying, "That would keep the dust down. We'd oil the floors with black oil. Then, of course, we would sweep the yard clean with brush brooms. They'd go out and cut them and sweep the yard. For a clean yard was a yard with no grass, with brush marks."[21]

Each fall the school held a fund-raiser "feast" to raise money for supplies, according to Sister Smothers. Women would cook baskets of food to be auctioned among the men for up to $2, she explained. "The women would cook it, and most of the time the men would buy it. My box would be sold to your husband, for example. Some would eat it right there, and some would take it home."[22]

School at Little Zion was in session from 8 A.M. to 3 P.M., Sister Smothers recalled, noting that most students walked a couple of miles to and from school until the 1950s, when the principal's husband began driving the children who lived farthest away in a covered pickup truck. "That was the school bus. The kids sat on a bench around the back of the truck," Sister Smothers said. Before the school day began, children collected drinking water and carried wood to fuel the heater. Since the school had no running water and no well, children brought pails and jugs to fill at the nearby spring, the teacher remembered. "Water was a problem at the school for a long time," she said. But she also noted that the need for firewood posed an even greater challenge: "I think the hardest thing was getting the fire going. The parents used to haul the wood there, sometimes in these great big logs. The kids had to cut it into lengths to fit the heater. We had to go out and get the wood, even if it was raining. Sometime we'd have coats and shoes drying all around the room. Sometime the parents in the community or the church would buy a load of coal from the truck when it came around, and they'd say, 'Put a load up at the school too.' Then we'd put a great big lump of coal in the heater with the wood. But most times we just burned the wood." Several former students spoke wistfully of foraging for kindling in the woods. Rev. Willie Carter said, for instance, "Oh, it was a beautiful time. The young boys had to go out around the hillside, pick up sticks, get pieces of wood and bring them back for them big old wood-burning heaters. We kept the school warm. We didn't have no gas at that time, and didn't have no coal. So the young boys would go out and break the sticks and bring them in to keep the young girls warm." Laughing, he added, "And to keep the teacher warm. That's what we done. Ooh, it was beautiful."

The school day officially began with prayer. "Each morning we would have devotions," Rev. Williams said. "Unless the weather was bad, we would line up outside the school, sing a song, do a pledge of allegiance, then file in by grades." Sister Smothers said morning devotions often were conducted in the principal's classroom, where "we would sing and read a verse or two from the Bible. Sometimes the kids would recite a Bible verse. Usually, we recite the Twenty-Third Psalm every day." Then the kids would file into their respective classrooms. "It was just a long straight building with three classrooms lined up," she added. "The principal taught in the middle room and we were on either side."

The teachers conducted lessons on a flexible schedule, usually with math, reading, and science in the morning, and spelling, history, and geography in the afternoon, according to Sister Smothers. The school offered instruction in arts and crafts and music once a week, she added. With limited supplies and without the aid of technology such as mimeograph machines, teachers relied heavily on the repetition of copying and memorization as educational techniques, Sister Smothers said. "You'd read it off to them or put it on the blackboard and they would copy it down. Of course, until about third grade they're writing slow and some of them are still using that big writing. It took a long time."

As explored in Chapter 2, the need for children to help with farm and household tasks also hampered education. Sister Smothers remembered, "Quite a few parents would keep kids at home to plow or help plant or cultivate. We had to tell them, 'Baby, you just try to come when you can.' They'd bring their homework in late and fall behind. Sometime you could tell the smaller brothers or sisters, 'Tell John I want him to do this page or that at home,' to help them keep up." Rev. Williams noted, "In the early spring when it came time to plant cotton and corn, very few students went to school. They had to stay out and plant. During September and October, very few students were in school. They had to pick cotton and get the corn in. They would start coming to school in the latter part of October, first part of November." Sometimes parents even kept children out of school to meet the mailman, Sister Smothers said, explaining that since the mailman didn't deliver to every house, people had to walk to meet him. "So sometime the kids were just sitting up there waiting on the mailman: 'Mama said I had to go to the mailbox.'"

Rev. Williams noted that education was in a "very pitiful state" during his childhood, which he attributed not only to limited supplies and poor attendance but also to a lack of extensive formal education among teachers. Sister Smothers said she obtained a two-year college degree before teaching at Little Zion, and later returned to university to complete a bachelor's degree. Rev. Willie Carter remembered vividly, however, that when he left Little Zion to attend Greene County Training School, now Paramount High School, he found himself far behind in many subjects. "That time was really heavy for me," he said. "It looked like I didn't know *nothing*. Lord, I was so far back. I was just like a fellow that was blindfolded, couldn't see nothing, didn't know nothing" (9/7/98).

Almost everyone interviewed remembered the strict discipline teachers employed to keep kids focused on their schoolwork. Sister Smothers said teachers and parents knew each other well in this tight-knit community and worked together to maintain order in the classroom. Corporal punishment was accepted and expected, with parents telling teachers, "If mine cut up or he don't do what you say, let me know. Or you go ahead and spank him," Sister Smothers said. Rev. Williams added, "Yeah, we got whippings. The teacher would send you out to get your own switches. It was not something she was afraid to do. If she needed to whip you, she'd whip you. And when she got through whipping you and told your mama about it, then you'd get another whipping when you got home." Mrs. Busby Jackson recalled:

> One day when I was about nine or ten, we were all out on the playground, and we were talking crazy. You know, I just wanted to be part of things. I was the sort of kid the rest would deal with only

if they had to. I thought if I did something different, I would be "in." So I told this girl a certain joke with some bad words in it, and what does she do but go back to the teacher and tell it. And I got a whipping for it. She whipped me, and there was blood. She drew blood.

So when I get home, oh, I'm all puffed up and everything. "Mama, she whipped me! Mama, she did this to me! Mama, she did that to me!" I knew I was gonna get another whipping if I said why she whipped me. So I didn't say that. Mama asked why and I didn't say.

Mama said, "I'll find out."

The next day, Mama's at school to find out what happened. That was the worst part. The teacher had to tell my mom what I said. Now, we don't talk like that. No! So Mama thinks it over and she says to the teacher, "Now, any time my kids do something wrong, you have my permission to whip them. You can whip them all right, just don't draw blood."

And that was that. I never said those words anymore for a long time, and I won't say them now. I tried to do something to get "in," but after I got that whipping, I said, "If this is what getting 'in' is gonna get me, I think I'll just get 'out' and stay 'out!' "

Many people recalled vividly having to gather their own switches. Mrs. Busby Jackson noted, "When we would gather the wood, we had to gather a switch for ourselves. You brought the switch up and you put it in the corner, as if to say, your switch had your name on it. And that switch was used as often as *you* liked. So if you didn't want the switching, you stayed in line. You came in, you did your work, and that was that." Many described their childhood fears of corporal punishment with exaggeration. Rev. Williams noted that the classroom walls were lined with "long switches, about, maybe the length of this room," and Mrs. Busby Jackson described one teacher who, "when she would whip you, she would almost jump in the air, she would hit you so hard! She really would!"

Church members spoke with awe of their teachers' power and emphasized how this motivated them to learn. Sister Courtney Porter said,

Mighty few kids didn't learn back then. I can tell you that, because those teachers didn't play.

I never had a whipping about my lesson but one time. I was in third grade and we was doing fractions. The teacher put a three on the board and a one-half on the side. Told me to subtract one-half from three whole numbers. I didn't quite understand how you done that.

Then she got her paddle and she told me what to do. She got my hand and she was spanking it with that paddle. She say, "You have to borrow one number from the whole number." Smack. "Take the half number from the other number." Smack.

When she got through, I learned fractions *that day* in school.

Mrs. Busby Jackson said she still fears her elementary school teacher, Mrs. O'Neal [phonetic spelling], decades later. She recalled a chance meeting after thirty years: "She said hello and I said, 'Yes, ma'am.' In that moment, I think everything she ever taught me came back. I couldn't answer her, 'Yes.' I said, 'Yes, ma'am.' She could walk past you and take a chunk out of you just like that and never crack a smile. She really could. But you got her lessons. You sure did. She was beautiful as a teacher."

In fact, several people expressed regret that corporal punishment is no longer permitted in public schools, asserting that order cannot be maintained without physical punishment. Rev. Willie Carter said, for example, "Now the teachers can't whip them no more. You can't even discipline them. I think that's a little wrong, because they gonna need discipline sometime" (9/7/98).

Of course, kids who behaved well and completed lessons quickly enjoyed comparable rewards, most memorably, according to Rev. Williams, the chance to run an errand outside of school. "Every now and then the principal might need a few pencils, or might want to mail a letter. They would send some of the students they thought were smart and mature down to the store about a mile or so away. That was a joyous gift."

Lunch was served in an adjacent building, many church members recalled. One woman did all the cooking, with ingredients supplied by parents and supplemented with USDA-issued products such as orange juice, peanut butter, canned fruit, and dried beans, members said. "In the early days, even the milk in the lunchroom was provided by parents," Sister Smothers noted. Later, the local milkman delivered to the school. "Most of us ate whatever the lunchroom served," Rev. Williams said. "I think it cost maybe fifteen cents a week. But there were some who could not afford that, who brought their own, for the average family may have made a dollar and a half a day when I was growing up."

After afternoon lessons, the school day closed with prayer. Rev. Williams recalled how the entire student body would line up outside the school: "The teachers would do a watchword and then they'd dismiss us. We'd take off under the hill running, heading home."

Occasionally, Little Zion sponsored special performances to show parents what students were learning, Sister Smothers remembered. For example, the Christmas program and the May concert were regular features each school year. The children recited poems and sang songs, and parents occasionally gave them gifts for performing well, she said. She also recalled that toward the end of the school year, another local school would host an art exhibit, and students would display items such as embroidery, soap carvings, bookends, or ashtrays. The school limited the number of evening activities, however, out of consideration for hardworking parents. "The parents would have to walk up to the school at night, and some were just too tired to do that very often," she said.

Little Zion's elementary school closed several years after the Supreme Court's historic *Brown vs. Board of Education* ruling declared segregated school systems illegal. Greene County finally consolidated local church school populations and provided busing for students to attend Greene County Training School. The move did not eliminate segregation, however. White parents withdrew their children from the public school and paid for admission at an all-white private school.

Though it operated on a very limited budget and provided what some called a limited education, Little Zion Preprimer School is still honored by church members for giving them resources under difficult circumstances. Rev. Eddie Carter summed up the feelings expressed by many when he said, "The school was historical. My father attended that school. My mother attended that school. The whole community attended Little Zion School. It was just a blessing to the community, not only educationally but spiritually too. People learned how to read and people learned how to write. People learned important lessons in that little school."

And people say they are still learning important lessons at Little Zion. Even though for much of its history the building was leaning to the right, that's where the congregation would go, Sunday after Sunday, shoring up the physical structure on the foundation of tradition. Perhaps in the act of attending service and going to school, in the participation in countless weddings, funerals, and other special events, Little Zion's members have absorbed the church's "leaning" as a cultural perspective, as much as they have absorbed the more easily identifiable practices of the religion and the belief system stated neatly in the Sunday school catechism. In these repeated gestures of religion at Little Zion, members have created, as Ann Hawthorne asserts, "an identity and a world to live in."

*And ye shall know that I am in the midst of Israel, and that I am
the Lord your God, and none else: and my people shall never be ashamed.
And it shall come to pass afterward, that I will pour out my spirit upon all
flesh; and your sons and your daughters shall prophesy, your old men shall
dream dreams, your young men shall see visions;
And also upon the servants and upon the handmaids in those days
I will pour out my spirit.*
—*Joel* 2:27–29

CHAPTER FIVE

Little Zion All in the Soul

My conversion was around '59. I confessed one Saturday night
under Rev. Lewis. To me, it's different the way children are
confessing now. Back then, we just couldn't be still. They don't
believe in all these testimonies now like in the old days. You ask
the Lord to show you all those things, and you feel the Lord
has freed your soul. Children nowadays just have a belief. But
back then we were testing it.

I had asked Him for a sign. You go out in the woods and pray,
go to yourself. They always told us you need to be by yourself
when you're praying. So I would go out in the woods, sit there
and ask the Lord to move a certain star in the sky. These things
would happen. You would see the star start crossing.

The star moved. I still didn't believe it. I knew I'd seen it, but
I still didn't believe that the Lord moved it.

I confessed Christ that Wednesday night, but I didn't really
believe it. So I came back and just asked the Lord for some
more testimony. I still wanted the Lord to show me a sign. I
say, "I've seen people have the Holy Ghost so they shake and
can't be still. I want you to just shower me with the Holy
Ghost."

It was the last night of revival. Something came in me this
night, saying, "You must believe." It just kept telling me that.

"You must believe that you are a freeborn child. You must believe."

Still, I sat there. I was crying just uncontrollable, couldn't keep the tears away. All of the sudden, something just lift me up off that seat. I tried to sit there and couldn't. I couldn't stay on that seat. I can remember just like it was yesterday.

I started talking, and it just looked like words was coming from everywhere. I just felt so light. I just felt so good. I was screaming and hollering.

It's a feeling that you could never forget if you once had it. It's an experience that you would never forget.

— Mrs. Mary Constantine

In this chapter the exploration of Little Zion's traditions continues its inward trajectory, focusing not on the church's role in the larger communities of Greene County and even the nation, or on the activities shared among members as they gather for church-related events, but rather on individual religious experiences and their expressions in this faith community. Until recently, folklorists have not concentrated heavily on matters of personal belief, as many scholars have pointed out.[1] Leonard Norman Primiano noted, for instance, "The folkloristic study of religious belief and believers should emphasize the integrated ideas and practices of all individuals living in human society. Indeed, while such an interest in the individual would seem to be a major concern of the scholar of religious folklife, it, in fact, has been the least examined element."[2] He went on to call for the field to "enlarge its focus to emphasize the individual as the creator and possessor of a single folkloric world view, who constantly interprets and negotiates his or her own beliefs."[3]

During my fieldwork, church members responded most enthusiastically to questions concerning their personal experiences of religion at Little Zion. From the initial conversion that gave the believer full membership in the church, to the signs, voices, and visions that provided evidence of God's continuing care and protection, to the call to preach experienced by some as the responsibility to carry their spiritual experiences back to the community in the spreading of

God's Word, talk of faith moved immediately beyond a recounting of church history to become a dramatic witnessing of the power of the Spirit in people's lives. It is important to note that my status as an outsider to this community probably served to encourage this transformation, the conversational nature of the interview easily accommodating testimony by the saved for the benefit of the unsaved.

Indeed, I actively pursued this transformation of the interview. As a Quaker, the personal experience of God speaks directly to my own religious faith in the Light Within. Quaker scholar and teacher Thomas Kelly described this belief memorably in *Testament of Devotion*: "Gladly committing ourselves in body and soul, utterly and completely, to the Light Within, is the beginning of true life. It is a dynamic center, a creative Life that presses to birth within us. It is a Light Within which illumines the face of God and casts new shadows and new glories upon the face of men. It is a seed stirring to life if we do not choke it. It is the Shekinah of the soul, the Presence in the midst. Here is the Slumbering Christ, stirring to be awakened, to become the soul we clothe in earthly form and action. And He is within us all."[4]

Quaker religious expression, both in the formal worship setting and in the informal conversations surrounding it, is highly personal but very restrained, a single, small voice in a quiet community. Kelly continued, "The basic response of the soul to the Light is internal adoration and joy, thanksgiving and worship, self-surrender and listening. The secret places of the heart cease to be our noisy workshop. They become a holy sanctuary of adoration and of self-oblation where we are kept in perfect peace, if our minds be stayed on Him who has found in us the inward springs of our life."[5]

By contrast, testimony at Little Zion is often highly expressive, as members move into the elevated chanted speech of the African American performed sermon tradition, artfully describing transcendent experiences of God's power. As in Mrs. Constantine's description of her conversion, believers receive signs such as the star that moves in response to human request, or the voice that breaks into the consciousness and commands, "You must believe you are a freeborn child." But in many instances, the very description of transcendence triggers its experience for both teller and hearer, and I have participated in such moments when the difference in Baptist and Quaker worship styles falls away and interviewee and interviewer need no further words to communicate understanding. (See the beginning of Chapter 3.) As Mrs. Constantine described it, "It's a feeling that you could never forget if you once had it. It's an experience that you would never forget."

My intention here is in no way to exoticize this community, where individual expressions of belief pack a greater dramatic punch than my own. Rather, I attempt to capture the artistic aspects of testimonial speech to honor the conviction among Little Zion members that this elevated language communicates the awesome Word of God. This sacred communication goes beyond secular efforts to explain and analyze belief, privileging listeners and readers instead to witness its transforming power in the lives of believers. Glenn Hinson pointed out a long history in the African American religious tradition of the "telling" of belief as integral to its development:

> Even as early as the 1790s, African American saints were articulating their faith in the language of experience. Indeed . . . they had already stretched the definition of "experience" beyond its reference to the ongoingness of everyday encounter to embrace the experiential singularity of conversion and then to denote the *telling* of that experience. In the conversational world of the saints, one "experienced" life, had "the experience" of conversion, and told (rather than told *of*) one's experience to the gathered faithful. Already saints were setting aside special assemblies for public testimony, "experience meetings" where the focus was not preaching or singing, but "giving experiences."[6]

And, as scholar Patrick Mullen has asserted, the telling of religious experience also reconnects the saved with their own conversion experiences. For many people interviewed by Mullen, "telling of their religious experiences was a ritual occurrence, reliving the original ritual through narrating it, reestablishing the link between their present selves and their new selves after conversion."[7]

Many folklorists have explored "performative" aspects of religious speech, notably Gerald Davis in his study of the poetics of African

American sermons. But in the past decade some scholars have expressed reservations about this model, because the word "performance" suggests an inauthenticity in the speech — as if the believer were merely playacting at worship. Diane Goldstein has cautioned scholars not to secularize religious speech with a concentration on elements of its "performance." She based her argument on Richard Bauman's landmark definition of the performed word: " 'a mode of spoken verbal communication [which] consists in the assumption of responsibility to an audience for a display of communicative competence.' "[8] Given the believer's attribution of religious speech to divine inspiration, and the sense that its ultimate evaluation lies beyond human understanding, the performance model proves inadequate, Goldstein says. In fact, "the characterization of acts understood by our informants as divine, under the rubric of performance, becomes an insult to native interpretations. The secular model does not serve to clarify the ethnographic situation, it simply secularizes it."[9]

I found the same discomfort with the idea of religious expression as performance among Little Zion members. Rev. James Carter said blacks preaching or praying in church are not performing for a human or a divine audience. Rather, he asserted that worshippers allow themselves to be vessels for the Holy Spirit's expression, without control over dramatic effect. When preaching, he noted, "even though you understand and you hear the congregation responding, you're not tuning in to the congregation. You're tuning in to the Holy Spirit. That's the only way you can allow the Holy Spirit to flow through you. If you're tuning in to the congregation, you're not being controlled by the Spirit. Then you're performing." He asserted the same lack of control in the heightened expressions of shouting by the congregation: "The shouting, people don't have any control of it. Sometimes people think folks are performing, but they're not. For the most part, in the black rural experience, I don't think people are performing." For Rev. Carter, religious expression that remains aware and in control of itself becomes an empty show.

But for Rev. Oscar Williams, the self-conscious artistry of religious expression can signify an immediate, personal relationship with a God "who deserves the best in terms of words." Williams explained:

Now, when you talk about praying, you ain't heard no praying until you hear black Baptist praying. If the Lord's up there, they'll get His attention. Black Baptists *know* how to put words together. I've heard them say, "Lord, just poke your head out of Zion's window and hear your servant's prayer one more time before death or early judgment." Now they're just getting wound up. Though I say that with a bit of humor, they mean every word of it. They mean every word of it. . . .

They pray in a way that some might call pretentious; some may even say it's phony perhaps. But not to blacks who are praying. For they want the Lord, who we look at as being a right-now God, to address these problems. . . .

So at a prayer meeting people bring their burdens to the Lord. Now whether they leave them there or not may be questionable. But they sure enough bring them, and they'll outline them in as eloquent a fashion as they can. For they feel that the Lord they serve deserves the best in terms of words that they can bring. This stirs the emotions of those who hear it.

Rev. Williams asserted that artistry in religious language need not imply *artifice*, an inauthentic, put on, or "phony" performance. Rather, the language of prayer becomes a human offering of respect and honor to the divine, made during worship in a way that "stirs the emotions of those who hear it," drawing others into the sacred experience.

Harris M. Berger and Giovanna P. Del Negro have offered insight into both scholarly and church member concerns about the performance model. They argue that all interaction includes an element of self-consciousness — even in situations where people pay no attention to themselves or others. For instance, they describe a jazz musician who loses himself in his music. He does not attend to his performance or the audience's reaction to it. But to do this he must narrow his focus; he must consciously move beyond himself: "On many nights, the Akron jazzers have to work to quiet the reflective voice, and some speak of learning to focus solely on the body and the sound as a lifelong project akin to meditation."[10] At Little Zion, quieting the self involves "tuning in to the Spirit," allowing God to move — and often speak — through the believer. Though the worship experience can be described with different degrees of self-awareness, what really matters is beyond the self. It is the contact with the divine that takes believers beyond the performance model or any other rational means of understanding.

CONVERSION: "I GOT SOMETHING TO TELL YOU"

For Little Zion churchgoers, full membership in the community begins with a conversion experience, traditionally a personal encounter with God that convinces them that their souls have been saved and that a new life of membership in the body of Christ has begun. Clifton H. Johnson described this experience in the introduction to *God Struck Me Dead*, a classic collection of African American religious conversion narratives documented through interviews with ex-slaves in Tennessee during the 1920s by A. P. Watson. Johnson wrote, "A conversion experience . . . is marked by a sudden and striking 'change of heart,' with an abrupt change in the orientation of attitudes and beliefs. It is accompanied by what can be described as an 'emotional regeneration, typically sudden in its advent and consummation.' Conversion thus affects radically one's outlook toward life and one's conception of oneself."[11] Rev. Williams noted of his conversion, "Now . . . that was a traumatic experience, in part because it indeed set you apart and made you think differently about the rest of the people. The conversion experience that I came through is a constant reminder to this day that there are some moral things that I know better than to do. I know better." Rev. Eddie Carter described the transformation brought on by his conversion experience: "I feel different. I feel like a burden has been lifted off of me." And Sister Rosie Lee Hendricks recalled how she felt new in both body and spirit. "I looked at my hands, / and my hands looked new! I looked down at my feet, / and my feet looked new!"

Members of the current generation of children at Little Zion, however, report their conversions to be the conclusion of a much more gradual development of religious understanding rather than a sudden, direct encounter with God. Rev. James Carter attributed the change in experience to an increase in education among community members: "The old way of being converted is that you got to be touched by the Holy Spirit. And you got to pray. It's not quite as straightforward as it is today. I think that's primarily because of an increase in education, a better understanding." Mrs. Johnnie Busby Jackson agreed, noting that members of previous generations, many of whom couldn't read, relied more heavily on emotional encounters with the divine than on rational study of the church's teachings in cultivating their faith. As noted in previous chapters, this shift in emphasis from emotional to rational understanding has left many church members with wistful memories of earlier, more devoted times. Mrs. Mary Constantine commented, for example, "You don't see any young people participating in the prayer service other than just singing. We used to pray just like the men. They didn't have to ask us; it just came natural."

Though churchgoers can experience conversion at any age and in any setting, Little Zion conducts a revival, usually each summer, aimed at saving souls. The church sets aside a "mourner's bench," which Rev. Oscar Williams described: "In that third row near the middle aisle, the first two, three, or four seats are reserved for those folks in the community who are not members of the church, who have not been saved. The revival is targeted at bringing folks, young and old, into the church, and through prayer and eloquent preaching, convincing them that they ought to be members." In fact, Rev. W. D. Lewis noted, "The revival depends on sinners. We ain't got no sinners, we ain't got no revival. Lord, I work sometimes to get them to come" (8/7/97). Revival marks "a sacred time," in the words of Rev. James Carter, when all efforts concentrate on winning everlasting life for these members of the community. Rev. Lewis explained, "Saving souls is the highest point of Little Zion's history. I don't care if we give up on everything else. If you save but one soul, that one soul's worth more than all worldly goods. If you can save one soul out of this world, that's the highest thing. Converting souls and adding to the church is the most important thing to me in my whole ministry. The church is to save the world" (8/7/97).

Little Zion's members looked back fondly on revivals from earlier times, asserting that those services reflected a deeper religious commitment in this community. As Rev. Williams explained, "During the 1950s and the years before, revivals were big things in the black Baptist Church. Every church had revival, usually two weeks. (Later on it became one week.) The first week was for prayer meetings to 'warm the church up,' to get ready for the preacher. Folks would come out and have prayer for two and three hours. This puts the folks in a different frame of mind, takes them away from the worldly cares of day-to-day living. For God is a God who — if we can just get him to listen for a little while — will take us out of our burdens." Mrs. Mary Constantine recalled, "We used to have the best revivals, all the old-time moaning and praying. People now, they're ashamed to even get down to pray. . . . We don't have that old-time revival anymore. It's spiritual, and I'm sure God is in the midst just like He was then, but the older people had taught us all these testimonies. We inherited them."

Rev. Lewis recalled practices that marked this time as sacred, such as "when the church had revival, there ain't no courting. For the whole two weeks, nobody courted" (8/7/97). Rev. James Carter remembered, "If you was on the mourner's bench when I came along, it was a serious situation. You didn't play. You've got no time for play. For those kids who are already converted, you don't run around the yard and play with them during that time. You put all playing aside. You got that serious. Very little eating. You're fasting. You would eat your meals, but there was an understanding that you didn't snick-snack all through the day. . . . You got sincere within yourself; you got sincere with God." Deacon Ed Carter reported that on the day of his conversion, for example, he fasted through dinner: "Now I always been greedy. Didn't never deny eating till that day. That evening, my grandma say, 'Your food is in the warmer.' (They had stoves then, cooked with fire, and up above they had warmers. You pulled the door open, put the stuff up in the warmer.) I said, 'Mama, I don't want none. I'll eat when I come back.' Denied my food one time. I'm praying" (8/7/97).

Mourner's bench participants were encouraged to pray constantly, both during and between revival meetings. Sister Hendricks said, "They told me to get down on my knees to pray. I did it. When people begin to advise me, whatever they say, I repeat it down in my heart. If you say, 'Rosie Lee,' I say, 'Rosie Lee.' You say, 'You do such and such a thing.' I say, 'You do such and such a thing.' I repeat whatever people told me, praying down in here [points to heart]. Girl, I sent up some prayers." Several members noted they prepared for their conversions by going out, as Mrs. Mary Constantine said, "in the woods to pray. You go to yourself."[12] Rev. Eddie Carter said, "I do remember my brother was telling me that I needed a praying ground. So I decided to make a praying ground out there in my father's barn," a private place to "pray on my knees." Rev. James Carter remembered "going up in the pasture and praying. I was nine years old. I just focused on hoping that the Holy Spirit overpowered me and I'd get converted." During the revival of her conversion, Sister Hendricks recalled that she stayed out all night: "There was a place with white dirt between my house and the church. And I went down in that white place, down in the ditches." In this private place, she prayed, "Lord, send somebody! Send somebody!" Deacon Dick Knott, a member of the church community, then joined the effort to help the mourner find God. "That morning before day, a deacon named Knott, Brother Knott, he came. . . . I heard him coming, singing, 'A charge to keep and a God to glorify!' "

Other members of the community play a role even in this "personal situation" of seeking religion, as Rev. James Carter called it, noting that "people are praying for you, and if you're not easily converted, you're asked to seek out those in the church who you believe could . . . help bring that conversion." Believers often use artfully performed metaphoric language in the battle to save their brothers and sisters. Deacon Carter remembered that during his conversion, "old man rode from up here . . . to see me. He said, 'Son, the Lord sent me up here, told me to tell you to pray for the Lord to overshadow you with the Holy Ghost and fix you where you can't hold your peace. And I want you to pray right now.' He said, 'If you pray this prayer like I told you, and the Lord don't free your soul, tomorrow I give my neck to the chopping block. . . .' This old man, he had *some* religion. He had some kind of religion" (8/7/97).

Rev. Lewis recalled his longtime efforts to convert Mrs. Mary Smith

and her family, citing a folktale that implied, humorously, his willingness to resort to any means possible to win this most important battle:

> Oh, I had a time getting Mae in there. Whenever I see her I said,
> "Mae, are you coming to church?"
> I would always talk to the children. They would tease me when-
> ever they didn't come to Sunday school, say, "You didn't get us."
> Back in slave time, the kids would tease the cook, say, "You didn't
> get us."
> The cook said, "I did too. I spit in your coffee every morning.
> Yeah, I did too. I spit in your coffee every morning."
> I'd tell those kids, "I spit in your coffee every morning."
> Then Mae and all the children came into the church together.
> Oh boy, it was like a duck going to the pond, Mae leading in all
> them children. (8/7/97)

When Mr. Henry Smith didn't join the family's conversion, Rev.
Lewis visited him at home, describing the encounter as similar to
trapping a wild animal: "He backed himself up under a tree. He
couldn't get past me. I caught him. I gave him a good talking, and
when I finished with him, he couldn't hold it, and he started hollering.
He was hollering like a panda" (8/7/97). Clearly, Rev. Lewis relied on
language as his overt weapon in the battle to save souls, giving the
sinner "a good talking." Arguably, he also relied on words as a covert
weapon, telling the story of the cook who spit in the children's coffee,
implying that his preaching was working on their hearts undetected
even while they shunned the church.

Seekers at Little Zion usually asked God for a sign that their souls
had been saved. As Rev. Williams explained, "There are those who
pray that, 'Lord, if you'll save my soul, I want to see a spot of cloud
disappear.' And they say, 'He did it.' Or, 'I want to hear a dove moan,'
and they heard it. Or they'll want something else to happen, and He
did it. I came up through that tradition." The very choice of which
sign to ask for seems highly dependent on tradition, as members
throughout the community asked for the same few signs — the star
moving, a cloud disappearing, the dove moaning, for example. In fact,
these signs correspond closely to those documented in *God Struck Me*

Dead. For instance, in one conversion recorded more than eight decades ago the seeker reported, "That night I said, 'Lord, if I am praying right, let me hear a dove mourn three times. . . .' and there I heard a dove mourn three times."[13] Another said, "I kept on until I asked the Lord, if he had converted me, to show me a beautiful star out of a cloudy sky. This was done, and I saw a star in the daytime shining out of a cloudy sky. I know I have got it, and hell and its forces can't make me turn back."[14] The imagery suggests seekers in this religious tradition have passed their requests for signs down through generations of churchgoers.

In praying for and receiving signs, members of Little Zion's community sought and experienced the supernatural transforming power of God in their everyday lives. Rev. James Carter noted, "You had to have a supernatural experience in order to be assured that God has changed you, that you've changed over." Many, such as Sister Hendricks, heard the voice of God speaking to them or saw a vision transcending human understanding, like the star that moves. Rev. Willie C. Carter, for instance, heard voices both while awake and while sleeping:

> I tell you it was a wonderful time when I confessed hope in Christ. I was at home, outside the house when I confessed, late one Saturday evening in July. I never will forget it. July on a Saturday evening, that's when He anoint me. I have heard voices talking to me on Friday. Telling me to get up and get on my job. There was rain coming and I dozed off. When I'm sleeping, a voice comes to me, say, "Get up and get on the job." So I got up and got on the job. Went back to praying, praying to the Lord. That Saturday evening, hey, I couldn't hold my peace. So I come and get baptized at Little Zion. (9/6/98)

Sister Courtney Porter experienced visions while sleeping, interpreted as far more significant than ordinary dreams:

> I asked the Lord to show me in a vision what he wanted me to do. He showed it to me. Every time I pray that prayer and go to sleep, I see myself on my knees praying. I wake up and tell my mother. She say, "Well, it's 'cause you have to pray."

I just prayed for the Lord to free my soul, to save me when I come in doubt. I said, "Now, if I got good religion that gonna save me when I come to die, I want you to show it to me."

He showed it to me. I was ten years old, sleeping, and saw myself dressed up in that white gown, going down in the water. The preacher way out there, Rev. Field, had his hand out. He said, "Come on."

I walk on out there and they baptize me. Then I woke up.

Often believers did not hear or see anything unusual but felt suddenly overwhelmed by the Spirit's presence. Mrs. Patricia Edmonds reported:

I confessed hope in Christ when I was eleven years old. During that time I was praying, and I asked the Lord, "If you free my soul from hell, I'll serve you till I die." That's the Word I had been taught. . . . So I asked Him to let me feel something, which He did.

We used to have a outside bathroom and when I was out there, it felt like I was just pushed off the seat onto the floor. I looked around to see was anybody in there with me. Nobody but Him.

So when I went back to the house, I peeped around the door at my grandmother, who was sitting on the porch. I didn't have to say anything. She seen me and knew. She hollered and I start crying. That let me know then that somebody else felt that beside me. She knew about it.

Sister Carrie B. Purse described a moment of transcendence in church, when she reached out to ask her mother to pray for her conversion. She said she "fell out," a moment later realizing that somehow she "was down on the floor." "I just had a feeling that I had never had before," she continued. "I was crying, and I didn't know what I was crying about. So I had to learn what I was crying about from the holy folks. It's a good feeling, a real good feeling. . . . I just got up and I went all over the church, testifying what the Lord had done. You don't think about what you're gonna say. You just be saying it. You don't think of it. The Lord speak through you. You open your mouth, and He'll speak through you. He do just that."

Deacon Ed Carter, in what has become one of the most repeated conversion stories at Little Zion, received signs as feelings other than those he sought. At seventeen years old, Deacon Carter said, he was a "hard believer," one who found it difficult to surrender to God. Though his grandmother had been trying to teach him to pray since he was twelve, as Deacon Carter put it, he "ain't got time to pray. I got to *play*."[15] While in his grandmother's presence, he was "going around with a hung down head like [he was] praying." But outside of her watchful eye was another matter. As Deacon Carter described his activities he began to hum, snap his fingers, and do a dance move. He recalled, "My granddaddy knowed it. He knowed what I was doing from twelve to seventeen. One day he was troubled, he was troubled about my soul. He said, 'Now look, Satan be at you every year. Pray, boy. Pray.' Now he had never said *nothing* to me about praying before. 'You go to praying, now, and get your soul in Christ. Because I need you to help tend to my business. Every year you go around fooling yourself. But you ain't fooling me. Now you go to praying.'" His grandfather's admonition touched Deacon Carter deeply. "That old man hurt me to my heart," he remembered. "He put a lot of Godly sorrow on me. In my soul, I went to praying to the Lord. Try to map my way out of nowhere." He began to pray: "Lord, I want You to free my soul. I want You to make it known to me. I want You to over-shadow me with the Holy Ghost, where I can't hold my peace."

Deacon Carter asked God for a sign: "I prayed and I prayed. I often heard my grandma say when she got converted, she had a burning in her breast, called a 'burning zeal,' that burned her so that she just confessed it. During that time we was raising a tater called a 'choker tater,' a very dry white tater. It wouldn't digest. Now, I'm praying for the Lord to let me feel that way in my breast and in my stomach. I call it a burning zeal."

Waiting for that sign, Deacon Carter began attending revivals, first at Little Zion, then at other area churches. He "mourned out" each church, moving on as each revival ended fruitlessly. Finally, he mourned out his mother's church, Shiloh Baptist, until the last night of revival.

Then Deacon Carter received help from other members of the community. Mr. Gullet [phonetic spelling], an old man from a nearby farm, rode over to pray with him, and staked his life on the certainty that, if the young man prayed as instructed, the Lord would free his soul.

In response, Deacon Carter heard a voice: "Something coming in me said, 'You're free. You're free indeed and you must believe.' . . . I said, 'I ain't got no religion. I know that I ain't got no religion, because I don't feel no burning zeal. I got to feel the burning.'" So the voice quieted.

At the advice of Mr. Gullet, Deacon Carter prayed for the Lord to meet him in Shiloh Church that night. "Overshadow me with the Holy Ghost and *fix* me where I can't hold my peace," he prayed. Throughout the day he continued to pray, and at dinnertime he fasted. "But when the sun went down, I hadn't felt the burning."

On his way to church, he recalled, "I burst out and went to laughing out loud to myself. Laughing just like a fool. And I jumped. I said, 'Lord, I ain't done nothing right.' I said, 'I ain't praying. I ain't done nothing. I'm laughing.'" Then he heard the voice again. "You're free. You're free indeed and you must believe." He responded, "Lord, I ain't got no religion. I ain't feeling no burning zeal. I ain't got nothing." Before he reached the church, Deacon Carter said the strange laughter came on him two more times, and both times his body jumped in response. "Lord," he thought, "what's wrong with me now? I'm going foolish, and I ain't got no burning zeal."

Here Deacon Carter paused in the narrative to explain: "I'm still trying to feel that burning. I'm trying to see if I can get that burning. But you don't come your way. You're gonna come God's way or don't come at all." He laughed at the memory of a young man who had not surrendered fully to God because he insisted in deciding just what form the sign of his conversion must take.

At church later that day, Deacon Carter recalled, he felt his body jumping and twitching in response to the preacher. "'Lord,' I said, 'what is this?'" The voice returned. "'You're free. You're free indeed and you must believe.'"

The preacher came down from the pulpit and said, "'Lord, I want you to shake him. Lord, shake him till he own you, Lord. I want you to shake him, shake him Jesus, till he can't hold his peace.'"

But, as is reported in many "hard believer" tales,[16] Deacon Carter held out against the conversion until the last possible moment. The congregation stayed into the night: "Twelve o'clock come, then one o'clock, them people all singing and praying over me, just singing and praying. Finally, they say, 'Well son, we got to go home.'" They told him to take the candidate's seat. "'That seat over there, you got to take that seat there. That's the seat set out there for you to sit in when you confess.'"

But Deacon Carter hadn't confessed. "I wasn't taking that seat. I got up to leave. I said, 'From this night, I never expect to go back to another mourner's bench.' I said, 'Where's my cap?'"

As Deacon Carter left the church, the congregation was totally silent. "You couldn't hear nothing. You couldn't even hear nobody whisper. And I got my cap and walked out of that church."

Outside, he looked up at the sky, saw the beautiful moon, and told the Lord, "'From this night, I ain't gonna pray another prayer.' I said, 'I prayed and done all I can do. I prayed and you wouldn't hear none of my prayers.'"

Pausing again, Deacon Carter explained, "This been the prayer I prayed standing on that porch. But you got to *give* yourself to the Lord."

Then one of Shiloh's deacons came out onto the porch and told him, "'I ain't saying you got religion. But if you believe the Lord has heard every prayer you prayed, give me your right hand.'" "Something [in me] say," Carter continued, "'You prayed for the Holy Ghost and you was shaking in there. That's what it was.' But something else say, 'You're gonna tell a lie.'" For some time he said he fought an inner battle, one voice saying he had been saved, the other saying it was a lie. "The devil stays with you till the last minute," he explained.

Finally, he touched the other man's hand, prepared to testify about the shaking that had come on him in the church: "I just touched that fellow's hand. Sister, something hit me up here at the top of my head, and I hit the ground on my knees. When I hit the ground, I said, 'Tell Daddy! Tell Daddy, come here! I'm so glad I got JESUS all in my soul!' I got up talking about it!" Laughing, he added, "I never did get that burning. But when that Holy Spirit hit me, it like knock me out of the world. That's something else. That Holy Spirit is something else. It's powerful. God got some *power*."

When Deacon Carter finally realized he had received a sign after all, and that God had freed his soul, he "got up talking about it." In fact, he concluded, "I *know* I got a witness for myself; that's what the Lord done for me. I got my witness. He knocked me to my knees and I jumped up. Yes, Lord. I know something about Him. That's my confession. Been telling it ever since."

The dramatic retelling of the conversion narrative continues to witness the power of God to transcend ordinary awareness, pulling the believer out of the mundane experience of the natural world and into a heightened encounter with the supernatural. It stands as an example to seekers, a kind of guide for those, as Deacon Carter described the mourner's bench challenge, trying "to map [their] way out of nowhere." Rev. Oscar Williams eloquently characterized the role of these witnessing narratives among churchgoers: "When those who had stayed on the mourner's bench a long time finally joined the church, they came off there shouting and falling out. They would talk about religion. That's the term they used. 'Talk about religion.' So when you'd ask those old fellows, you'd say, 'Let me hear you talk about religion.' They would go into a singsong kind of poem which would probably start off, 'I'm so glad I got Jesus.' Then they would take you on down through their travelogue. 'And I went on down to my praying ground. And I knelt down on my knees. . . .' Some of them could tell it in such a fashion that you would just love to hear them repeat it and repeat it."

Of course, as Rev. Williams pointed out, the most dramatic conversion narratives detailed the change of heart of the hard believer who had held out for years against God's redemptive call. These stories were, and still are, retold inspirationally not just by the one saved but by others throughout the community. Rev. James Carter, for instance, recounted his grandfather's experience of waiting on the burning zeal, noting that it served as an example for him as he sought his own conversion: "When I came along, just like my grandfather, I was waiting on that burning zeal." In fact, Rev. Carter's conversion took a

similar form, as the touch of the preacher's hand triggered a supernatural experience: "The preacher said to me, 'Do you believe that
Christ will save you when you come to die? Take my hand.' When I
took his hand, my mother said that I leaped in the air. I don't remember leaping. I don't remember jumping in the air at all. I remember
coming to myself and seeing that I was sitting on the other seat. I
had come off the mercy seat; I was sitting in the conversion seat. And
I was crying. So I truly believe that the Holy Spirit intervened and
took control of my mind, and gave me that assurance. That was my
conversion."

Many of Little Zion's members recall vividly a "camp meeting"
after the close of revival in 1981, which aimed at and succeeded in
saving the soul of a hard believer who had held out against joining the
church into his old age. Camp meetings, held in both black and white
Protestant communities since the late 1700s, took the revival tradition outdoors, with unlimited space for worshippers to preach, sing,
and pray in the hope of converting sinners. Eileen Southern offered
this description of the practice in *The Music of Black Americans*: "At
night the scene of the meeting was an awesome sight. Huge campfires
burned everywhere, so that it seemed as if the 'whole woods stood in
flames.' From three to five thousand persons or more were assembled
in the huge main tent, called a tabernacle, to listen to the preacher-
for-the-evening address them from an elevated stand. On benches
below the elevation sat other preachers. Then there were rows of
seats for the people."[17] Since Little Zion has a relatively small number
of members, its only camp meeting of recent memory did not approach the scale of that in Southern's description. But the fervor of
the meeting clearly impressed participants deeply. Mrs. Mary Smith
recalled how different church members hosted the worship service
each evening:

We were going around to the houses, just singing and praying and
preaching like we was at church. Everybody be sitting around our
door. We made seats for to sit them out there in the yard. People
from all places would come around, different preachers every night.
Every night at somebody else's house for about two weeks. . . . We

was having choir practice at night during that time, and everybody would leave from choir at Little Zion and head right over there to the camp revival. You could just stand out and see car lights coming in, coming in to that camp revival. It was a beautiful something to see, sure was; it was beautiful to see.

By the meeting's close, hard believer Mr. Thomas James Smith had joined the church, along with several other adult members of the community.

The story of Mr. Smith's conversion also testifies to the powerful role of community members in helping the seeker to find God. Many at Little Zion credited not only Rev. W. D. Lewis but also Mrs. Patricia Edmonds with softening this man's heart. Mrs. Bessie Smith remembered the years she spent trying to convert her husband, with Rev. Lewis visiting often. She recalled the preacher's exhortation, "You living here. You ain't gonna live here always. You don't want to die and go to hell. You got to make a change. You don't make a change here until you lift your eyes." Then, after the Friday night close of the 1981 summer revival, Mrs. Edmonds heard a voice. She recalled, "Saturday morning I had gotten up, a voice spoke to me and said, 'Why don't you call some of your members and go down to the Smith man house? Why don't you go down there and have prayer with him?'" She obeyed, organizing the camp meeting. Toward the end of this second revival, one of the deacons reportedly asked Mr. Smith if he would like someone to pray for him. Mrs. Edmonds said, "When he turn around and throw his hand out to me, that's when I hit the floor. When I came back to, I felt like his mouth was opened to confess. Before I knew one thing, he had ran out the door. That's when he confessed."

The long-awaited conversion inspired awe in many who witnessed it. Mr. Smith's daughter-in-law, Mrs. Mary Smith, described it eloquently:

We had a wonderful, wonderful camp revival! When my father-in-law had his conversion, we was all just praying, some of us in the house and some of us on the porch. Deacon Jonas Smothers was praying out loud, and all at once my father-in-law just jumped up and started hollering and crying and saying he believed in the Lord. Then he just ran out of the house and down the road. A lot of us were running behind him.

A lot of us was in the house, just jumping up and shouting. We was all up on my mother-in-law's bed, just jumping up and down! It was a wonderful time! . . . That man had been seeking Christ so *long*, so many years. That night he just gave up, and boy we had a time then. We was all up on her bed. Yes, yes, yes.

With regard to the validity of Mr. Smith's conversion, and of those experienced by other adults, community acceptance seems to have been automatic. But for children, the confession that the Lord had freed their souls was scrutinized closely and only accepted when elders in the church declared themselves satisfied that the child had, in fact, been saved. Mrs. Mary Constantine said that when her daughter said she had religion, the child's grandmother denied the assertion and sent her back to the mourner's bench. "That's what most old people used to do," Mrs. Constantine explained. "If you said you had religion, they would make you go back. You didn't get off that mourner's bench if those old people didn't say you could. If the Lord hadn't showed them something, they make you go back. . . . You had to really be a praying person for them to let you get off that mourner's bench." Mrs. Constantine continued: "Mama said she had prayed, and the Lord didn't show her that [my daughter] had religion. [She] had to go back. I think it was that Thursday night, she got religion again. I told my mother, 'If [my daughter] believes, then you should believe.' But my mother said she had to pray over it. Finally, I guess the Lord showed her that [my daughter] had been saved." Rev. Oscar Williams reported a similar reaction to his conversion at nine years old, saying that at first his mother and grandmother "didn't want to pay much attention," instructing him to "go back and think about that, son," and saying, "We've just got to pray over this ourselves for awhile." But "it didn't take them long" to confirm that the conversion was real, he noted, saying that they then cried more than he did at the joyous news.

Of course, church elders' scrutiny safeguarded the custom of testifying about supernatural encounter from abuse by children inclined to imitate the dramatic form without the sacred experience — the inauthentic performance discussed earlier. One church member still laughs about her own childhood conversion, when, tired of waiting on the Lord, she attempted to fake a moment of transcendence. When she fell from the mourner's bench to the floor, apparently overcome, she opened her eyes to find her mother standing over her. The child was promptly told — in no uncertain terms — to get back in her seat. Deeply shamed, she didn't move again until the Spirit truly struck her.

As already mentioned, the practice of waiting on a sign to confirm the conversion has waned in recent years, as Little Zion now emphasizes education more strongly than supernatural experience as crucial to religious development. This shift has also corresponded with a relaxing of elder scrutiny of young people's confessions. Sister Leola Carter, for instance, had been uncertain of her youngest children's religion, resolving to "find out whether they got anything." Then she had a dream in which she saw them going down in the water to be baptized. "When I woke up, I said, 'I'll never say no more what these little children ain't got. If they say they believe in God, say yes to everything the preacher asks them about whether they trust the Lord until they die, that's enough for me.' " Sister Carter saw the dream as a sign that today's children need not necessarily show evidence that they have received signs. She concluded, "It wasn't for me to believe [their confessions], for only they know and God knows. I had nothing to worry about." Mrs. Busby Jackson echoed these feelings, saying that older members have no right to question children's beliefs because this practice pushes young people away from the church. Sister Carrie Purse added, "It used to be, some of those kids would get off of the mourner's bench, and the next night they'd be back on there again. 'My mama didn't believe.' See, I think that's wrong. Because those parents can't save them. How can you save me? You can't save yourself. The Lord got to save you. I can't. I don't have nothing to do with that. Those kids think they saved, I think so too. If they believe it, I believe it."

Young people interviewed for this project confessed their faith simply as a statement of readiness to accept the church's teachings. One eight-year-old boy recalled, for example, "I said, 'I want to get baptized this year,' because I don't want to be ten and on the mourning bench, waiting and waiting, and then I never get baptized. I said, 'I'm ready now.' They said, 'Okay,' and let me get baptized." Another boy, age ten, asked his grandmother if he could be baptized. She said yes, so he went to the mourner's bench: "The preacher ask me, 'Do you want to be baptized?' I say, 'Yes.' And he ask me all this other stuff, and I say, 'Yes.'" In my experience, children often speak much less eloquently than adults in interviews, especially in those conducted by community outsiders. Children, after all, have not fully developed the language skills needed to articulate their experiences. However, the stark contrast in the simplicity of young people's statements with the detailed and dramatic confession narratives of Little Zion's elders seems to signify a change in attitude toward this rite of passage — from an overwhelming transformational experience to a public affirmation of belief by saying "yes" to the preacher.

Among candidates for baptism, the practice of proclaiming their conversion experiences from house to house throughout the community also has been abandoned, several older church members said. Mrs. Jane Anthony remembered, "So many got religion during the revivals, they would go in a group from house to house telling about their conversions. When I get through talking, you talk. They would do it from the first evening during revival, all through till they got baptized."

Although the emphasis on telling the details of the conversion experience throughout the community might have waned in recent years, the sense among Little Zion members of the importance of being saved has remained absolute. Rev. W. D. Lewis said he still regretted his inability to convert one man in particular, who, he said starkly, "died and went to hell." Sighing, he added, "I tried to save him so many times. He said, 'I'm coming. I'm coming.' He never did make it" (8/7/97). Mrs. Bessie Smith also emphasized the high stakes in the battle to save souls in describing her concern for her husband, Mr. Thomas James Smith, who didn't confess hope in Christ until late in life (at the camp meeting described earlier): "If you never confess, you can't be good enough to go to heaven. I don't care how good you is. Jesus say, 'If you ashamed to own me before men, I'll be ashamed to own you before my father.'[18] You got to make some open confession here. If you don't make no open confession here, the Bible says, to hell you lift your eyes." Rev. Lewis agreed, urging spouses, "You have a husband or wife. If they don't go to church, it's your job to take them there. You have to save that man or woman for the rest of his or her life. There's nothing wrong with marrying a sinner, but you've got an obligation to save them. . . . When they die, it's all over" (8/7/97).

Mrs. Smith said she never despaired that her husband's soul would be saved, however: "I figured my husband still had a chance. I felt like if he want to get it in his mind, it'll leave his mind and go to his heart, and he would confess. I wasn't afraid, because I know God is good. He'll send a change. He was giving him time." She cited the biblical parable of the laborers in the vineyard who all received the same pay, even though some started work early in the day and others began at the eleventh hour.[19] "You know the man that went at the eleventh hour, he got just as much pay as them that was there all the time. . . . So if you just make it in, you all right. If you just got in and die the next minute, you saved. It's just so simple you can't hardly understand it." Mr. Smith died in 1989, and Mrs. Smith said she looks forward to a reunion with him. "Now I know I'll see him again in heaven. Yes sir. Yes sir. I firmly believe that."

BAPTISM: "TALKING ON THE WATER"

At the close of revival, Little Zion baptizes candidates who have publicly confessed hope in Christ. The full-immersion baptism ceremony has changed over the past century as the church facilities have expanded, first incorporating an outdoor pool in the early 1970s, then providing an indoor structure behind the choir stand in the building constructed after the 1996 burning. While many agreed the changes had been made for "convenience," they also remembered fondly the baptisms conducted through most of the twentieth century in nearby creeks and cow ponds. As has been a theme in regard to other areas of church life, several people argued that today's more comfortable physical surroundings dull the edge of religious fervor among those participating in the ceremony. Mrs. Mary Smith said, for example, "I got baptized in what was called a creek baptism. You didn't have pools then. I wasn't dipping in no pool at no church. [She laughs.] Well, it's just more convenient at these churches now. But in my time,[20] people was going out on these rivers and ditches and getting baptized, and it was more spiritual. Back in time, people wasn't as dressy then. It wasn't so convenient then. People was serving and praising the Lord more in that time. People would just be shouting and hollering and rejoicing." She also pointed out that those standing outside on the banks of a creek or around a pond witnessing the ceremony remained active participants. But seated inside the church, witnesses become more passive observers. "It do something to you being outside; it be like you have more room where you could express yourself. That's what it was like, singing and praising the Lord. But after they got it so convenient, you could just sit down and watch." Sister Courtney Porter, one of the church's oldest members, reminisced about the feeling of togetherness present at the creek and pond baptisms: "I just wish you could have been born back then to see what it was like, standing outside around the water, singing those good songs, moaning good moaning and praying good prayers. It just look like it's more of a together feeling. We have baptism pools in the church now. It's good, but not as good as standing around out there."

Even the baptism pool outside the church represented a transformation of the ceremony, as candidates no longer faced physical danger in the murky water, for instance. Several people spoke of the death and rebirth symbolism of the baptism ritual, as the candidate dies to the worldly self and is reborn again in Christ.[21] Many of those baptized in natural settings said they literally faced their own mortality in the creeks and ponds, feeling vulnerable to the water moccasins common in this part of the country, and to their own inability to swim. Mrs. Patricia Edmonds noted, for example, "Getting ready for baptizing, you had a good fear. You had a good fear. Probably scared of drowning. You getting ready to go in the water, wondering how you're coming back out of it. But if you have Jesus, that will save you." In fact, Mrs. Edmonds said she didn't swim, and the day of her baptism was "the first time I was under water." Deacon Ed Carter laughed as he remembered learning later that his baptism in 1934 had been the first Rev. W. D. Lewis had ever performed. He said jokingly, "I'll tell you, if at that time, I'd have known he didn't know nothing about baptizing, he would have had to go get another preacher. I couldn't swim; I didn't want to take no chances!" (10/20/96). Mrs. Busby Jackson remembered watching, terrified, as the deacons prepared for her baptism by wading in the water, tapping the ground with tall sticks "to ward off the snakes." She said, "I think I prayed more that day than any day during my whole life. I asked God to save me from the snakes that I knew were just *waiting* in there for me. These are water moccasins I'm talking about, not some little garden snakes. These are some *snakes*." In the clear pool water outside the church, candidates no longer confronted the possibility of a snakebite or, for those unable to swim, the accidental loss of footing on the muddy pond bottom.

Though the baptismal setting has changed, many of the customary preparations have not, Little Zion members pointed out. Women in the community still sew the white gowns worn by the candidates into the water, for instance. Sister Courtney Porter said her mother made her baptismal gown early in the twentieth century: "My gown cost twenty-five cents. My mother was a seamstress, and the cloth was ten cents a yard. You paid for two yards and a spool of thread." Interviewed in the summer of 1997, Sister Porter said she and Mrs. Jane Anthony had sewn eighteen gowns for one recent baptism. "It wasn't too hard. I can make nine or ten a day, myself." Sister Porter could not recall how many gowns she has made in her lifetime, noting that she made all of her children's gowns. "Then I just let them sleep in that all winter." She also explained that if you buy your gown, you keep it. But if the church buys it, then it is washed and reused in future ceremonies.

The church's women also help the candidates dress for the ceremony, putting on their gowns and covering their heads with white scarves or caps. In 1997, Little Zion allowed me to witness the preparations in the hallways outside the baptismal chamber, conducted

Mrs. Felicia Davis helps candidates dress for baptism at
Little Zion in August 1997.

quickly and quietly, with the children waiting nervously and saying little. Older members remembered similar preparations, dressing in houses near the water or, in many cases, in a store at "the old Simm place,"[22] where the pond was frequently used for baptisms. Mrs. Edmonds spoke of a sense of continuity in participating in the ritual first as a baptismal candidate, now as one helping the children get dressed. "I feel good about [it]. Someone helped me get ready, and I have a feeling I need to help someone too. It's just like when they sent John to prepare the people for Jesus when He come. John got them ready for the baptism, but Jesus was gonna come and fill them with the Holy Ghost."[23]

The ceremony itself also appears to have changed little in recent years. Mrs. Jane Anthony summed up the events at her baptism decades ago, noting, "They prayed and had a song, and then they talked on the water and got ready for baptizing. So I went on down." Little Zion's August 8, 1997, baptism service opened with a short sermon, followed by the congregational singing of "Come to Jesus," and a brief prayer on behalf of candidates by Rev. Lewis. The ritual then moved to the pool behind the altar, visible to the congregation through a large mirror suspended on the wall over the water. Rev. Willie C. Carter then offered another prayer for the candidates:[24]

To do the will of God, / (Yes Lord)
Oh, help them, our Father. / (Yes Lord)
Throw your arm of protection around them. / (Please Lord)

. . . .

Father we thank you for these young candidates tonight. /
(Thank you Lord, thank you Jesus)
In the name of Jesus, / (Yes Father)
Oh heavenly Father we ask You to make them strong. /
    (Yes Father)
Oh Father lead them by the reign of their mind, / (Yes Lord)
Father that they obey thy will. / (Yes Lord)

. . . .

Oh Father let the church be able to teach them / (Yes Lord)
That You are the way. / (Yea)
Teach them to keep thy command. / (Yes Father)
Teach them to walk in thy footsteps / (Yes Father)
Every day of their lives. / (Yes Father)
Teach them to love one another, /
To love our God with all our heart /
And our soul and our mind [inaudible]. / (Yes Lord)
Love our neighbor as our own self. / (Yes Lord)
In the name of Jesus Christ / (In the name of Jesus)
We thank you Father. / (Thank you Lord)
Let them have a believing heart. / (Yes Lord)

. . . .

That You are the savior, / (Yes Lord)
The son of a living God, / (Yes Father)
All powerful in your hands. / (Yes Lord)
Thank you Jesus, / (Thank you Father)
Thank you Father / (Thank you Lord)

With this prayer the ministers continued the custom of "talking on the water," as Mrs. Busby Jackson explained. "They gonna do the same thing at tonight's baptism: 'Talking on the water.' You'll hear Reverend Carter when he starts preaching the Word of God on the water, preparing to go down in the water. Nothing has changed. Only now we're inside of a building at the inside pool, instead of on the banks of a pond."

Following another congregational song, "Must Jesus Bear the Cross Alone," the candidates were baptized, immersed one at a time with the words, "My sister [or brother], in according to the confession of your faith, we now baptize you in the name of the Father, in the name of the Son, and in the name of the Holy Ghost." While the community sang "Take Me to the Water," the children came up from the water quietly, without dramatic expression of any transcendence they might have experienced in the ritual. One child interviewed said of his baptism at an earlier ceremony, "I was in the spirit of God." Another said, "When I came out the water, I started crying because I was glad, and then my mama was glad, and my grandma was glad." But none on this evening shared their feelings with the congregation or in conversation with me.

This silence represents these children's major departure from the expressive worship style shared by their parents. As in the conversion stories, without exception, baptism narratives told by adults testified to the direct experience of God's power during the ritual. Some spoke of seeing a light or hearing a voice. Others just felt the Lord's presence. And many responded by witnessing to others; they emerged from the water thanking God, praising the change he had wrought in their lives. Mrs. Edmonds recalled of her baptism, "When they carry me under, I seen a big light. Your eyes is closed, but this light, I seen this light. I felt good." Baptized on the first Sunday in August 1914, Rev. Lewis recalled, "I was ready to go down in the water and I had a vision. I had a vision and heard a voice, said, 'Go down in there. Go on and come back.'" As late as the 1970s, Rev. James Carter recalled, "During that time, you had a confession. When you come out of the water, you had a confession of what God had did for you. It's a spiritual feeling, a spirit-filled feeling."

Baptism recipients often communicate this "spirit-filled feeling" with vivid imagery and metaphor, as the baptism has provided "a new path that we walked in, and it was beautiful," in the words of Rev. Eddie Carter. He elaborated on these memories of his baptism about four decades ago:

> I shall never forget, it was a beautiful Sunday, the third Sunday of the month. Back in 1962, around July 13. We had to walk there about half a mile to the pond. There was a store called Simm's Store, where we dressed out. A black man was overseer, James Bragg. We dressed out in his house in our garments and walked to the pond to be baptized. I shall never forget.
>
> We came down to the pond where cows drank water from; it was a cattle pasture. They had cleaned it all off. The deacons had sticks; they carried them out to test the footage of the water. They test how deep it is, according to the height of the minister, so he can baptize you.[25]
>
> So I told myself that I wasn't going to go down in the water without holding my breath. "I'm gonna hold my breath if I go down in the water." I never did be trained up in swimming. I always stayed away from water. I had never swam in my life. And it was a fearful thing at first. But I prayed about it, and I asked God to meet me at the water.
>
> I made it to the water; they had us all lined up in our white garments, with a cap or something like a towel around the head. And they carried me in the water. My father was there and my brother. Seemed like they carried me in the most deepest part. And that water was cold, but it soon kind of relaxed me.

In facing his fear, and in asking God to be present with him, Rev. Carter experienced transcendence as the physical surroundings literally changed, were purified, in his eyes: "There were no snakes or anything around the water that day; the water had turned completely blue. It had purified. It was clean. Then sort of like a breeze came by, and you could see the waves, small waves rolling in the water. Then the waves moved back and it became calm. It was amazing to me how it got so calm around that pool. Everybody was singing. All I can remember they were singing a round of, 'Take Me to the Water:' 'Take me to the water. Baptize me.' All I can remember was the minister saying the ritual word, 'I baptize you in the name of the Father, Son, and the Spirit.'"

Like many others, Rev. Carter saw a light, and he marveled at how his surroundings had been cleansed:[26]

That man carried me down deep into that water. And I know that I had forgot about holding my breath and everything. When I went down in the water, it seemed like I saw a light. It seemed like I saw a light with me. It seemed like I saw a light just shining around the lake. I thought many times, "Snakes ought to be here, water moccasins." I've seen them around my father's barn. But they weren't around the lake. It was clean. It was pure. The water had turned blue and clean. God had purified the water. The grass, the trash had just been pushed away. It was a new path that we walked in, and it was beautiful.

As was customary in every generation as far back as the Little Zion community recalled, Rev. Carter witnessed to the power he had experienced. "When I came up, I was shouting. I was shouting. 'I'm so glad I got Jesus to take care of me always!' I was thankful. I was shouting and rejoicing as I went to the bank. I felt renewed. I felt new all over." Mrs. Busby Jackson also described this spiritual rebirth, and the bond it creates among those who share the experience: "You become special on that day. That's how it was then. You became special. It's like God has pushed away everything else except only you. That's my own personal feeling about it. My brother and myself and four other candidates were baptized together. And we had a closeness there, a bond that has lasted all these years. We still remember back, and nobody can ever take that away from us."

ADULT FAITH: "I FEEL HIS PRESENCE PRETTY MUCH ALL DAY"

For many who remain rooted in Little Zion's community, the personal relationship with the divine that began in the conversion and baptism experiences continues through the trials and tribulations of a lifetime. Church members said regular prayer and communion with

God remain central to their lives. Sister Rosie Lee Hendricks noted, for example, "I have to pray. If I don't pray, things'll go messed up. But if I talk to Jesus every day, through the night and through the day, things go right. I don't have no certain time to look up and say, 'Lord, have mercy.' He's a wonderful God; He's worthy to be praised. He's a good God." She also spoke poignantly of a house she and her husband had built together: "He nail a nail and I nail one. . . . We had some money; we put it on the house. We didn't have no money, he lay his hand on the wall and pray to God." In Mrs. Patricia Edmonds's memory, regular prayer became central to her life early in childhood: "They used to teach me things when I was growing up; it stick with me now. The way they taught me, in the morning time when we get ready to have breakfast, we have to thank God for the blessing that He have given us, and thank Him for the night that we lay down, get up and continue on through life. We would gather round the table. Most time my grandmother or grandfather would ask the blessing. At night we say our prayers, thanking Him too." Sister Porter described her prayer life in practical terms, saying, "You know I had to pray a lot to raise seven kids. I had to pray. And He answered. He was good to me."

Most adults interviewed said they sometimes receive clear, direct answers to their prayers, hearing a voice or, less frequently, seeing a vision in which the Lord offers guidance or comfort. Many members described these direct encounters happening during life's challenging moments, such as when they were in dire need of money, during illness or preparation for surgery, or through the grief of surviving a loved one's death. Rev. Lewis downplayed the drama of these experiences, noting that God is always present in an active spiritual life. He said, "I feel His presence pretty much all day. I feel God pretty much all day. He'll guide and protect you all day long. You ain't planning for tomorrow, just living through the night, starting out on that day with God guiding you" (9/5/98).

As an outsider to Little Zion's religious practices, I was most surprised not by the ongoing supernatural encounters described by church members, but by the matter-of-fact tone in which these narratives were delivered. The voice of God does not break into the everyday routine so much as emerge from it — anticipated and expected.

Clifton Johnson's *God Struck Me Dead* narratives abound with believers' descriptions of moments of transcendence emerging seamlessly from mundane experience. One narrative begins, "One day while in the field plowing I heard a voice. I jumped because I thought it was my master coming to scold and whip me for plowing up some more corn. I looked but saw no one."[27] Then the narrator realizes he has been transported far from the familiar reality of plowing: "Again the voice called, 'Morte! Morte!' With this I stopped, dropped plow and started running but the voice kept on speaking to me, saying, 'Fear not, my little one, for behold! I come to bring you a message of truth.' "[28] Then the experience evolves into a vision: "Everything got dark and I was unable to stand any longer. . . . I looked up and saw that I was in a new world."[29]

Rev. James Carter told a humorous story that underscores the rhetorical power of these adult faith narratives in the Little Zion community:

> My granddaddy [Deacon Ed Carter] said there were three things he ask the Lord for: He wanted religion, he wanted a family, and he wanted some land. He figured if he get those three things, he was gonna be all right. He said later on when he retired, he went to the mailbox and said, "Well Lord, I need some money." The Spirit spoke to him, said, "I gave you everything you asked me for. You asked me for a conversion. I converted you. You asked me for a family. I done gave you a wife and three children. You asked me for land. I done gave you all this land you built this house on. You didn't ask me for no money! Go on now!" He said, "Yes, Lord!"

The moral of the story? "We have to set our goals higher," Rev. Carter said, laughing. "God will give you the desires or your heart, and you have to believe that. In Hebrews, eleventh chapter, in the first few verses, it says that faith is the substance of things hoped for, the evidence of things not seen. And it says that without faith it is *impossible* to please God.[30] So anything you want, you ask the Lord," — and you believe.

Many at Little Zion testified that hearing the instructive voice of God fundamentally changed their perception of their lives. Sister

Hendricks, for instance, felt despair after her husband died, describing how she piled all of her favorite china in the middle of the dining room one day. After years of collecting the beautiful dishes, suddenly, she said, "It meant nothing." But, she continued, "that's the day the Lord spoke to me, told me He was too holy and too righteous to make a mistake. I start back to living. He say, 'I'm too holy and too righteous to make a mistake.' He let me know that John's time was up and he had to go. And that I should continue to live."

Similarly, Sister Leola Carter grieved when, after raising her granddaughter for seven years, her son called to say he would be taking his daughter home to live. "Then," she recounted, "a voice came to me and said, 'Stop crying. Stop crying. You just only raised that baby. You know she wasn't yours in the first place.' I stopped crying. I told my son to come and get her." Sister Carter said God also mitigated her grief by letting her son move home from Tuskegee, where he had been going to school. "So I still didn't lose my baby," she explained.

Anxiety kept Mrs. Bessie Smith awake the night before her trip to Birmingham for eye surgery. She professed faith in the medical establishment, noting, "Doctors is wise now, wiser than they used to be. They study and they read. They know best how to go about things, with new techniques and everything." But that trust in human power could not comfort her like her personal relationship with the divine. Dressed for the operation, rolling on a stretcher toward the operating room, Mrs. Smith said, "I could hear a voice, saying, 'Everything gonna be all right. Everything gonna be all right.' I was going on down the hall and I was just as satisfied as if I could get up and go out that door right there now. I went on in the operating room. Something was just telling me, everything gonna be all right. When he [the doctor] did the operation, I ain't had nary a pain or any more than I'm paining now."

Sometimes, in Little Zion members' experience, God's direction provides the cure for the ailment modern medicine cannot heal. Rev. Lewis, for instance, said once he injured his arm while fixing a woman's heater. "It swelled up to my elbow. It was feeling strange; I went to the doctor on Monday. They x-rayed it, but couldn't find nothing there. Tuesday, they x-rayed that hand three more times. I was hurting. They didn't know what to do" (9/5/98). But where human healing failed, God's intervention did not, Rev. Lewis said. "That evening I was talking to the Lord, and He told me what to do. He told me to urinate on it. That's what I done Tuesday night, and Wednesday morning it was healed like it is now. After one night the Lord had cured me" (9/5/98). When asked whether he was skeptical about God's instruction, Rev. Lewis replied, "I ain't never done nothing like that before, ain't never heard of anybody else done it before.[31] But the Lord told me what to do. I don't question about it. If God tells me to urinate on it, I urinate on it. I don't question God" (9/5/98).

In times of material want, Rev. Lewis and several others at Little Zion said the voice of God directed them to much-needed money. Decades ago as a student of religion at Selma University, Rev. Lewis recalled, "I didn't have a dime in the world. Here it's noontime, and I'm down to my last meal. Then the Spirit told me, 'Get up. Go downtown.' I went downtown to the bank, prayed on the way. They gave me a loan. I went back to the car where my friends is [waiting], told them, 'Get up, while I tell my God thank you'" (8/7/97). In fact, Rev. Lewis noted that as recently as the day before I interviewed him, he got out of his car to go into a store, checking his wallet for money. He noticed he was missing a $20 bill. Then, he said, "the Lord speak to me: 'Go back out where you drive that car.' I turn around and went back. It was laying on the ground" (9/5/98). Rev. Lewis explained, "He let me drop it now, but he didn't let me get too far from it. It was right there when I went back, just laying there" (9/5/98).

Mrs. Bessie Smith described a similar experience:

When I was going to Spring Hill[32] times was kind of rough with money. They had on a fund-raising drive down there; it was a luncheon and we were being asked for $20. That $20 look like a million to me at that time. I said, "Lord, I ain't got no way to pay no $20." With the little money that I did have, I got the food and cooked it for the luncheon. It was Saturday, and the next would be Sunday for to pay the $20, and I didn't have it.

Went on down the road, and I cast my eye over there. I said, "That's something." I looked over there, saw $20 wrapped around a dog fence. It had been there a long time. It had some prickers on it, but you could see it still. I walked over there and I thought, "Oh Lord, here are $20!"

Like Rev. Lewis, Mrs. Smith immediately knew God had provided. She noted that divine intervention works in many ways. Sometimes He puts you at the right place at the right time, or sometimes He "just works through people. He don't come down Hisself and do things, but He work through other people, through you. If you got any common sense at all, you *know* that it had to be God, because this couldn't happen unless God permit it." But the day Mrs. Smith found the money, God spoke directly to her: "He said, 'That's your money for tomorrow.' Just like that. I said, 'Thank you, Jesus! Thank you!' I said, 'Because I know it wasn't nobody but You.' I heard it. He just spoke so loud, it looked like somebody was standing there. Said, 'That's your money for tomorrow.'" Of course, the encounter confirmed her faith: "Oooh Lord! Don't be talking about God, saying there ain't no God. God's dead and all. Don't tell me that. God ain't dead and never will die. Oh yeah. I done experienced a lot in my life."

While many at Little Zion said God had spoken to them in answer to their prayers, only a few said He had revealed himself in visions. Sister Hendricks remembered older church members from her childhood, some of whom would "go to heaven every night." Her mother would sit and shell peas with Cousin Tilly [phonetic spelling], who would recount her visions. Sister Hendricks continued, "I don't know if she was sleeping or what. I imagine she was dreaming. . . . She says heaven is a beautiful place. She says everything up there is white. She'd say, 'I went there last night. Sure did.' And she'd talk about it." After finishing the peas the two friends would walk each other home. "Mama walk her home a little piece with her. They'd turn around, walk a little piece this way, turn around, walk a little piece back." All the while, they'd, "keep talking about heaven. She'd tell Mama it was beautiful up there. Everything is white. . . . She'd tell you about angels, watch over you all night while you sleep."

Many of the *God Struck Me Dead* narratives include descriptions of visions of heaven in which everything is white. One narrator reported, for instance, a vision of heaven in which he saw Jesus, "standing in snow — the prettiest, whitest snow I have ever seen. . . . Everything seemed to be made of white stones and pearls."[33] Another even described himself and God in terms of white images. "My soul took to the air and having wings like a bird I flew away into a world of light with thousands of other images like myself. . . . I didn't see anything but myself and the other white images like me."[34] In a later vision, angels around a white table with gold-tipped wings informed the narrator, " 'This is heaven,' " and "I saw the Lord in the east part of the world and He looked like a white man. His hair was parted in the middle and he looked like he had been dipped in snow and he was talking to me."[35]

Sister Hendricks also testified to a vision in which God healed her of a crippling paralysis. Her perception of the experience seems to blend mundane, physical reality with supernatural encounter because she does not make a distinction between seeing herself healthy again and physically experiencing that return to strength. She said, "I got one time where I couldn't walk. You could point at that foot and it wouldn't move. I couldn't move it myself. I said, 'Lord, is You gonna let your child live in the world, won't be able to walk no more?' I said, 'If I be able to walk, Jesus, show me a sign. Show me so plain that a fool can understand.' And when I saw myself (in my mind's eye), I saw myself running. And I began to run. And it come to me, it said, 'Is this me running?' I looked at my foot and said, 'Lord have mercy. This is me running.' I been running ever since." Does she literally mean that she began to run? It remains unclear, as she continues to meditate on her condition as if still witnessing God's power in her mind's eye: " 'Lord have mercy. This is me running.' " With her statement "I been running ever since," Sister Hendricks seemed to be speaking rhetorically, indicating that she has remained strong in faith ever since this vision.[36] In fact she followed up with a statement to that effect, saying, "And Little Zion, I love it. I always will love it." Thus, the physical return to health remains an obvious outcome of spiritual healing. She had been lame earlier, but God had shown her a vision of herself running. Professing strong faith and clearly physically mobile during this interview, she indicated that in the aftermath of the vision, she has been running ever since — both symbolically and literally.

For Rev. Lewis, the blending of the mundane and the supernatural had literally changed his perception of time and space, allowing him to foresee future events, for instance. He said matter-of-factly, "Sometime He shows you what's gonna happen. I see it. Anytime I ask Him, that's what He gives me. . . . Ain't nothing to do but to go to work then. Go to work in harmony with what He showed you gonna happen" (9/5/98). Sometimes, though, nothing can be done to avert upcoming events. Rev. Lewis said once as a young man he had a vision predicting that his house would burn down:

> Don't nothing slip up on me. Must have been sixty or seventy years ago, I come in the house, sat down. The devil jumps up and tells me, 'It's gonna burn. Your wife's gonna burn your house. Your wife's gonna burn your house *up* tonight.' I went back out and finished working, come in, sat down just like every other night. I inquire about everybody. The children not in the house. I asked, 'What about the baby?' My wife said, 'Mama got the baby tonight.' I sat down there and prayed. The devil come to me, the Lord come to me, the Spirit come to me again. 'The house is gonna burn tonight.' Just like that. 'The house is gonna burn tonight.' That was the Lord. He told me, 'It gonna burn tonight.' " (9/5/98)

Though his wife did not cause the fire, Rev. Lewis reported, "At nine o'clock, [the house] was in ashes. I was waiting for it to happen. It just caught fire; I couldn't stop it. If I went in there, I get trapped. But everybody got out; nobody got burned." Notably, this narrative marks the community's only description of an encounter with the devil, and even here, God was the overriding power in warning the family of the upcoming crisis: "That was the Lord," Rev. Lewis asserted. "He told me, 'It gonna burn tonight.' "

As touched on earlier, many at Little Zion regarded Rev. Lewis as a prophet with a direct connection to the Lord. He said of the ability to see future events, "It's common in my life, this knowing. All we need to do is trust in God. Just trust in God. Ask Him to tell you what to do, and when it's done you can thank Him. You can do anything on faith" (9/5/98).

CALL TO PREACH: "PICK UP THE BIBLE"

For some men in Little Zion's community, the awesome experience of God's power shapes their lives even more profoundly than the expressions of guidance and comfort outlined above. For them, the inward encounter with the Lord turns their spirits outward again, with the life-changing command to go and preach the Word to others. Rev. Willie C. Carter remembered:

The day when He called me in 1985, I had that feeling. Early in the morning, I was getting ready to go to work. Looked like He was on my house roof, like the voice was coming from the roof of my house.

The voice said, "Pick up the Bible and go to Proverbs, 16 and 16." I opened the Bible; it was a miracle. I was on Proverbs, 16 and 16. I read it, and it was telling me that wisdom is better than gold. Understanding is better than silver.[37]

I said, "Yes Lord." Seemed like I want to say, "Give me a little more time." Seemed like I want to say that.

But He said, "This is not all. Turn to 16 and 15 in Mark." Mark 16 and 15 said, "Go ye in all part of the world and preach my gospel to every creature. He that believes in me shall be baptized. He that believe it not shall be damned."[38] (9/6/98)

Rev. Carter had never wanted to be a preacher, because "everybody look like give the preacher a bad name," he said, laughing. "I ain't never had no idea that I would be a minister till the Lord called me. I liked teaching Sunday school and being in the church. I was leading the service all my life. But I just didn't want to be a preacher" (9/7/98). But in receiving the call, Rev. Carter said, he literally was transported by the will of the Spirit. After reading the Bible verses, he recalled, "I don't know how I got out of the house, but it seemed like I had two wings. I had two wings. I got up and went on through. My kid was getting ready to go to school and he said, 'I don't know what's the matter with Daddy.' I landed out there by the car of some men that were working for me. . . . When I come down on the ground, I was preaching God's word" (9/6/98).

Rev. Carter's family members elaborated on his experience, recalling that when he reached the front yard he had a vision. His wife, Sister Leola Carter, said, "The angel, or God, or whoever, told him to come outside. There was what looked like a ship parked out here in front of our house, big and long, white as snow. The voice told him to come on board." His father, Deacon Ed Carter, remembered: "One morning he come running over here, say, 'Daddy, God told me to go preach, go preach His Word. I'm a preacher. God told me, "Go preach! Go preach!" I want you to come on and go with me around to tell the folks what the Lord told me!' Right out here at the back door. He went outside and saw a white boat, a shining white boat in the front yard and God told him to preach His word. So me and him got in the truck and he went all around preaching" (8/7/97).

Like the children who witnessed their conversion to faith by going from house to house spreading the good news, Rev. Carter felt moved to go public with his message. Filled with the Lord's power, he spoke in the local black and white communities, knocking on doors to spread the Word in people's homes: "I preached for five days without stopping. I preached from that Monday morning all that week before I reconsidered. I didn't reconsider if I even had a job; I was doing God's work everywhere I go. I just went all around, all in the country, all in Forkland, all in Eutaw, up and down the street. Wherever I stopped, I was preaching God to white and black. That's the way he traveled me" (9/6/98). Sister Carter said, "We drove around all day and half the night. When he went to people's door, a lot of them looked like they had just gotten the Holy Ghost themselves. I went in with him. Every time he preach, look like he go a round higher each time."

Days later, Rev. Carter prayed for another experience to confirm his new path in life. With his family at a football game and the house to himself, he asked the Lord, "I want you to do me as you did to peoples on the day of Pentecost, and you fill the house. I want my house to be filled, my rooms to be filled."[39] After praying for a few minutes, Rev. Carter said, "all of the sudden, the curtains came out and the wind from the curtains was so warm. It hit me and I had the Holy Ghost. I went from one side of the room to another. I said, 'Thank you, Lord. I do hear you now' " (9/6/98). Comparing himself to the children of Israel at Mount Sinai, to whom God issued the Ten Commandments out of a cloud of thunder and lightning, Rev. Carter said he now heard clearly God's will: "He went to talking to them through thunder and lightning. And they say to Moses, 'We obey your God. We hear your God. Your God is *the* God.'[40] That's the way I was. I said, 'Lord, you don't have to do it to me no more. If I don't feel it no more, I will accept your Word, just like I did' " (9/6/98). He concluded, "This happened in *one* week, 1985. I was called" (9/6/98).

Others who received the call to preach described similar transcendent events. Rev. Willie Carter's son, James, received his calling on a Friday afternoon, while singing with the choir in his college chapel. He said, "And then all of the sudden, I just had this change come over me. I thought it was just a great moment with the Holy Spirit. And I went on." But on his way home an hour later, Rev. Carter realized the encounter had held more significance. "I just got out of my car and preached. I preached my first sermon in a housing project, where there was a party going on. I knew nobody there. I preached. They just listened. They stopped the party and listened." He remembered clearly the message of his sermon — that God wants us to deny ourselves. Rather than testify personally about his spiritual life, Rev. Carter spoke more broadly, citing the Word in exhorting and advising others. For Rev. Carter, the gesture of taking God's message outward in this way confirmed the supernatural encounter for him as a vocational calling. He noted, "I had no control. It's a spiritual experience. I have a vivid memory of it; I was watching it happen."

The experience lasted for three days. "Three days before I came out of it, or before it came out of me," Rev. Carter said. Late one night he was preaching loudly, and someone called the police. "There was two cops. One of them thought I was on drugs. He went to push me." But the other recognized the young preacher's state of mind. "He said, 'I know what's wrong with him.' " When he telephoned Rev. Carter's family home, "he told [Rev. Carter's] father, 'He's in good hands.'" His mother immediately recognized that her son had received the call to preach. Sister Leola Carter said, "The police thought he was going crazy, but when they gave him that phone and he start talking to me, I just start shouting. I call to my husband, 'He preaching! He preaching!' I said, 'He preaching!' I just kept saying it." Upon hearing him spreading the Word, Sister Carter said the Spirit struck her too: "Yeah, I'm gonna tell you that was a time of my life. I felt it. I felt it in here. It looked like something just *hit* me. It made my hair stood up on my head." Rev. and Sister Carter immediately went to visit their son, "and that boy preached and preached and preached," she concluded. "Now that was a joyous time in my life."

God's call to preach traditionally has qualified the preacher for the role of leading local congregations in this region. Churches looking for pastors invite new preachers to conduct "trial sermons," offering permanent positions to those well-received by the church community. But in recent decades, preachers have prepared themselves beyond the customary practices of growing up in the faith community and heeding the call. Now formal education plays a large role in many preachers' spiritual journeys, with several men at Little Zion noting that the call to preach prompted them to begin serious theological study. Rev. Eddie Carter said he was called to the ministry around 1994. But, he went on, "I knew that I didn't know much about Jesus Christ biblically. I decided to, through the grace of God, pray to Him, and He showed me that I was going to school, going to reside somewhere." When he was given information on Birmingham Theological Seminary, Rev. Carter laid it down somewhere. "The Spirit said, 'Pick it up and read it.' So I read it. I applied and was given a scholarship. . . . The Lord blessed me financially to be able to grow in the call . . . until I earned a Masters of Ministry."

Rev. Oscar Williams said he used his education to wrestle with his calling, attempting to explain it away. At nine years old, he said, the Lord came to him in the night, saying, " 'Go ye therefore into the world, preaching and teaching.'[41] It came to me just as plain, just as plain as I'm talking to you. . . . My formal ministry now is a surrendering to what I know that I was destined, called to be. I have known since I was nine years old. I just did not formalize that until years later." He added, "Whether I ran from it or not, I knew it, and I have no doubt in my mind that I am called. Even if I would doubt it, I would have to come back to the very fact that He said to me, 'Go ye therefore . . .' Then, most importantly, He said, 'And lo, I will be with you always, even to the end of the world.'" Rev. Williams said he simply can't get around that plainly stated divine command. "Now other folks may try to wiggle around it. But I don't have no wiggle room. I could intellectualize it, you know: [Speaking in an affected voice,] 'Well you were in a high state of excitement.' [Returning to a normal voice,] Yeah, He told me, 'Lo, I'll be with you always. Even,' He said, 'until the end of the world.'"

Though he turned to education to rationalize his experience, Rev. Williams finally concluded that he could not explain away the divine encounter that called him to serve in the ministry. "I'm talking about having wrestled with that question for forty-nine years. I still can't get around it. I wore out a B.S. degree wrestling with it. I put a stranglehold and a body slam on a masters, and I got a choke on a doctorate; I still can't get around it! No matter what I say or do, I have no doubt in my mind of my call." He also noted of the courses he has taught at seminary, "We can talk about how far away the sun is, and the moon and the planetary system, explore the heavens up and down. . . . We get into some theological discussions, but you still can't shake us out of that basic conviction." For the call to preach "is as real to me today as you sitting here. I can go where I want, still, He did say that to me. 'Lo, I will be with you always, even to the end of the earth.'"

MINISTRY: "I DON'T WORK FOR MONEY. I WORK FOR HEAVEN."

For those called to preach in the Little Zion community, formal theological training serves as only part of the minister's preparation to lead the congregation. In preaching almost always without written notes, ministers rely on a lifetime lived in the oral tradition, in which sermons are delivered with the rhythmic cadences of the performed African American sermon. All those interviewed for this project indicated that the act of preaching becomes a transcendent experience, with God speaking through them to His people. Thus, extensive preparations for oratory, such as outlining or note-taking, are unnecessary. Instead, the preacher must ready his spirit to receive God's Word.

Rev. Willie Carter noted, for example, "I can't hop up and just preach a sermon. If the call is unexpected, I can preach for them, but I won't want to. I be praying all the week anyway, but I just want to dedicate myself to the sermon" (9/7/98). He prays over his sermon all week: "I concentrate on it, and pray over it every day. If I've got free time on Sunday, I just meditate and pray over it before I do it" (9/7/98). Then, when he rises to preach, Rev. Carter said, "I talk till I can feel God; I can feel God's Spirit coming. It's just all on the inside of me. Oooh! When it come, it bring all my remembrance. . . . Mostly I don't have to write it down, because God gives it to me" (9/7/98).

His son, Rev. James Carter, agreed, saying, "Every sermon I preach, I get this cognitive flow. I meditate and I ask God, 'What it is you want me to say? What it is you want me to preach about? What message do you want me to preach?' I just wait, and that's the way it happens." Rev. Carter pointed out that "it is very important to remove yourself from this as much as possible and just allow the Spirit to flow." In focusing beyond the self, the preacher allows God to perform the sermon through him. Rev. Carter also cited the Pentecost story as a model for his preaching, saying he hopes to emulate the disciples who prayed and waited until they were filled with the Holy Spirit and the voice of God spoke through them.[42]

Both father and son described their preaching as a vehicle for the Spirit to move outside of themselves and touch others in the community. As discussed earlier, the traditional call-and-response format of sermons at Little Zion relies on the congregation's response to help drive the sermon forward rhythmically. And these preachers said that the Word gains power as the Spirit moves through the church's believers. Rev. Willie Carter explained: "It just goes on, goes on, goes on till I get deep in it, and touched with the Spirit. And the whole church will just about get like me. The people, some of them start moaning and groaning and singing songs. When I'm standing there I can see the reaction, and it just makes me feel good too. It gives me the energy to preach" (9/7/98). He compared the experience to rabbit hunting with his father: "We used to have some dogs, and the more we whooped at them, looked like the better they get. They get to running rabbit, and the rabbit would go to running and come all around our feet. Well, when you're telling the Truth, and they know the Truth, and when they all join in with you, whew, it gets good! [Here he rubbed his hands together.] It gets wonderful!" (9/7/98). His son agreed, describing how the preaching becomes a vehicle for each person in the congregation to come to God. But he also cautioned, "I can't really convince you; you have to convince yourself" and added that though the sermon moves forward on the congregation's responses, the preacher must remain "tuned in to the Holy Spirit. . . . It's not a concert. You're not thrilled because of the applause or 'amens.'" Rather, he said, the preacher serves as a watchman. "My responsibility is to keep the people awake, and to keep the people clearly focused on the fact that the God we serve, even though he is a God of love, a God of grace, will one day be a God of judgment."

The seven preachers interviewed for this project also emphasized that their ministry extends beyond speaking God's message outward to the congregation.[43] They also must live out His will in the larger community. Rev. W. D. Lewis spoke succinctly of his calling, noting, "I don't work for money. I work for heaven," and asserting that God works through him to save souls beyond the boundaries of the church (8/7/97). In fact, the role of the church "is to save the world," he said. "People talk about them bad people not being saved. Well, if the church ain't gonna save them, who is?" (8/7/97). Preachers associated with Little Zion perform this community outreach not only by spreading the Word but also by providing a living example of Christ's teachings. For instance, even after Sunday services that often extend into the afternoon, Little Zion's preachers and deacons routinely stop by the local hospital to visit ailing church members, friends, and neighbors. Rev. Willie Carter noted that he tries to live "a good life." "I try to live by the commandments of God, the Bible," he explained.

"I have the love for the peoples, and I do things for peoples. I just love and keep on. I do it every day and keep on doing it" (9/7/98). For Rev. Oscar Williams, the essence of his ministry is community service. Citing a career as varied as participating in the Peace Corps, creating affordable housing in Greene County, establishing credit unions, setting up Ruritan Clubs, and coordinating the vo-tech program at Tuskegee University, Rev. Williams said, "My life has been one that is dedicated to the service of others." He added, "My ministry is service to others to help others help themselves. If there's anything I would want on my tombstone, it would be that I tried to do right by all persons, regardless.... As long as I can help somebody, then my living will not be in vain. It will not be in vain."

Finally, Rev. James Carter pointed out that an effective preacher also turns the church congregation outward, teaching them that the fruits of their conversion experiences, their membership in the church, and their continued personal relationship with the divine should be shown in the work they do in the communities in which they live. Slipping into the rhythms of preacherly oratory and citing the words of Jesus (Matthew 25:34–40), Rev. Carter easily transformed the interview into a forum for urging church members to put their beliefs into practice:

God will judge us according to the deeds we did in this life. He'll say, "When was it that you fed those that was hungry? When was it that you took in those that was outdoors? When was it that you went and visited the sick? When did you go to see about those who were in prison? When did you give somebody water when they were thirsty? Bread when they were hungry? When did you do these things?"

When you did it to anybody, it's just like doing it to God.... We have a responsibility to people as we grow.... If I know my neighbor is cold, I have a responsibility to be concerned. If I know my neighbor is naked, I have a responsibility to clothe him. It's something that you have to make a part of your life. You have to practice it, and once you practice it, it becomes a part of you.... You can reach in your pocket and hand somebody your last dollar, knowing that God is gonna give you another.

In this way, the very individual experience of religion at Little Zion remains strongly tied to the outward community in which it is practiced — both within the walls of the building and beyond them, in any setting where these people live out the beliefs and traditions wrought by lifetimes of activities at the church on the hill, once a brush arbor, once a log cabin, once a frame church leaning to the right, and twice now a brick church. Since the burning of the first brick structure in 1996, Little Zion's members, collectively and individually, have incorporated that event into a belief structure that recognizes "our God *is* a consuming fire" (Hebrews 12:29) and maintains that "they that trust in the Lord *shall be* as mount Zion *which* cannot be removed, *but* abideth forever" (Psalm 125:1).

*And be not conformed to this world; but be ye transformed by the
renewing of your mind, that ye may prove what is that good,
and acceptable, and perfect, will of God.*
—*Romans* 12:2

CHAPTER SIX

Recollections by Rev. Michael Barton

I interviewed Rev. Michael Barton at Little Zion on Sunday, July 20,
2003, after he'd led a powerful worship service that had run until
midafternoon and packed the church with about seventy-five people
—about double the usual attendance in my experience. We settled in
the pastor's study, having just met for the first time moments before.
I was concerned that Rev. Barton would not feel comfortable during
this interview. His predecessors, Rev. Lewis and Rev. Williams, had
participated in this project during its much earlier stages, clearly giving both men the chance to shape the direction of this work. But this
interview came near the end of research and writing. I was afraid Rev.
Barton would not feel free to guide this narrative as I always hoped
Little Zion's members would do.

My fears were unfounded. Although Rev. Barton had little to say
about Little Zion's past, as is discussed in the rest of this book, he
outlined a vision for the future and spoke eloquently of his efforts to
move the church according to God's will. Our conversation seemed to
complete this book, moving forward from the collected memories
toward the ministry of a rebuilt and revitalized church.

As did Sister Rosie Lee Hendricks (see Chapter 3), Rev. Barton
narrated a life story with the church at the center. But this much
younger man did not look back over a long lifetime's spiritual journey

shaped by the church. Rather, he spoke of "the old time church," which provided his religious foundation, in contrast to "the newer ways," which he now felt called to bring to Little Zion — with a strong emphasis on youth ministry and adult fellowship. In a much more overtly powerful position than Sister Hendricks enjoyed, Rev. Barton was more self-conscious of his role in shaping tradition at Little Zion.

That self-awareness also points to a major difference in the two narratives. While Sister Hendricks surrendered herself to the Spirit during her interview, transforming it into testimony, Rev. Barton did not. Though he provided a detailed account of his own struggles to surrender his "hardheaded" ego to God's plan, he did not experience that letting go during this conversation. As church pastor, Rev. Barton had another venue for that surrender: the pulpit. In fact, he spoke with me just after the delivery of a Spirit-filled sermon. Sister Hendricks, as a woman not called to preach formally, lacked such an outlet for sacred speech. For this reason, perhaps, the interview gave her a chance to witness the power of God in her life.[1]

Rev. Barton presented his calling as a preacher, and his early experiences in God's service, as a struggle "to let go of the worldly things." But those worldly things seem mainly to include his awareness of himself, as he elaborated, "I just wasn't ready, and I had a fear of how people would receive me, knowing the lifestyle that I had lived, and now here I am presenting myself as a preacher." Finally, Rev. Barton said, "I surrendered" and accepted the calling. Yet his self-consciousness remained a challenge: "The first time I preached was a moment of nervousness like never before. I was thinking a lot on the task that I was getting ready to step into. I was trying to look down the road, even while sitting there waiting to get up to preach. I tried to look into the future." Flustered, Rev. Barton dropped the notes to his sermon, and in that moment learned to let go fully. He prayed for the Lord's guidance and was given the words (Word) to preach the sermon. Now, he said, "as the Lord speaks to me, I share. I love listening to the Spirit."

Rev. Barton also recounted an instance when nobody attended his Sunday service. Without an audience, he "was moved to go through the worship service anyway." Thus, he had learned to perform the

On July 20, 2003, Rev. Michael Barton discusses his vision
for Little Zion's future.

service not, as Rev. James Carter distinguished, for an audience's benefit, but out of God's leading, and he gave lie to the saying, "You can't preach to an empty church."

Still, outside of the immediate experience of God's presence during his interview, Rev. Barton was willing and able to dissect the performative aspects of his calling. He noted candidly, "I try to make the services interesting; You notice I use humor. I try to make it exciting, and at the same time make sure you're getting some good Word, something to help you. I'm very mobile in my preaching. I walk, I move, I jump, I run sometimes." Perhaps the very formality of Rev. Barton's preaching venue gives him space to reflect on his spiritual encounters in this way, whereas Sister Hendricks's informal testimony meshes more seamlessly into her personal religious journey and does not trigger such reflection.

With differing degrees of self-awareness and self-analysis, the narratives of Sister Rosie Lee Hendricks and Rev. Michael Barton provide excellent examples of the artful use of religious language to touch the sacred in these two believers' life stories.

I grew up in the Forkland area, which is about ten miles adjacent to this community. But I had never even visited Little Zion. During my school-age years, I was at Ebenezer Baptist Church in Forkland. That's where William McKinley Branch, first black probate judge, was pastor. I grew up under his teaching.

My brother and my sister and I were raised by our great-great-aunt. I'm the oldest of the three, and she was seventy when I was born. She taught us what she knew about the Lord in the home, at the church. We always knew about the Lord Jesus growing up. Every Sunday we were drug to church. Once, I heard a preacher say that he's been on the "drugs." And what he was referring to, was, "I was drug to church!" We were drug to church.

There was never a time that I can remember not wanting to go. In my church there were a lot of youths, and we were able to get involved. Every year, we would go down to Selma to the

Baptist convention. That was like a reward for us. We were able to be with peers, and at the same time sit down with the church's leadership. It was exciting. So even after I grew up and moved away, I never moved away from the church. I always went to church. It was just instilled in me.

We had a great growing up. My brother and sister and I had a great teacher in Feignroe Robinson. Lord, have mercy. She was the oldest of eight, and her mother's health failed when she was young. My aunt had to be the mother of the house and raise all of her siblings, even take care of her mom. She would tell us how hard it was, how they didn't have food to eat, how she would go into the cotton fields from sunup until sundown, and may sometimes get a nickel a day. She would tell us about how hard it was even after she became grown and began to have children herself, providing for her family and her children, even her brothers' and sisters' children. She took care of family. She raised my great-grandmother, she raised my grandmother, she raised my mother and she raised me, four generations.

At that time the community believed in, "It takes the whole village to raise the child." In the community, I could sit around and listen to the older people just talk about the Lord in visitation. They told how they came up in the church, and I was able to experience some of that myself. I experienced the old-time church that they were saved in, the wooden floors, the wooden pews, the pot-bellied stove in the corner. My aunt would tell us how they had to walk for miles to church. How they already knew what they were gonna wear to church every Sunday because there was only one outfit. How they would pull their shoes off in the walking to the church, and put them on when they got there. She would tell about how they would have to walk in the cold, then build the fire once they got there. She would tell about how the people were so unified and so loving; they really believed in just praising God and thanking God. I was able to experience a lot of that. Sometimes now, churches here remind me of her stories.

We walked to church every Sunday, rain, shine, sleet, or

snow, a little less than a mile away. Then there were times when my aunt was not able to walk the distance because of age and health. So she would take us to the road, and she would stand there, watching, until we had gotten to where the road went down in the little ditch. When I was seven, eight, we would have to walk up to the church like that. There would be someone standing at the church — Deacon James Belton, a great man. He would be standing outside, greeting people, waiting for us to come. He would stand and wait at the door.

My aunt taught us the fear of God. That was first and foremost. To the point where we were almost afraid of God, you know, thunder and lightning. She taught us the fear of God, and then she taught us how to love ourselves as brothers and sisters, the three of us, and love each other. We would sit down and eat together, and we would talk. She would pray with us, and pray before us. She would sing songs, especially "Amazing Grace" and "Precious Lord," those type songs. She would make us sometimes sit down, and just listen to her sing, and just listen to her pray. She whipped us when we had different little spats. She would whip us, and then she would tell us the right way, what we should do.

She raised us, but she always taught us that mom and dad should be respected as mom and dad, even though they were not there much during the growing up. She taught us how to clean. She taught us how to cook. Of course, there were chores. My brother and I would have to go with her, learn to chop wood, farm. She taught us how to work.

My first Christmas present that I can remember was a lawn mower. My brother and I were like, "Okay, where are the boxes? Where are the toys?" (I just shared this with some young boys that I talk to quite often.) She said these words to us: "Now, when you do what's right with this, you'll be able next Christmas to have the toys."

We tried to figure out what was right. We would cut grass in the neighborhood, and we would make five dollars here, ten dollars there. She taught us how to put back. And when next Christmas came around we were able to purchase our toys.

We grew up in a home where we received welfare. She received SSI, and I can remember exactly how much it was: She only received $163 a month. And then we received like $76 in food stamps. And for a long time, that was all the finances that were coming into the house. But I cannot remember a day going without clothes on my back, going without food.

She lived until I was twenty-two. Her health had begun to fail her after she was about eighty-five, eighty-six. Her daughter and son-in-law, Pastor Thomas Gilmore, first black sheriff, helped a whole lot in the raising of us. We've had some great teaching.

Pastor Branch had a love for the children and for the people of the church. He was a great teacher, and church was just instilled. It was just instilled. The Sunday school classes. Singing in the choir, the Easter and Christmas programs, being able to go to BTU [Baptist Training Union]. BTU gave us the opportunity to come back and stand before the church, to tell what we had learned. Man, it was just a great time. Those things are very fond memories.

My aunt would tell me about times of segregation, when they were afraid sometimes in having church. But they had it anyhow. Because even though they were scared, they knew that the Lord would still be with them and take care of them.

A lot of the mass meetings during the civil rights movement were held at the church I grew up in. One deacon there lived right across the street from me. Deacon Blocker Carter: He was 101 when he passed a few years ago. He would remind us quite often of one night when they were having a mass meeting in church, when there were Klansmen coming to the church. Some of the men from the church hid out back in the woods with their guns during the service — to scare off the Klan.

They had to fire their guns and run the Klansmen away. But they did not interrupt the service. The service went on.

I accepted the Lord in 1979 and was baptized outdoors. The pool is still there. I've even experienced pond baptisms and lake baptisms, but mine was in the pool outside of the church.

At the revival in the third week of August, 1979, I was nine years old. My aunt had been preparing us. She would read the Bible with us, pray with us, and just tell us about the Lord. She would ask questions like, "Do you want your soul to be saved?" and "Do you believe that Jesus is your savior?" They had had two weeks of prayer service before the revival, every evening, just praying at the church. The preacher would open the service, and then the people would just come and just pray. It was something to see the people all bending on their knees, bowing and praying, and travailing to the Lord in spirit, praying for sinners, praying for souls to be saved.

That Monday night of the revival, there were twenty-two of us on the mourner's bench. Our pastor opened the church, extended the invitation, and I was the third person on the bench. The gentleman that was sitting on the very end got up and went to shake the pastor's hand. He said that he wanted to be baptized, and he believed. And people started coming around, the older mothers of the church and deacons, bowing and bending before the mourners, praying that the Lord would touch our spirits, touch our hearts, move us.

That night myself and about six other people came off the mourner's bench. I was very hesitant because a lot of people said you needed a sign: You needed to hear something, needed to see the sun rise in the east, all types of little signs before you could really come forth. I believed that at that time, and I was hesitant. But I got up because my friend had gotten up. I think a lot of us got up because we didn't want to be the last one on the mourner's bench.

Years later, I actually went before God in repentance. I acknowledged that I had believed and wanted to be saved. I wanted to know Him as Lord and Savior. But at the same time, I didn't see a sign, and I didn't want to be the last one on the pew. "Lord, just forgive me for stepping out in that fashion. But I honestly wanted to be saved."

Thank God, even after all of that, I never lost a love for the church. I was able to really experience salvation. The peace came years later.

I don't believe that you must see a sign, that you must hear the dove or what have you. I'm not in agreeance with the signs, but because I was taught that as a child, that stuck with me. I'm often reminded of the scriptures, and the writings of Paul to the Romans, 10th chapter, around verse nine,[2] that thou shall believe in thy heart, and confess with thy mouth on Jesus, that He died and God raised Him from the dead. He says, "Thou shall be saved." I don't recall reading where there must be a sign. And then there's another passage: The wicked and perverse generation seeketh out the signs.

Salvation is something that you accept, and it comes through your belief and your confession. I'm not in agreeance with the signs, because I've learned and read and studied since then for myself. In talking with a lot of older people, I've come to the realization that back in those days a lot of them couldn't read and write. They needed something tangible. I can somewhat understand that, but I have seen and studied in the Word for myself.

Shortly after I graduated from high school, I moved to Columbus, Ohio, for a few months, and then back to Huntsville. I went to Alabama A&M University, a child- and adolescent-development major. I joined the Primitive Baptist Church in Huntsville in '89.

Then around '91 the Lord began to work with me and deal with me spiritually, as far as moving into the ministry. He worked a lot with me through visions. There was an unction God had placed in my spirit to preach. He had called me to the purpose and showed me what He wanted me to do in the ministry.

But I was fighting it. I didn't want to have to let go of the worldly things. I just wasn't ready, and I had a fear of how would people receive me, knowing the lifestyle that I had lived, and now here I'm presenting myself as a preacher.

Because of my disobedience to what I knew that the Lord wanted me to do, I went into a phase of whippings from the Lord. The whippings came. I went through being homeless, out on the street. There, you have time to really meditate. I tried to figure out, how can I get off the street? How can I be restored with shelter and a job? The Lord spoke to me, "It's because of your disobedience."

But I was hardheaded. I not only contemplated suicide, I even attempted it. While I was sitting waiting for my demise, the spirit of God spoke to me, said that my life is in His hands, that there's a work He wants me to do. And I was not going to leave this life until I'd done it.

I surrendered. It had got to a point where I really was just tired of the whippings. I said, "Okay, let's do what I know I need to do." I surrendered unto the Lord and I accepted the calling on June 25, 1995. I began to work in the ministry.

Approximately a month and a week later, I did my first sermon. I began preaching. I had been sitting under my pastor and studying, because I wanted to be prepared. I had spent most of my time at home, just studying and praying and meditating. Just spending time with the Lord.

The first time I preached it was a moment of nervousness like never before. I was thinking a lot on the task that I was getting ready to step into. I was trying to look down the road, even while sitting there waiting to get up to preach. I tried to look into the future.

I had written out my sermon, about seven pages. But here's the interesting thing. I began to preach. Before I got finished with the first page, I knocked all of my papers on the floor. My pastor just reached down, picked them up and put them back for me. But I didn't want to further embarrass myself by trying to put the pages in order.

So I stopped and I just prayed. I just asked the Lord to guide me. It was like the Lord just answered. I never got past page one, but I finished the sermon. The Lord really blessed that, and I haven't been nervous since.

I've had seminary experience. I've taken notes, and I've tried several times since my first sermon to preach from my notes. But I find myself speaking more from what the Lord puts within me. It's hard for me just to use the notes. My preaching is expository; I deal directly with what I see in the scripture. As the Lord speaks to me, I share. I love listening to the Spirit.

There have been times that I've studied all week to prepare for a sermon. And I've gotten up and the Lord just puts something else in my spirit. Sometimes I question, "Okay, Lord, I didn't prepare for this passage of scripture. I'm totally surrendering to You and what You put in my spirit." I love that type of preaching. It comes from previous study, from meditation time, from listening to God and from personal experiences. It's exciting. Sometimes I get up wondering, "Okay, Lord, what will You have me say today? I really need to hear from You. People are waiting."

We must understand as ministry men, as teachers, we have to be led by the Spirit. Sometimes God may be wanting to reach someone who's not fitting in with what we've prepared in our own intellect — what we write and what we say. We have to understand that we're really just vessels for the Lord to work through us. We must prepare, but at the same time we must yield to the Spirit. I try to do that every time I mount the pulpit.

Under my pastor's leadership I served as interim pastor in Athens, Alabama, at a small church that had been closed for almost four years. There were only five members, just one family that did not want to lose ties with that church. I was assigned to work with them.

There were Sundays that I went and there was no one there. There was no one in the church. Believe it or not, I was moved to go through the worship service anyway. And no one was there. I would get up and preach. I would sing. I would pray. And I would preach. And then I would extend the invitation, and no one was in the church but me.

There were some Sundays when I left the doors wide open, and all the windows wide open. And I would preach to anyone who might hear.

One day three young men had been walking past the church. They came in. I ministered to them. And they accepted the Lord as their Savior.

They did not join that church, but we were able to send them back to their home churches, their family churches, to be baptized.

My life was so comfortable for me in Huntsville. I was working on a special juvenile training program, I supervised at a detention center, and I was working part time in the barber shop. I was loving my church; the ministry was going good.

But the Lord moved me, gave me the vision to come back to Greene County, come back home. He showed me a church in the vision. It was like an out-of-body experience. I could just see the church in my spirit, and how the church was growing. There were dreams; they were just awesome. I can remember waking up, and it just felt like people were flooding my apartment. One night, I just got up and went into the front room. I stood in the middle of the room, and I just invited them, just said, "Come on." I had a roommate at the time. He said I was sleepwalking.

This happened one Friday night, about three o'clock in the morning. By three thirty I had packed everything in my car and moved home. I didn't know where I was going to stay; the home I grew up in was being rented. I just started driving home. I was crying and praying and talking and crying and praying. The Lord just assured me that everything was going to be okay, even though I would suffer great loss.

I went back to my home church, Ebenezer. That Sunday there were fifteen people in the church. Members had just fallen away.

I talked with the pastor about starting a youth ministry and a young adult choir. I went from door to door, talking to old friends, old classmates, just encouraging them, "Look, come on back to the church." There were twenty-seven people in the young adult choir, and only one of those people had already been coming to church.

There had been about three to five kids in Sunday school. Within the next three Sundays, we had sixty-two kids in Sunday school. The Lord was saying, "The vision is being fulfilled."

We started the children's ministry on Wednesday nights. It started out with twenty-five kids the first Wednesday night. That second Wednesday night there were seventy-six kids. I'll never forget it. By the fourth Wednesday night, we were up to 119 kids.

My pastor said that was starting another church within the church. So they canceled the children's ministry, and they stopped me from teaching.

The Lord spoke to me. "I got a place for you."

By that time, I had been asked probably by seven different churches to pastor. But I never would go, because I never felt that unction to pastor. Shortly after that, I was working with Americorps one Saturday morning. I was singing, "Let your light from the lighthouse shine on me." We were not supposed to be singing church songs because of separation of church and state, but I was singing that.

A young lady from this community said, "Why're you just singing that song like that?"

I said, "For some reason, I just feel that the Lord is getting ready to place me into a church."

She said, "Well why you wait until all the churches in Tishabee have a pastor?"

I said, "Well, I had to wait until the Lord put that unction into my spirit." I wasn't going looking for a church. That's God's work.

I was supposed to preach here at Little Zion the next morning. When I got here and drove around the church, it just hit me. A church that sits up on a hill. It's like a city that cannot be hid.[3] What about pastoring here?

At that moment, I literally said, "No!" I was like, "Devil, you're a liar! How are you gonna present this to me when you know that I just said yesterday that I feel like it's time for me to pastor? This church *has* a pastor. So I *know* you're lying."

When I walked in the door, the deacons called me back here and said, "Yesterday, Pastor Williams turned in his resignation. How about putting your name in the hat?"

I was sitting right there in that corner. Right there. And tears just began to flow. I said, "Sure, I'll put my name in the hat. But God just told me a few minutes ago, when I was driving around the church, that I was gonna be the pastor here."

The chairman of the deacon board, Morris Turner, began to shout. He said that just a few days before, he woke his wife up and told her that the Lord said I was gonna be the next pastor here.

So, ooh, wow! That's how we got here.

I began pastoring here on the first Sunday of July 2000, perhaps a month after Rev. Williams had stepped down. The gentleman that preached at my installation service gave as his subject: "Going places you've never been, and doing things you've never done." And he prophesized over the church. Ever since then, we've been going places — and doing things — that we've never been or never done before.

That first Sunday was an amazing day. I can remember the shouts over the finances alone! Since I've been here, the finances have gone from somewhere between $200 and $300 a week to around $1,800 to $2,000 a week.

In the first year and a half, we took eighty-nine people into the baptism. And over the three years, we've lost count. The Lord has blessed us tremendously. I would estimate Little Zion has about 200 members now, and I would say at least 75 percent of our congregation are twenty-five and under.

In January 2001, we started having services every Sunday. The people had a fear because for the fifty years under Pastor Lewis and the time that Pastor Williams was here, they had a first and third Sunday schedule. There was a fear about participation and church expenses. I think we were one of the first churches in this community to go to an every Sunday schedule. But right away, our second and fourth Sunday services were larger than the first and third.

I'm heavily in activities with the youth. I served as park and recreation director for awhile, I coached three teams of softball, coached basketball. I do a lot of volunteer work at all of the schools here. The Lord has blessed me in giving me the gift of youth ministry. A lot of the youth have joined because of the rapport, the relationship that we have outside of here. I play ball with them. I've been criticized a lot because, traditionally, it's not pastorly. Throughout this whole county, there's one other pastor, myself, and my assistant, Christopher Stephney, who actually get involved.

We also have an interesting group of young adults. Most of the churches will normally have older senior citizens, middle-aged people, forties, thirties, and then teenagers and smaller. But we have a wonderful group of twenty-somethings. It's been surprising to me.

We have Bible study and mission classes on Wednesday nights now. Surprisingly, we've gotten up to sixty people at the Bible study, and it's on a week night. I'm really looking forward to turning that into a midweek service.

The Lord has blessed us with transportation. We got a van less than a year ago, and normally we have four designated drivers to pick people up for Sunday service or take people to a special program in another church. We use the van to do our mission work, hospital visits, nursing home visits. We have a ministry at the county jail on Tuesdays, and we sometimes go to the Hale County jail on Wednesdays.

We use the van for our youth ministry, which we organized a little over a year ago. We have at least forty kids actively participating in things like bowling, pizza, movies. And we have adult fellowship, things like getting all the fathers and the senior citizens and the choir members and going to a restaurant in Tuscaloosa to eat together. That brought joy to a lot of people.

We've made a lot of changes. We just got a telephone in the church since I've been here.

If we had stayed with all of the old traditions, then we would not have the congregation that we have here now. I was fortunate enough to grow up in between the old traditions and the newer ways. Most of the congregation that we have now grew up after the old traditions. It's like another world to them. So we are blessed to be able to hold on to the old; at the same time reach and grab forward. The Lord has blessed us in that way.

I've walked away from some of the teachings I've gotten over the years, now after being able to read and study and understand and listen to the spirit of God myself. I can understand why it was taught in that way, but I disagree. As a young pastor,

I'm having to deal quite often with the dress code. I was told that a preacher must always wear a white shirt, necktie, and a suit coat. I can understand why, because it was used as an identification piece. But I disagree. I was always told that women must dress in a certain way, distinguish themselves as young ladies. When it comes down to your salvation, it's not about the dress. The Book asks, "Who is thee adorning?" Is it the braids? Is it the apparel? Or is it the inner man? I'm not so concerned about how a person dresses; I'm concerned about how they live.

When I first got here, it was understood that you would dress up for church. That has been an obstacle for me — getting people to understand that our job, as Jesus did with James and John, is to be fishermen of men. It's not our job to clean the fish; it's our job to catch the fish. We try to clean the fish before we catch the fish. We can't do that. Because of the dress code, we've put stipulations, restrictions, on allowing God to deal with the inner man.

When I got here, we were broken up into separate Sunday school classes for men, women, and children. I brought everyone together. For one reason, I was learning the members, and I wanted the members to learn me. I would do the teaching, and I wanted to make sure that we were getting the Word. Recently, since I started the children's ministry, we have allowed the kids to go to Sunday school in the classrooms. But we won't split the women and the men out again.

The people were accustomed to sitting in different parts of the church, the men over here, the women there, the children back there. That really bothered me, because I understand that the church goes as the family goes. If I have broken the family up, how am I really helping? I am teaching a division.

Right now in our Bible study we're teaching on the strength of the family. I've asked for family to sit together in church. Husbands, sit with your wives. Sit with your children.

When I first got here, I taught heavily against women preaching from the pulpit or anywhere else. I'll never forget. I was teaching from the book of Esther in Bible study. And there was a conviction that came over me in regards to the women in the ministry. I fell before God on hands and knees and face; I apologized to God and asked God for forgiveness. I went before the people and apologized to the church. Because my understanding was off.

Since then, I've allowed the women the opportunity to teach, to preach, and to use whatever gift God has given them, in the church. I'm not the one who does the calling. That's not my job or my responsibility. I cannot dictate who God uses.

It's interesting that when I preached against women in the ministry, there was acceptance. And then when I publicly said I was wrong, it was also accepted. I've explained to the church, when I'm wrong and God convicts me, I've got to come back and say I'm wrong. I'm not too big and too proud; I can't continue to preach something that I know I'm wrong about.

I try to make the services interesting; You notice I use humor. I try to make it exciting, and at the same time make sure you're getting some good Word, something to help you. I'm very mobile in my preaching. I walk, I move, I jump, I run sometimes.

We've been able to move into the tape ministry, where we record the services and allow church members to purchase them. We use that money to buy tapes to keep the ministry going.

We've had drums in the service for about four months. We did a session a while back on how praise and worship should go, what instruments should be used. I just said one day, "Look, I'm gonna get some drums."

It's been wonderful, wonderful. We had our second annual homecoming this year. I was told that we did not have homecoming celebrations before, but now we invite everybody from far away to come and visit.

We've pretty much done away with second programs whose main purpose was to raise money. We did those programs when I was young, but I'm not a firm believer in them. I continuously go back to the Bible. I was instructed that the Lord's house would be taken care of through tithes and offerings. If we are to rightfully do what we are supposed to do with tithes and offerings, then the church will be funded. It was proven in the finances.

When I got here, I never understood all of the different collections. Why so many? To me that's almost *making* you give. If I just send the collection plate around one time, you give your tithes and offerings, just what you want to. Give the people the opportunity to give one time, and they're gonna give what they want to give. We stopped the reading out of the amount collected because I just believe that when I'm giving to God, that's between me and God, and everybody else doesn't have to know. So we've made a lot of changes.

It's been an experience. I've had to go through a lot of things since I've been here. This church has been placed out of fellowship with a lot of churches. We've literally been told by other pastors that they have no fellowship with us because of some of the changes that we've made. I've been threatened to be removed from this place by the association of pastors. My life has been threatened.

Oh, Lord. If you notice, there are no chairs in the pulpit. One day I was teaching, preaching, on distractions in the worship service. I was talking about how pastors come into worship services and just walk straight up to the pulpit, just sit down and begin to speak, even if the preacher's preaching. That's a thing here that pastors do, and I don't agree to it. The moment I was teaching that, three pastors walks in and walks into the pulpit. The very moment I was saying it. They began to shake hands with the choir members and talk.

I was down on the floor. The whole congregation did this [turns his head] to look at them. Then I heard the talking. I turned around. There they were. I said, "Let me help you all understand what I'm preaching and teaching. I'm preaching and teaching distractions in the worship service. And this moment, I was talking about us as pastors, how we walk in and distract the service. You all have just proven it.

The Lord had just given it to me to say: "From this day forward, no more chairs in the pulpit."

We have used the pulpit to make ourselves bigger than we really are. We're not more than the people, even though God has called us into a different calling. I can't say that I'm more than you. You can't say that you're more than this person. I was teaching that.

When they decided to meet with me, the Peter of the pastor's crowd, the spokesperson, said, "Well, this is why we sit in the pulpit — because God has elevated us. The pulpit, that's what it is. It's to reach down and *pull* people out of the *pit*."

I said, "I don't agree." And, I said, "If that's your teaching, I really wouldn't mind if we didn't fellowship."

I have to learn to just give a little at a time. Yeah. Because when I first started out, I was ready for change. I was used to that church in Huntsville, and coming back down here, it's totally different. It's like night and day. I was trying to hurry up and get Little Zion there, so that I could feel a little bit more comfortable. But actually, this move was to bring me out of my comfort zone, so that I can learn — and then bring others up.

Pastor Lewis gave the church — and gave me — his signature, if I can say it like that. He said, "Out of the years that my health has been failing, and I know that it has been time for me to step down, I couldn't really give it up. Because I wanted to make sure that you all would get the right person." He shared with us, and with me. He said, "I'm now satisfied; I'm now happy with who you all have chosen as pastor." He gave us his signature of approval and his blessing.

And that blessed my spirit. He and I grew really close. He would still come every first and third Sunday, even when he came in a wheelchair. He told me, "Pastor, make sure that — even if they have to bring me in here in a bed — they get me to the church." When he was here, I would make sure that he was able to just take the mike, to just say something, if it was nothing but, "Good morning."

I always knew him from a little boy, working with his watermelons and his peas. But I never had the opportunity to hear him preach. Never had the opportunity to hear him preach. Yet when I came here as pastor and I introduced my vision for the church, Reverend Lewis almost stood up. Because his vision and my vision for the church were the same. We wanted to see some of the exact same things for Little Zion.

When we did get the chance to really sit and talk, I was constantly just thanking God for Pastor Lewis. I learned so much in a short time under him. I didn't quite understand him word for word, but I learned so much under him.

In the last few years at Little Zion, we've had some wonderful experiences. We've grown and done some things that we thought we would never do. We've gone quite a few places. We've been to Detroit for a revival the past two years and this year. This was something that had never been done. The Lord has brought this church a long way.

It gets kind of emotional sometimes for me.

I find myself sometimes coming here to Little Zion, and I will sit and meditate. I'm waking up late in the night, coming up here on the hill. Yes, I will come up here and just sit.

I have always shared with the people that we're growing together. That's where we've been. We've been growing together.

EPILOGUE

Sitting with Rev. Barton inside Little Zion on a Sunday afternoon in July 2003, I realized that my effort to contribute something to the rebuilding of Little Zion Baptist Church had been completed. I had collected some memories of this church, recorded its baptism by fire, and returned to see it begin to grow with new life.

Upon returning from that last fieldwork trip, I reflected that I had spent seven years trying to understand Little Zion Baptist Church from the inside. During the 1996 rebuilding effort, we hung the drywall that literally enclosed the sacred spaces that would become the sanctuary, the pastor's study, the baptismal pool. I took the part of the title of this project from an inscription scribbled on that drywall — words written, ironically, by one of the volunteers, an outsider like me.

And yet the church has embraced the inscription, allowing the words to remain inside its very structure upon completion of the building. When I shared this finished narrative with Rev. Barton and members of the church, I was gratified to see my work received in the same way, accepted as something of value to this community.

Over the years I have learned one thing from my perspective: I was correct in the realization that Little Zion is not just the church that was built and rebuilt over several generations, and then burned and

Part of the title of this project was taken from an inscription
inside one of the walls of the church.

was rebuilt in 1996. The building itself stands as a symbol for a living
faith. And in the narratives people share about that faith, in the stories
they tell to their children and grandchildren — even to and through
outsiders like me — the foundations of something life-giving and sus-
taining are revealed.

If I could begin again and re-record these narratives for the first
time, I would change only this: I would trust more fully in the welcome I received at Little Zion and move forward with greater con-
fidence in my sense of doing what I felt led to do. I would understand
that the multiple purposes of this project — from that of the activist
attempting to contribute to the rebuilding effort, to that of the folklife student working toward a graduate degree, to that of the Quaker
seeking "that of God" in this religious community — could be fulfilled
in a way that enriched each other with the understandings of multiple
traditions. The knowledge that this book catches something of Little
Zion's long history has, to quote Rev. Barton, "blessed my spirit."

But the church was not rebuilt to look backward. The structure provides a place of worship for those who gather here today, and for those who will come in the future. When this second brick building was finished in 1996, for instance, the sanctuary held pews for far more than the approximately thirty worshippers who at the time regularly gathered on Sundays. When the Sunday school classrooms were built in 1998, they offered much more space than the small group of children attending at that time needed. Yet under the leadership of Rev. Barton from 2000 to 2004, the rooms were filled.

And of course Little Zion's story doesn't end here. Rev. Barton left Little Zion in 2004 amid questions about whether the change he brought in the past several years had pushed the church too far, too quickly. What happens to your traditions when, as a community, you are "going places you've never been before?" Will this group of people, as they continue to "act in common," return to some of the church's old ways? Or will Rev. Willie Carter keep some of the new practices begun by Rev. Barton?

The questions remain, because the tale given to me has ended. So I must do what Quakers in meeting for worship always do when finished giving a message: Simply sit down and listen to the silence.

APPENDIX

Past Leaders of Little Zion Baptist Church

Pastors	Deacons	Trustees	Secretaries
Steve Burnett	Corgan Smothers	John Braggs	John Braggs
Saul Brown	Dick Knott	Isikiah Hubbard	Marshall Anthony
Samon Bryant	Ennis Earley	Dick Knott	Henry T. Carter
Rev. Terry	Sam Underwood	West Murphy	Oscar M. Williams,
William Field	Jessie Paul	Boz Hubbard	Treas.
Woodson D. Lewis	Mack Davis	Forris Watson	Bessie Carter
	C.H. Develle	Charley Hubbard	Tony Carter
	John Davis	Ike Paul	Leroy Smith
	Jonas C. Smothers	Ennis Davis	
	Ed Henry Carter	John Hubbard	
	Henry T. Carter	Paul Brown	
	Willie C. Carter	Joe Braggs	
	Henry Smith	Sid Murray	
	Tommie J. Smith	Peter Newman	
	Leroy Smith	Rufus Branch	
	Thomas Bell		

NOTES

PREFACE

1. Video link in "Handprint Could be Key to Church Fire Probe," from Rusty Dornin, February 9, 2006, <http://www.cnn.com/2006/US/02/09/alabama.churches/index.html> (accessed February 14, 2006).

2. Rev. W. D. Lewis served as Little Zion's pastor from 1950 until his retirement in 1999 at the age of ninety-six. Rev. Oscar Williams then led the church until mid-2000, when his failing health forced him to step aside. Rev. Michael A. Barton served as Little Zion's pastor from July 2000 until early 2004. In September of that year, Little Zion named lifelong member Rev. Willie C. Carter as its new pastor. He remains Little Zion's leader as of this writing. After continuing to attend, and often to preach, at Little Zion until the end of his life, Rev. Lewis died on October 26, 2002.

3. On his birth certificate and the deed for Little Zion, Mr. Smaw's name appears as written here. Most church members recalled his name, however, as Mr. Dick Small.

4. Luke 3:16: ". . . He shall baptize you with the Holy Ghost and with fire."

CHAPTER ONE

1. Deacon Ed Carter is speaking to his grandson, Rev. James Carter, here, in a videotaped family history documented on July 26–27, 1987. Rev. James Carter shared the video with me on September 6, 1998.

2. Eutaw is the county seat, about 10 miles from Boligee.

3. Smith and Holmes, *Listen to Me Good*, 10.

4. According to federal census data, blacks comprised 80.3 percent of the 9,923 people living in the county in 2000, while whites numbered 19.1 percent (U.S. Census, *State and County QuickFacts*). In 1999, per capita income totaled $13,686, with 34.3 percent of residents living below the poverty line. This figure is one of the country's highest, as 40 counties nationwide reported a higher percentage of impoverished citizens that year (U.S. Census, *Census 2000* Summary File 3 — Sample Data).

5. Smith and Holmes, *Listen to Me Good*, 11.

6. Press, "Town with 'Two of Everything,'" 10.

7. Richard Bauman has explored the elevated roles of speaking and silence among early Quakers in many of his writings, including (but not limited to) "Aspects of Quaker Rhetoric" (1970), "Quaker Folk-Linguistics and Folklore" (1975), "Speaking in the Light" (1974), and *Let Your Words be Few* (1983). In the last publication, Bauman argued: "By making the speaking of God within man the core religious experience of their movement, the Quakers elevated speaking and silence to an especially high degree of symbolic centrality and importance. Victor Turner has suggested that iconoclastic religions, by eliminating iconic symbols, place ever greater stress on the Word (1975: 155). Again, the early Quakers carried this tendency close to its extreme among contemporary [seventeenth century] radical puritan sects by the symbolic weight they attached to speaking and silence" (30). (The Turner reference is to "Symbolic Studies," published in *Annual Review of Anthropology*, vol. 4, Bernard J. Siegel, ed. Palo Alto, Calif.: Annual Reviews.)

8. In the nineteenth century, the Religious Society of Friends struggled, in part, between the impulse to continue meeting in the old, unprogrammed style, listening to what they called "that of God in everyone" without the need for a clergy or set doctrine, and the desire of many people to revitalize the worship experience with such elements common in other Protestant churches. The Society eventually split into several branches. In the United States, many unprogrammed monthly meetings now are associated with the Friends General Conference, and many programmed monthly meetings are aligned with Friends United Meeting. Programmed meetings, while filled with longer periods of silence than other Protestant services, are led by paid clergy and include elements such as a sermon and hymns throughout the service.

9. This move is grounded in the examinations of other folklife scholars, notably José Limón and M. Jane Young ("Frontiers, Settlements, and Development"), who argued as early as 1986 that we must examine both the "micro" and "macro" dimensions of the performance of folklore; Amy Shuman ("Dismantling Local Culture"), who considered a connection between the "local" and "larger-than-local"; and Dorothy Noyes ("Group"), who postulated that relationships between groups of people can best be described as interconnected and extended social networks.

10. This structure is modeled on Lawless, *Holy Women, Wholly Women*. She also suggested her work could be read in several ways: "I have invited the reader to read the life stories at a point in the text of my chapters where the reader 'meets' a particular woman or 'hears' her voice. But the reader also has a choice. If you would rather read all of the life stories of the women in this study first, before venturing into the discussion of them, the way they are presented in the book will make it easy to do so. If, on the other hand, you would rather read the ethnographic and analytical material first and then read the life stories, that, too, will be easy to accomplish" (6).

11. Some of the Greene County Historical Society's publications include *A Goodly Heritage*; Lancaster, *Eutaw*; *Welcome to Black Belt Pilgrimage 1972: Greene County and Gainesville*; and *The Heritage of Greene County, Alabama*.

12. Greene County Historical Society, *Visitor's Guide to Historic Greene County*.

13. U.S. Census Bureau, *Eighth Census, 1860*, Agricultural and Slave Schedules.

14. Miller, ed., *"Dear Master,"* 27. The text notes, "Most eighteenth-century and early nineteenth-century Southern liberals, including Cocke, [Thomas] Jefferson, and James Madison, advocated the colonization of American blacks as a solution to the race problem in America and indirectly as a way of promoting gradual emancipation."

15. Ibid., 142.

16. Ibid., 150.

17. Ibid., 156–57.

18. In *Civil War and Reconstruction in Alabama*, Walter Fleming described the various sharecropping arrangements common throughout the state:

the usual designations were "on halves," "third and fourth," and "standing rent." The tenant "on halves" received one-half the crop, did all the work, and furnished his own provisions. The planter furnished land, houses to live in, seed, ploughs, hoes, teams, wagons, ginned the cotton, paid for half the fertilizer, and "went security" for the negro for a year's credit at the supply store in town, or he furnished the supplies himself, and charged them against the negro's share of the crop. The "third and fourth" plan varied according to locality and time, and depended upon what the tenant furnished. Sometimes the planter furnished everything, while the negro gave only his labor and received one-fourth of the crop; again, the planter furnished all except provisions and labor and gave the negro one-third of the crop. . . .

"Standing rent" was the highest form of tenancy, and only responsible persons, white or black, could rent under that system. It called for a fixed or "standing" rent for each acre or farm, to be paid in money or in cotton. The unit of value in cotton was a 500-pound bale of middle grade on October 1st. (723–24)

19. Ibid., 725.

20. Ibid., 733.

21. Trelease, *White Terror*, 246.

22. Lancaster, *Eutaw*, 27.

23. Trelease, *White Terror*, 259.

24. Daniel, *Shadow of Slavery*, 22.

25. Cooper, "The Damned," F6.

26. U.S. Commission on Civil Rights, *Fifteen Years Ago*, 43.

27. U.S. Census Bureau, *Census 1980*; U.S. Census Bureau, *Census 2000*.

28. I intend here to give only a brief overview of relevant trends in folklife studies during the past half century for readers unfamiliar with the discipline. Therefore, this analysis risks oversimplification of the many complex debates of among scholars during this time.

29. Shuman and Briggs, "Theorizing Folklore," 123.

30. Ben-Amos, "Toward a Definition of Folklore," 13.

31. Shuman and Briggs, "Theorizing Folklore," 121. Though Ben-Amos deliberately omitted the concept of tradition from his definition, later folklorists would reincorporate this idea, noting, as Shuman and Briggs put it, that "characterizing cultural forms as 'traditional' constitutes a powerful means of imbuing them with social value and authority" (ibid., 116). Thus, traditions came to be seen, on one level, as social and political constructs employed "for empowering particular groups, rhetorics, and interests" (ibid., 116).

32. Dance, *Shuckin' and Jivin'*, xii–xiii.

33. Ibid., xix.

34. Seward, "Legacy of Early Afro-American Folklore Scholarship."

35. Roberts, "African American Diversity," 157.

36. As Roger Abrahams pointed out in "After New Perspectives," "Our practices have reflected the analytic habits derived from folkloristic and anthropological isolationism, and from the kind of politically correct paradigms which regard African American or Mexican American or Native American or women's or children's discourse as operating separately from 'the mainstream,' whatever that may mean (Bauman and Abrahams: . . . *And Other Neighborly Names*)" (388–89). This isolated cultural zone, according to Abrahams, often is portrayed without specifics of time and place, "maintaining the impression that folklore connects us with some kind of timeless past. Groups of children, Indians, African Americans, and Mexican Americans thus are given this aura of timelessness, fostering the impression that somehow the tradition-bearers of these groups have maintained some of life's deeper truths" (389).

37. Roberts, "African American Diversity," 169.

38. U.S. National Church Arson Task Force, *Fourth Year Report*, Chart T.

39. Mitchell Duneier pointed out the dangers inherent in the white liberal scholar's attempt to generalize about African American culture based on fieldwork with a small number of informants. He described a "power of innocence" dynamic; the scholar's ethos of goodwill obscures his or her assumption of the power to make unfounded generalizations about the population under study. In *Slim's Table*, Duneier said:

> The sociologist's success at conveying his or her "essential goodness in relation to others," most commonly by simply advertising that his or her books present a less stereotypical view of blacks, or by embracing a liberal political program, has afforded a license to make generalizations about the black population that are not supported by firm evidence. What is most surprising about these studies is that the elevation of innocence over evidence as an entitlement to generalize has not even led to a more positive image of blacks. Yet, because these books are written by scholars who so successfully establish their innocence, it has largely gone unnoticed that as a body of work they confirm inaccurate stereotypes that happen also to be demeaning. (139)

40. This narrowing of focus might give readers unfamiliar with black church practices an unfair and unrealistic sense of Little Zion as wholly unique in the powerful traditions that sustain generations of churchgoers here. In fact, the church shares many of its practices with African American houses of worship nationwide, especially other small, rural southern congregations. The call-and-response sermon style, for example, can be heard in black churches of many denominations and demographics, as Gerald Davis explored in *I Got the Word in Me*. Davis also beautifully documented the oratorical power of many African American ministers who preach in a chanted sermon style, often without any notes. The Little Zion practice of allowing worshippers to choose songs during the service by lining them out for other members has been noted by observers in black worship services for centuries. See Eileen Southern's *Music of Black Americans* and C. Eric Lincoln's *Black Experience in Religion* for more. As documented in Chapter 5 and elsewhere, Little Zion's traditionally dramatic conversion experiences bear much in common with those reported as far back as under slavery in the Federal Writer's Project narratives collected in Johnson, ed., *God Struck Me Dead*.

Readers interested in more general considerations of African American church traditions might also turn to Fulop and Raboteau, eds., *African-American Religion*. Raboteau's *Fire in the Bones* also offers a great introduction to black church history. A few other important texts include Lincoln and Mamiya's *Black Church in the African American Experience* and Gayraud S. Wilmore's *Black Religion and Black Radicalism*. Intellectual documentations and analyses such as those listed above provide only a limited understanding of religious practices, however, because religious experience happens in the heart and soul as much as, or more than, in the mind of the believer.

41. And, sometimes, the conversation with one outside our own cultural landscape allows us to reflect on and appreciate anew our own environment. When called to explain and consider practices and traditions that we have always taken for granted, sometimes we deepen our awareness of their meaning. I believe many of those interviewed understood this dynamic better than I did at the outset this project.

42. Two meals at the home of Rev. James Carter on September 6, 1998, and November 14, 1999, are particularly noteworthy. During the first, my mother, infant daughter, and I were invited to a late lunch of baked chicken and cabbage, pork chops and sweet potatoes with several men of the Carter family. During the second, my husband and I were privileged to share with Rev. Carter and his children a meal of chicken and venison in gravy, collard greens, cornbread, biscuits, grits, and homemade pear preserves with allspice. Rev. Carter emphasized that having come all the way from Washington, D.C., to Greene County, Alabama, we should experience local home cooking. This self-conscious sharing of foodways helped develop and maintain a connection between Little Zion insiders and me as an interested and appreciative witness to this culture. The interaction recalls the transmission of foodways at festivals, where members of an in-group allow others to experience their culture through food prepared especially for this purpose. In *Ethnic and Regional Foodways in the United States*, Linda Keller Brown and Kay Mussell point out: "When members of different groups come into contact in a multi-cultural society, the sharing of traditional food items may take on a variety of new meanings, depending on the motivation of the giver and the response of the recipient. In the context of a festival . . . members of ethnic or regional groups offer delicacies to an audience that comes prepared to appreciate it" (7).

43. Recognition of this bias abounds in contemporary folklore. Patrick Mullen addressed the issue succinctly, pointing out how folklorist John Lomax's use of dialect when quoting an African American interviewee in 1947 "creates a definite distance between him [Lomax] and Henry Truvillion since there are no dialect spellings in Lomax's speech" ("Dilemma of Representation," 162). Mullen asserted, "Representations of dialect in literature and scholarship, derived largely from the minstrel and plantation traditions, underlined negative valuations" (162). He also cited Henry Louis Gates Jr., who said in *The Signifying Monkey* that by the late 1800s, "dialect had come to connote black innate mental inferiority, the linguistic sign both of human bondage (as origin) and of the continued failure of 'improvability' or 'progress,' two turn of the century keywords" (176, quoted in "Dilemma of Representation," 162).

44. I've chosen to represent the use of "gonna" literally, for instance, since

changing the form to "going to" significantly changes the tone and flow of the speaker's statement.

45. Lawless, *Women Preaching Revolution*, 7.

46. II Kings 19:12.

47. Richard Bauman, in *Verbal Art as Performance*, glossed the connection between African American religious expression, including "elaborate and highly marked" (19) sermons, and Quaker worship, severely circumscribed by the propensity toward silence (29), when citing both as examples of performative cultures.

48. In the transcriptions of sermons, line breaks are used to approximate the oral experience of the preacher's rhythmic pauses during delivery. Forward slashes and parentheses indicate the congregation's responses that complete the rhythmic lines.

49. Note that when the collection context for this sermon is considered, it becomes obvious that the words were directed pointedly at me. Just before making these comments, Rev. Carter asked the congregation to open their Bibles to the second chapter of Philippians and the eleventh chapter of Ecclesiastes. Easily visible in a front row, I knew many people would witness my struggle to find the correct passages. (Neither my Roman Catholic nor Quaker education has emphasized Bible study to the extent practiced at Little Zion.) Embarrassed, I left my Bible in my lap and busied myself with my tape recorder. The preacher looked directly at me, paused significantly, and repeated his directions. When I still didn't respond, he repeated his directions three more times, pausing longer between each cue, until at last he spent forty-seven seconds staring at me. Finally, he read the passages aloud, both of which focused on teaching youth to live uprightly in the eyes of God. But before turning his attention directly to the text, Rev. Carter spoke about the shortcomings of a predominantly secular education. Whomever else he addressed in that moment, the preacher clearly spoke to me, the scholar unschooled in the Good Book: "People with degrees are broken today / Because they have missed the understanding that / All is vanity, / Except / When God is at the front / Of all of what you do. /"

In admonishing me, Rev. Carter also reversed a potential class difference between us, with my secular graduate work serving a lesser purpose than his undergraduate degree spent in the Lord's service. Patrick Mullen explored this same interaction in a narrative by lay preacher Quincy Higgins, recounted in *Listening to Old Voices*. In conducting a funeral service with a more formally educated preacher, Higgins recalled singing "Amazing Grace" with such spiritual power that "the educated preacher admits his inferiority to Quincy Higgins in terms of divine inspiration" (183). As Higgins asserted, the other preacher would "'give everything he possessed if he could just lay them handbooks down, them prayer books and things, and depend on divine spirit' " (183). Mullen concluded, "This sacred story . . . prov[es] that Mr. Higgins, despite his rural uneducated background, is equal to or better than people with higher social status" (183). The tension between divine inspiration and formal education in the preacher's vocation is considered further in Chapter 5.

CHAPTER TWO

1. Deacon Ed Carter, seventy-nine at the time of the burning, was generally regarded as the keeper of the church's oral history. Until his death on December 2, 1997, church members deferred to his recollections of church events, repeatedly advising me, "Deacon Carter can tell you more about that."

2. In a 1995 *Journal of American Folklore* article, Dorothy Noyes declared that "acting in common makes community" (468). I find this definition insightful in its simplicity.

3. Williams, *Community in a Black Pentecostal Church*, 9. The references here are to E. F. Frazier's *Negro in the United States*, R. A. Billings's "Negro and His Church," and E. de S. Brunner's *Church Life in the Rural South*.

4. Williams, *Community in a Black Pentecostal Church*, 9.

5. In this book the titles "Brother" and "Sister" will be used instead of "Mr." and "Mrs." or "Ms.," according to preferences expressed by individual church members.

6. This is a retelling of "A Father and His Sons." According to *Aesop Fables*, the father of a "contentious Brood of Children" gave them a bundle of sticks and asked each to try to break it. They could not. Then he unbound the sticks and the children broke the sticks easily, one by one. "The Reflection" states, "This is the intimate Force of Union, and the Danger of Division. What has it been but Division that has expos'd Christendom to the Enemies of the christian Faith? And it is as ruinous in private as 'tis in publick. A divided Family can no more stand, than a divided Commonwealth; for every individual suffers in the Neglect of a common Safety" (L'Estrange, trans., *Aesop Fables*, 137–38).

7. According to *Bartlett's Familiar Quotations*, this quote originated with John Dickinson's *The Liberty Song* in 1768: "By uniting we stand, by dividing we fall" (46ob). Dickinson, however, was paraphrasing the moral of the Aesop's fable above. The phrase was later picked up by George Pope Morris in *The Flag of Our Nation*: " 'United We Stand, Divided We Fall' " (600a). Of course, all of these quotes echo Matthew 12:25: "And Jesus knew their thoughts, and said unto them, "Every kingdom divided against itself is brought to desolation; and every city or house divided against itself shall not stand."

8. Du Bois, *Souls of Black Folk*, xii.

9. Raboteau, *Slave Religion*, x.

10. The *New York Times* ran Smothers, "Black Church Fires," on page 7, while the *Washington Post* ran Pressley, "Church Fires Rekindle Pain," on the front page.

11. Smothers, "Black Church Fires."

12. Booth, "In Church Fires," A1.

13. Davis, *I Got the Word in Me*, 64. Of course, Davis and others have noted that the transformation of the political to the spiritual can be used for opposite purposes — to mobilize a congregation to take action in the secular world or to pacify people with the promise of future rewards in heaven. As is explored in Chapter 4, Greene County's leadership role in the civil rights movement was established, at least in part, by local preachers who fought from the pulpit for their visions of justice and equality.

14. Hinson, *Fire in My Bones*, 11.

15. Ibid., 19.

16. Smothers, "Burning of Black Churches," 14.

17. "Arson Could Be Cause of Churches Burning." Lankster is black.

18. Ibid.

19. Parker, "Authorities." Lavender, who is white, served as mayor of Boligee from 1976 until 1996. By "these churches," Lavender was referring to Little Zion, Mt. Zoar, and Mt. Zion.

20. "Ashes and Ashes."

21. Ibid.

22. Smothers, "Black Church Fires."

23. Pressley, "Church Fires Rekindle Pain," A8, A1.

24. Ibid., A8.

25. This project is, of course, a similar effort by an outsider to gain extensive cultural understanding through a relatively short period of interviews. In my case, those interviews were conducted almost exclusively within the African American community, as only one white person attended Little Zion regularly during my research.

26. See Fletcher, "U.S. Investigates Suspicious Fires"; "U.S. Investigates Fires"; and other newspaper reports.

27. Fields and Watson, "Arson at Black Churches."

28. U.S. National Church Arson Task Force, *Third Year Report*, 1.

29. Smith and Peyser, "Terror in the Night down South."

30. Booth, "In Church Fires," A1.

31. Parker, "Funds Rebuilding Churches," 2.

32. See Fletcher, "No Linkage Found," and other newspaper reports.

33. Booth, "In Church Fires," A7.

34. Sharn and Fields, "White Churches Equally Subject to Arson."

35. Day, "Missed Chance to Examine Race Relations."

36. U.S. National Church Arson Task Force, *Fourth Year Report*, Charts Q, R, S. The Arson Task Force's *Fourth Year Report*, issued in September 2000, was the latest report available as of this writing.

37. Ibid., 1, Chart B.

38. Rev. Eddie Carter is the son of Rev. Willie and Sister Leola Carter.

39. Matthew 12:25; Luke 11:17.

40. Ezekiel 37:1–3: "The hand of the Lord was upon me, and carried me out in the spirit of the Lord, and set me down in the midst of the valley which was full of bones.

"And caused me to pass by them round about: and, behold there were very many in the open valley; and, lo, they were very dry.

"And he said unto me, Son of man, can these bones live? And I answered, O Lord God, thou knowest."

41. See Appendix for the listing of Little Zion's trustees through 1996.

42. Greene County Historical Society, *Goodly Heritage*, 85.

43. Sister Porter died on February 22, 2002.

44. Carter interview with James E. Carter.

45. Kolchin, *First Freedom*, 108.

46. Carter interview with James E. Carter.

47. Ibid. Deacon Carter drew a distinction here between sharecropping arrangements, which included various levels of landowner provisions in return for proportionate crops. See Chapter 1, note 18, for further explanation.

48. Ibid.

49. Ibid.

50. U.S. Commission on Civil Rights, *Fifteen Years Ago*, 49.

51. Carter interview with James E. Carter.

52. Boykin, "Emergence of a Black Majority," 235–36.

53. Ibid., 234.

54. Moody, *Coming of Age in Mississippi*, 302–3.

55. U.S. Commission on Civil Rights, *Political Participation*, 224.

56. Ibid.

57. Rev. William McKinley Branch's name did make the ballot because he ran for two state offices, candidates for which are approved by the secretary of state. Rev. Branch lost in both races, however.

58. Boykin, "Emergence of a Black Majority," 1, 275.

59. Ibid., 237.

60. U.S. Alabama Advisory Committee, *Burning of African American Churches*, 3, 14. Quotations from this meeting on July 2, 1996, are taken from my notes. However, a transcript was later released by the Alabama Advisory Committee to the U.S. Commission on Civil Rights, so citations refer to this more readily available document.

61. Ibid., 7.

62. Ibid., 9.

63. Ibid., 36.

64. Ibid., 39.

65. Ibid., 57–58.

66. Ibid., 12.

67. Ibid., 24.

68. Ibid., 13.

69. Ibid., 46.

70. Ibid., 43.

71. Ibid., 45, 14.

72. Ibid., 7.

73. Ibid., 15.

74. Carter interview with James E. Carter.

75. U.S. National Church Arson Task Force, *Fourth Year Report*, 6.

76. Before it burned, Little Zion featured a front facade and two side wings, making the shape of a capital T. As Rev. Carter saw in his vision, a fellowship hall at the rear of the building would change Little Zion's shape to a cross, such as is made by a lowercase t. The church was rebuilt in this shape.

77. James 2:14–26, especially verses 22 and 26. Verse 22: "Seest thou how faith wrought with his works, and by works was faith made perfect?" Verse 26: "For as the body without the spirit is dead, so faith without works is dead also."

78. Reference to the gospel song "He's Right on Time." (Refrain lyrics: "He may not come when you want Him, but He's right on time.")

79. WQW volunteers worked on Little Zion and Mt. Zion. A group of Mennonite volunteers helped in the rebuilding of Mt. Zoar.

80. Castaneda, "Teens Toil to Rebuild Black Churches," A1.

81. Ibid., A17.

82. If Little Zion was founded as an African American church during this time, it almost certainly would have served the slave community, for federal census records show few free blacks in antebellum Greene County. The 1860 census counted 10 free blacks in the county (U.S. Census Bureau, *Eighth Census*, Slave Schedule).

83. The rededication date is incorrect. This was the date originally planned, but the church was not officially rededicated until January 19, 1997.

84. 2 Corinthians 12:9: "And he [Jesus] said unto me, My grace is sufficient for thee: for my strength is made perfect in weakness."

CHAPTER THREE

1. The term was defined in "The Life Story." I have quoted Titon's succinct restatement of that definition in *Powerhouse for God*, 410. Titon advocated the

reproduction of the interviewer's questions and responses in the collected life story. As elsewhere in this book, however, I've chosen to remove my presence to keep the focus on Little Zion's members. But I have heeded Titon's advice in remaining a "sympathetic" listener, whose "responses are encouraging and nondirective" (283). I asked very few questions during this interview; Sister Hendricks seemed very certain about what she wanted to share for this life story of Little Zion Baptist Church.

2. Titon, "Life Story," 278.

3. Ibid., 290.

4. Ibid., 291.

5. Titon, *Powerhouse for God*, 410.

6. Mullen, *Listening to Old Voices*, 46.

7. Titon, *Powerhouse for God*, 409–10.

8. Bauman, *Story, Performance, and Event*, 3.

9. These added details were worked into the original conversion narrative as presented in the text that follows. As discussed in the introduction, I have used editorial judgment in stitching together narratives told at intervals during the flow of conversation.

10. Hinson, *Fire in My Bones*, 1.

11. Mullen, *Listening to Old Voices*, 60.

CHAPTER FOUR

1. Hawthorne, "Method and Spirit," 5.

2. It is important to recognize that this privileging of intellectual over emotional understanding plays into historical stereotypes of highly charged worship styles as unsophisticated and uneducated. Certainly, it is not my intention to promote such a stereotype, nor do I believe Rev. James Carter is unequivocally implying such a judgment, as evidenced throughout this project by his great respect for his ancestors' religious fervor. For me, these comments reveal mixed feelings in this community toward education, which can be "the rolling wheel for success" (Deacon Ed Carter, interview with James E. Carter). Yet, according to Rev. James Carter, "People with degrees are broken today / Because they have missed / The understanding that / All is vanity, / Except / When God is at the front / Of all of what you do" (sermon, October 18, 1996).

3. Davis, *I Got the Word in Me*, 46. Davis further defined these terms as follows:

Formulaic: Milman Parry, whose work Albert Lord completed, defined "formulaic" as "a group of words regularly employed under the same metrical conditions to express a given idea." The essential element in the

Parry definition is the unit concept of meter. In this discussion the meter concept is shifted from its accustomed literary environment to a quasi-musicological environment in which qualitative units of tempo and tone contours are more applicable. . . .

Theme: Lord defines "theme" as a "commonly used incident, description, or idea which, regardless of content, uses many of the same formulas in approximately the same sequence." My use of "theme" is a bit more conventional than Lord's and includes subformula statements identifying the topic of a sermon, in addition to Lord's units. (ibid., 45–46)

4. Interestingly, switches were not present in any of the church services I attended as part of a large group of Quaker visitors during the rebuilding of Little Zion. Though the congregation appeared largely unfamiliar with Quaker traditions, perhaps they were familiar with the widespread commitment to nonviolence, and for those services the switches were put away. As an outside observer I would never have noticed the absence, except that in my many subsequent trips to Little Zion as a lone Quaker visitor, I saw many women carrying switches.

5. At Little Zion, ministers traditionally are chosen on the basis of a spiritual experience during which God calls them to preach the Word. Though today most follow up with formal theological training, education alone cannot make the preacher. His claim to leadership rests on his direct experience of God's call to preach. This concept is explored in much greater detail in Chapter 5. In Rev. Porter's case, God had originally called him ten years earlier, but he had not been ready to accept the challenge. The congregation, filled with family and friends, heard news of Rev. Porter's acceptance of the call in the context of this ten-year journey, with no need for reminder or explanation by the preacher.

6. As discussed previously, Little Zion held full worship services every week from 2001 until 2004.

7. Lincoln and Mamiya, *Black Church in the African American Experience*, 346.

8. Hinson, *Fire in My Bones*, 3.

9. Jackson, "Music of the Black Churches."

10. Psalm 98:4: "Make a joyful noise unto the Lord."

11. Hinson, *Fire in My Bones*, 3–4.

12. After the arrival of Rev. Barton in 2000, the church also purchased a drum set for use in services.

13. Lomax, *Land Where the Blues Began*, 47.

14. Ibid., 81.

15. Mrs. Anthony died on May 28, 2004.

16. The hostesses, identified by matching aquamarine dresses in contrast to

the bridesmaids' fuchsia, were appointed to help at the reception dinner, several guests pointed out. Though repeatedly invited, I did not attend the wedding reception at a nearby club.

17. The sexton is responsible for church maintenance duties. Sister Gladys Smothers remembered that early in the twentieth century, the sexton's duties included "make the fire [in the pot-bellied heater], ring the bell when someone dies, tote water from the spring for service, light the kerosene lamps." Rev. James Carter added that the sexton's job still includes taking care of the building and grounds, including digging graves in the cemetery.

18. When Little Zion was rebuilt in 1970, the bell was not included in the steeple design. Neither was the bell restored in the 1996 rebuilding following the burning. As Rev. Williams explained, the community no longer needed a bell for communication after telephones became commonplace in this rural area.

19. After her death in 2002, Sister Porter was buried at Little Zion.

20. In the 1940s and 1950s, Mrs. Mary Bell Smith Hubbard served as Little Zion's principal and Mrs. Beatrice Gilmore was the other teacher, according to Sister Smothers.

21. Alice Walker and John Lewis both have described beautifully this southern custom of sweeping a dirt yard clean. In "Everyday Use," Walker wrote: "I will wait for her in the yard that Maggie and I made so clean and wavy yesterday afternoon. A yard like this is more comfortable than most people know. It is not just a yard. It is like an extended living room. When the hard clay is swept clean as a floor and the fine sand around the edges lined with tiny, irregular grooves, anyone can come and sit and look up into the elm tree and wait for the breezes that never come inside the house" (23). In *Walking with the Wind: A Memoir of the Movement*, Lewis recalled, "The yard encircling our house was nothing but dirt — no grass, no weeds. We weren't allowed to let weeds grow out there. My brothers and sisters and I had to get out there and pull every weed, pick up every leaf and every pecan that had dropped from those trees — hundreds of pecans. Finally, we had to take out the brooms — homemade brooms fashioned from small bundles of slim tree branches — and sweep the entire yard. When we were done, the place looked immaculate, as manicured in its own way as the finest gardener-tended lawn" (19).

22. Through the mid-twentieth century, this practice of box socials as fund-raisers was widespread, with women filling the boxes and then decorating them elaborately, so that the men would bid on the food sight unseen. Charles Camp's *American Foodways* features a description of one such event, which was collected between 1939 and 1941 by the Nebraska Writers' Project as part of the Works Progress Administration Federal Writers' Program: the "America Eats" manuscripts. Here the box meal sparked courtship interest, as young men competed to buy the food provided by the young women they

wished to impress (66–67). A recent Internet search for boxed-meal auctions revealed that that event remains a fund-raiser for churches, schools, and other community groups in many regions. But most of today's meals seem to be served up with nostalgia, as part of local history festivals or senior center activities, for instance.

CHAPTER FIVE

1. Belief scholars such as David Hufford, Marilyn Motz, and Patrick Mullen have attributed the subject's lack of appeal among twentieth-century folklorists to an overfascination with scientific analysis. Motz urged the field to focus on "believing as a practice rather than belief as an entity," noting that "the usefulness of folklore scholarship lies not in its ability to collect and categorize beliefs but in its ability to explore how people believe" ("Practice of Belief," 349). Finally, Glenn Hinson argued in *Fire in My Bones* that overlooking matters of personal belief fails to address the concerns of the faith communities in which students of religious folklife work: "Speaking of soul, Spirit, and experience draws talk into a realm rarely explored by academic inquiry. Yet these are the topics that dominate conversation among those who call themselves 'saints,' believers who have professed Christ as their personal savior, been saved by His holy power, and now walk the 'set apart' path of sanctification. To ignore these matters is to deny the saints' experiential world, and thus to craft a portrait that speaks more to academic understandings than to the lived reality of believers" (2).

2. Primiano, "Vernacular Religion," 47.

3. Ibid., 48.

4. Kelly, *Testament of Devotion*, 3.

5. Ibid., 4.

6. Hinson, *Fire in My Bones*, 15.

7. Mullen, *Listening to Old Voices*, 270.

8. Goldstein, "Secularization of Religious Ethnography," 28.

9. Ibid.

10. Berger and Del Negro, "Bauman's Verbal Art," 75.

11. Johnson, *God Struck Me Dead*, xvii.

12. Going out unaccompanied into the natural world (especially the archetypal unknown of the forest) is a common motif in conversion narratives, as the individual must prepare alone for an encounter with the divine. The *God Struck Me Dead* narratives abound with examples of people being converted after experiencing visions or hearing God's voice while alone in the woods and fields. (See references on pages 12, 22, and 65).

Patrick Mullen took the association between the woods and the supernatural one step further in documenting the conversion narrative of African

American deacon Leonard Bryan. Bryan reported that in seeking Christ he'd often stop in the woods to pray on the way home from church: " 'And seemed like the boogerman,' he laughed, 'get me out there and I couldn't pray. I had to come out of them woods,' " retreating to a nearby field to pray (*Listening to Old Voices*, 91). Mullen asserted, "He [Deacon Bryan] must confront the devil directly in the form of the 'boogerman,' who is associated with the woods" (92). Thus, going to the woods to pray exposes the seeker to potential supernatural encounter with not just the divine but also the devil. For Deacon Bryan, God is to be found at the edge of the wildness — in "the safer setting of the cultivated field" (92).

13. Johnson, *God Struck Me Dead*, 20–21.

14. Ibid., 128.

15. The conversion narrative that follows was recorded on August 7, 1997.

16. Many conversion narratives reported in this project began with the assertion that it was the last night of revival, that everyone on the mourner's bench had already been converted, or that the seeker was about to be left unsaved at the close of revival.

17. Southern, *Music of Black Americans*, 94.

18. Paraphrase of Luke 9:26 and Matthew 10:33.

19. See Matthew 20:1–16.

20. Mrs. Smith was in her mid-fifties at the time of her interview. She died on August 30, 2005.

21. Mrs. Johnnie Busby Jackson summed up several others' descriptions of the baptism ceremony: "And then the Reverend would raise his voice and say, 'I baptize you in the name of the Father, the Son, and the Holy Ghost.' And down you went. And up you came. That's the Baptist faith. You went down in your old self, and you came up again new."

22. According to Rev. Willie C. Carter, the property was about three miles from the church.

23. This story is told throughout the Gospels. See Matthew 3:1–7, Mark 1:2–9, Luke 3:15–18, John 1:6–36, and John 3:26–30.

24. With the congregation removed from the immediate activity at the baptismal pool, Rev. James Carter assumed full responsibility for the traditional community responses, included here in parentheses.

25. Mrs. Busby Jackson recalled that the deacons waded in the water before baptism, tapping the ground with tall sticks "to ward off the snakes." In fact, many at Little Zion remembered this practice but did not agree on its purpose. Like Rev. Eddie Carter, Rev. Oscar Williams asserted that the sticks simply checked the water's depth. It's possible, however, that the sticks also served a symbolic purpose, ridding the area of the influence of the devil — often portrayed as a snake. As Rev. Eddie Carter elaborated, "I thought many

times, 'Snakes ought to be in here, water moccasins. . . .' But they weren't around the lake. It was clean. It was pure. . . . God had purified the water."

26. Rev. Lewis said of water in the baptism ceremony: "Water is the symbol of salvation. It washes you clean."

27. Johnson, *God Struck Me Dead*, 15.

28. Ibid.

29. Ibid.

30. Hebrews 11:1, 5–6: "Now faith is the substance of things hoped for, the evidence of things not seen. . . .

"By faith Enoch was translated that he should not see death; and was not found, because God had translated him; for before his translation he had this testimony, that he pleased God.

"But without faith *it is* impossible to please *him*; for he that cometh to God must believe *that* he is, and that he is a rewarder of them that diligently seek him."

31. Urine traditionally has been used for curative power among rural African Americans in the South. According to *Folk Beliefs of the Southern Negro*, for instance, weak eyes could be cured by bathing them in the sufferer's urine (383), and headaches could be eased by rubbing urine on the head (379). Interestingly, this book also documented the use of peach leaves to relieve headache. In the early conversion narratives of *God Struck Me Dead*, a believer reported that God had directed him to heal swellings in his limbs with peach leaves. As in other narratives in this collection, the speaker's voice seemed to echo Rev. Lewis's: "Later that misery came back and I asked God to heal me. The spirit directed me to get some peach-tree leaves and beat them up and put them about my limbs. I did this and in a day or two that swelling left me and I haven't been bothered since" (60).

32. The reference here is to the nearby Spring Hill Baptist Church.

33. Johnson, *God Struck Me Dead*, 59.

34. Ibid., 73.

35. Ibid., 74–75.

36. The phrase echoes language in a *God Struck Me Dead* conversion narrative, where the believer notes, "I waited on the Lord till my change came. . . . He set my feet in the path and told me to go, and I have been traveling ever since" (169). Sam Cooke's 1964 soul hit, "A Change is Gonna Come," used even more similar phrasing: "I was born by the river in a little tent. / Oh, and just like the river I've been running ever since."

37. Proverbs 16:16: "How much better is it to get wisdom than gold! and to get understanding rather to be chosen than silver!"

38. Mark 16:15–16: "And he said unto them, Go ye into all the world, and preach the gospel to every creature.

"He that believeth and is baptized shall be saved; but he that believeth not shall be damned."

39. Acts 2:1–4: "And when the day of Pentecost was fully come, they were all with one accord in one place.

"And suddenly there came a sound from heaven of a rushing mighty wind, and it filled all the house where they were sitting.

"And there appeared unto them cloven tongues like as of fire, and it sat upon each of them.

"And they were all filled with the Holy Ghost, and began to speak with other tongues, as the Spirit gave them utterance."

40. Exodus 19:10–24:3.

41. Matthew 28:19–20: "Go ye therefore, and teach all nations, baptizing them in the name of the Father, and of the Son, and of the Holy Ghost.

"Teaching them to observe all things whatsoever I have commanded you: and, lo, I am with you always, even until the end of the world."

42. See note 39, above.

43. Preachers interviewed are Rev. W. D. Lewis, Rev. Willie Carter, Rev. Oscar Williams, Rev. Eddie Carter, Rev. James Carter, Rev. Frederick Porter, and Rev. Michael Barton.

CHAPTER SIX

1. Jeff Todd Titon similarly speculated about the role of women in a white Appalachian Baptist church: "Testimony affords women one of the few avenues of attention for solo verbal performance in the church. Denied the right to preach, or to hold office, yoked by the Pauline admonition that women must keep silence in church, some of the women . . . take full advantage of the opportunity to testify" (*Powerhouse for God*, 359).

2. Romans 10:9: "That if thou shalt confess with thy mouth the Lord Jesus, and shalt believe in thine heart that God hath raised him from the dead, thou shalt be saved."

3. Matthew 5:14: "Ye are the light of the world. A city that is set on an hill cannot be hid."

WORKS CITED

ORAL SOURCES

Anthony, James (Jane) E. Personal interview. August 8, 1997.

Barton, Michael A. Personal interview. July 20, 2003.

Busby Jackson, Johnnie Mae. Personal interview. October 19, 1996.

Carter, Ed Henry. Interview with James E. Carter. *Untitled*. 1987. Video-
cassette. Not distributed.

———. Personal interview. October 20, 1996.

———. Personal interview. August 7, 1997.

———. Personal interview. August 12, 1997.

Carter, Eddie L. Personal interview. August 12, 1997.

Carter, Henry T. Personal interview. August 11, 1997.

Carter, James E. Personal interview. August 7, 1997.

Carter, Leola B. Personal interview. August 11, 1997.

Carter, Willie C. Personal interview. September 6, 1998.

———. Personal interview. September 7, 1998.

Constantine, Mary. Personal interview. August 8, 1997.

Edmonds, Patricia. Personal interview. September 4, 1998.

Eight-year-old boy. Personal interview. September 6, 1998.

Hendricks, Rosie Lee. Personal interview. August 9, 1997.

Lewis, W. D. Personal interview. August 7, 1997.

———. Personal interview. September 5, 1998.

Porter, Courtney. Personal interview. August 6, 1997.

Porter, Frederick D. Personal interview. November 14, 1999.

Purse, Carrie B. Personal interview. July 22, 2003.

Smith, Bessie. Personal interview. August 10, 1997.
Smith, Mary V. Personal interview. August 10, 1997.
Smothers, Gladys O. Personal interview. November 13, 1999.
Smothers, Jonas. Personal interview. November 13, 1999.
Ten-year-old boy. Personal interview. September 5, 1998.
Williams, Oscar M. Personal interview. November 12, 1999.

WRITTEN SOURCES

Abrahams, Roger D. "After New Perspectives: Folklore Study in the Late Twentieth Century." *Western Folklore* 52 (1993): 379–400.

Alabama Advisory Committee to the U.S. Commission on Civil Rights. *Burning of African American Churches in Alabama and Perceptions of Race Relations.* Transcript of a Community Forum held July 2, 1996, Boligee, Alabama. Copy available through U.S. Commission on Civil Rights Web site: <http://www.usccr.gov/pubs/pubsndx.htm>.

"Arson Could Be Cause of Churches Burning." *Greene County Democrat*, January 17, 1996, 1.

"Ashes and Ashes." Editorial. *Greene County Independent*, February 14, 1996, 4.

Bartlett, John. *Bartlett's Familiar Quotations.* 14th ed. Edited by Emily Morrison Beck. Boston: Little Brown, 1968.

Bauman, Richard. "Aspects of Quaker Rhetoric." *Quarterly Journal of Speech* 56 (1970): 67–74.

———. *Let Your Words Be Few: Symbolism of Speaking and Silence Among Seventeenth-Century Quakers.* Cambridge Studies in Oral and Literate Culture 8. Edited by Peter Burke and Ruth Finnegan. Cambridge: Cambridge University Press, 1983.

———. "Quaker Folk-Linguistics and Folklore." In *Folklore: Performance and Communication*, edited by Dan Ben-Amos and Kenneth S. Goldstein, 117–39. The Hague: Mouton, 1975.

———. "Speaking in the Light: The Role of the Quaker Minister." In *Explorations in the Ethnography of Speaking*, edited by Richard Bauman and Joel Sherzer, 144–60. Cambridge: Cambridge University Press, 1974.

———. *Verbal Art as Performance.* 1977. Prospect Heights, Illinois: Waveland Press, 1984.

Bauman, Richard, and Roger D. Abrahams, eds. *And Other Neighborly Names: Social Process and Cultural Image in Texas Folklore.* Austin: University of Texas Press, 1981.

Ben-Amos, Dan. "Toward a Definition of Folklore in Context." *Journal of American Folklore* 84 (1971): 3–15.

Berger, Harris M., and Giovanna P. Del Negro. "Bauman's Verbal Art and the Social Organization of Attention: The Role of Reflexivity in the Aesthetics of Performance." *Journal of American Folklore* 115 (2002): 62–91.

Billings, R. A. "The Negro and His Church: A Psychogenetic Study." *Psychoanalytic Review* 21 (1934): 425–41.

Booth, William. "In Church Fires, a Pattern but No Conspiracy: Investigators Say Climate of Racism, Not Hate Groups, Drives Arsonists." *Washington Post*, June 19, 1996, A1+.

Boykin, Milton Lee. "The Emergence of a Black Majority: An Analysis of Political Participation in Greene County, Alabama." Ph.D. diss., University of Alabama, 1972.

Brown, Linda Keller, and Kay Mussell. *Ethnic and Regional Foodways in the United States: The Performance of Group Identity*. 1984. Knoxville: University of Tennessee Press, 1997.

Brunner, E. De S. *Church Life in the Rural South: A Study of the Opportunity of Protestantism Based upon Data from Seventy Counties*. New York: George H. Doran, 1923.

Camp, Charles. *American Foodways: What, When, Why and How We Eat in America*. The American Folklore Series, ed. W. K. McNeil. Little Rock: August House, 1989.

Castaneda, Ruben. "Teens Toil to Rebuild Black Churches: Area Volunteers Hammer Away in a Rural Alabama Town." *Washington Post*, June 30, 1996, A1+.

Cooke, Sam. "A Change is Gonna Come." Rec. January 30, 1964. *Ain't That Good News*. Abkco, ASIN B0000O9PJPA, 2003.

Cooper, Len. "The Damned: Slavery Did Not End with the Civil War. One Man's Odyssey into a Nation's Secret Shame." *Washington Post*, June 16, 1996, F1+.

Dance, Daryl Cumber. *Shuckin' and Jivin': Folklore from Contemporary Black Americans*. Bloomington: Indiana University Press, 1978.

Daniel, Pete. *The Shadow of Slavery: Peonage in the South, 1901–1969*. Urbana: University of Illinois Press, 1972.

Davis, Gerald L. *I Got the Word in Me and I Can Sing It, You Know: A Study of the Performed African-American Sermon*. 1985. Philadelphia: University of Pennsylvania Press, 1987.

Day, Katie. "A Missed Chance to Examine Race Relations." *Philadelphia Inquirer*, November 21, 1998, A15.

Du Bois, W. E. B. *The Souls of Black Folk*. 1903. New York: Signet Classics–New American Library, 1982.

Duneier, Mitchell. *Slim's Table: Race, Respectability, and Masculinity*. Chicago: University of Chicago Press, 1992.

Fields, Gary, and Tom Watson. "Arson at Black Churches Echoes Bigotry of Past." *USA Today*, February 8, 1996, 3A.

Fleming, Walter L. *Civil War and Reconstruction in Alabama*. New York: Peter Smith, 1949.

Fletcher, Michael A. "No Linkage Found in Black Church Arsons: Justice Department Lists 28 Attacks in 17 Months." *Washington Post*, May 22, 1996, A8.

———. "U.S. Investigates Suspicious Fires at Southern Black Churches." *Washington Post*, February 8, 1996, A3.

Forkland, Alabama. Map. Reston, Virginia: United States Geological Survey, 1979.

Frazier, E. F. *The Negro in the United States*. New York: Macmillan, 1968.

Fulop, Timothy E., and Albert J. Raboteau, eds. *African-American Religion: Interpretive Essays in History and Culture*. New York: Routledge, 1997.

Goldstein, Diane E. "The Secularization of Religious Ethnography and Narrative Competence in a Discourse of Faith." *Western Folklore* 54 (1995): 23–36.

Greene County Historical Society. *A Goodly Heritage: Memories of Greene County*. Edited by Mary Morgan Glass. Eutaw, Alabama: Greene County Historical Society, 1977.

———. *A Visitor's Guide to Historic Greene County*. Eutaw, Alabama: Greene County Historical Society, 1991.

Hawthorne, Ann. "Method and Spirit: Studying the Diversity of Gestures in Religion." Introduction to *Diversities of Gifts: Field Studies in Southern Religion*. Edited by Ruel W. Tyson Jr., James L. Peacock, and Daniel W. Patterson. Urbana: University of Illinois Press, 1988.

Hinson, Glenn. *Fire in My Bones: Transcendence and the Holy Spirit in African American Gospel*. Philadelphia: University of Pennsylvania, 2000.

History for Meridian NAS, Mississippi. Chart. N.p.: Weather Underground, n.d. <http://wunderground.com> (accessed September 17, 2003).

Holley, Joe. "Anatomy of a Story: Who Was Burning the Black Churches." *Columbia Journalism Review* 35.3 (1996): 26–33.

Holy Bible: Authorized King James Version. Grand Rapids, Michigan: Zondervan, 1994.

Hufford, David J. "The Scholarly Voice and the Personal Voice: Reflexivity in Belief Studies." *Western Folklore* 54 (1995): 57–76.

Jackson, Joyce Marie. "Music of the Black Churches." <http://www.louisianafolklife.org/LT/Virtual_Books/Fla_Parishes/book_florida_gospel.html> (accessed July 5, 2005).

Johnson, Clifton H., ed. *God Struck Me Dead: Religious Conversion Experiences and Autobiographies of Ex-Slaves*. Philadelphia: United Church, 1969.

Kelly, Thomas. *Testament of Devotion*. 1941. Paperback ed. with a biographical memoir by Douglas V. Steere. New York: Harper Collins, 1996.

Kolchin, Peter. *First Freedom: The Responses of Alabama's Blacks to Emancipa-

tion and Reconstruction. Contributions in American History 20. Westport, Connecticut: Greenwood, 1972.

Lancaster, Clay. *Eutaw: The Builders and Architecture of an Ante-Bellum Southern Town.* Eutaw, Alabama: Greene County Historical Society, 1979.

Lawless, Elaine J. *Holy Women, Wholly Women: Sharing Ministries of Wholeness through Life Stories and Reciprocal Ethnography.* Edited by Patrick B. Mullen. New Series. Philadelphia: University of Pennsylvania Press, 1993.

———. *Women Preaching Revolution: Calling for Connection in a Disconnected Time.* Philadelphia: University of Pennsylvania Press, 1996.

Lester, Julius. *Black Folktales.* New York: Grove, 1992.

L'Estrange, Roger, trans. *Aesop Fables.* 1692. New York: Everyman's Library Children's Classics–Alfred A. Knopf, 1992.

Lewis, John, with Michael D'Orso. *Walking with the Wind: A Memoir of the Movement.* 1998. 1st Harvest ed. N.p.: Harvest Books-Harcourt, 1999.

Limón, José, and M. Jane Young. "Frontiers, Settlements, and Development in Folklore Studies." *Annual Review of Anthropology* 15 (1986): 437–70.

Lincoln, C. Eric, ed. *The Black Experience in Religion.* Garden City, New York: Anchor-Doubleday, 1974.

Lincoln, C. Eric, and Lawrence H. Mamiya. *The Black Church in the African American Experience.* Durham: Duke University Press, 1990.

Lomax, Alan. *The Land Where the Blues Began.* New York: Pantheon, 1993.

Miller, Randall M., ed. *"Dear Master": Letters of a Slave Family.* 1978. Athens: Brown Thrasher–University of Georgia Press, 1990.

Moody, Anne. *Coming of Age in Mississippi.* New York: Dell, 1968.

Motz, Marilyn. "The Practice of Belief." *Journal of American Folklore* 111 (1998): 339–55.

Mullen, Patrick B. "Belief and the American Folk." *Journal of American Folklore* 113 (2000): 119–43.

———. "The Dilemma of Representation in Folklore Studies: The Case of Henry Truvillion and John Lomax." *Journal of Folklore Research* 37.2–3 (2000): 155–74.

———. *Listening to Old Voices: Folklore, Life Stories, and the Elderly.* Urbana: University of Illinois Press, 1992.

Noyes, Dorothy. "Group." *Journal of American Folklore* 108 (1995): 449–78.

Parker, Leewanna. "Authorities Have No Suspects in Fires That Burned Three Black Churches." *Greene County Independent,* January 18, 1996, 1.

———. "Funds Rebuilding Churches." *Greene County Independent,* June 26, 1996, 1+.

Press, Robert M. "A Town with 'Two of Everything.' " *Christian Science Monitor,* August 5, 1996, 9+.

Pressley, Sue Anne. "Church Fires Rekindle Pain: Specter of Racism Rises with the Smoke." *Washington Post,* January 23, 1996, A1+.

Primiano, Leonard Norman. "Vernacular Religion and the Search for Method in Religious Folklife." *Western Folklore* 54 (1995): 37–56.

Puckett, Newbell Niles. *Folk Beliefs of the Southern Negro*. 1926. New York: Dover, 1969.

Raboteau, Albert J. *A Fire in the Bones: Reflections on African-American Religious History*. Boston: Beacon, 1995.

——. *Slave Religion: The "Invisible Institution" in the Ante-Bellum South*. New York: Oxford University Press, 1978.

Roberts, John W. "African American Diversity and the Study of Folklore." *Western Folklore* 52 (1993): 157–71.

Seward, Adrienne Lanier. "The Legacy of Early Afro-American Folklore Scholarship." *Handbook of American Folklore*, edited by Richard M. Dorson, 48–56. Bloomington: Indiana University Press, 1983.

Sharn, Lori, and Gary Fields. "White Churches Equally Subject to Arson." *USA Today*, June 18, 1996, 8A.

Shuman, Amy. "Dismantling Local Culture." *Western Folklore* 52 (1993): 345–64.

Shuman, Amy, and Charles L. Briggs. "Special Issue: Theorizing Folklore: Toward New Perspectives on the Politics of Culture: Introduction." *Western Folklore* 52 (1993): 109–34.

Smith, Margaret Charles, and Linda Janet Holmes. *Listen to Me Good: The Life Story of an Alabama Midwife*. Women and Health Series. Columbus: Ohio State University Press, 1996.

Smith, Vern E., and Marc Peyser. "Terror in the Night down South: A Rash of Church Fires Confounds the Feds." *Newsweek*, June 3, 1996, 34.

Smothers, Ronald. "Black Church Fires Are under U.S. Review: Link between Eight Cases in Alabama and Tennessee Is Considered." *New York Times*, January 20, 1996, A7.

——. "Burning of Black Churches Tries the Souls of Southern Towns: Out of Ashes, Many Blessings." *New York Times*, June 23, 1996, 14.

Snedecor of Greene County: Garrett's Shop. Map. Mobile, Alabama: Strickland, 1856.

Southern, Eileen. *The Music of Black Americans: A History*. New York: W. W. Norton, 1971.

Titon, Jeff Todd. "The Life Story." *Journal of American Folklore* 93 (1980): 276–92.

——. *Powerhouse for God: Speech, Chant, and Song in an Appalachian Baptist Church*. Austin: University of Texas Press, 1988.

Trelease, Allen W. *White Terror: The Ku Klux Klan Conspiracy and Southern Reconstruction*. Edited by Kenneth B. Clark. The Urban Affairs Series. New York: Harper & Row, 1971.

U.S. Bureau of the Census. *Census 1980*. Characteristics of the Population,

Chap. C, General Social and Economic Characteristics, part 2, AL, Table 186.

——. *Census 2000* Summary File 3 (SF 3) — Sample Data. P155A. Median Family Income in 1999 (White Alone Householder). <http://census.gov> (accessed September 17, 2003). Path: American FactFinder; Census 2000 Summary File 3 (SF3).

——. *Census 2000* Summary File 3 (SF 3) — Sample Data. P155B. Median Family Income in 1999 (Black or African American Alone Householder). <http://www.census.gov> (accessed September 17, 2003). Path: American FactFinder; Census 2000 Summary File 3 (SF 3).

——. *Eighth Census of the United States, 1860.* Agricultural Schedule.

——. *Eighth Census of the United States, 1860.* Slave Schedule.

——. *State and County QuickFacts.* N.p.: n.p., 2003. *Greene County, Alabama.* <http://quickfacts.census.gov/qfd/states/01/01063.html> (accessed September 17, 2003).

U.S. Commission on Civil Rights. *Fifteen Years Ago . . . Rural Alabama Revisited.* Washington, D.C.: GPO, 1983.

——. *Political Participation: A Study of the Participation by Negroes in the Electoral and Political Processes in 10 Southern States since Passage of the Voting Act of 1965.* Washington, D.C.: GPO, 1968.

"U.S. Investigates Fires at Black Churches." *New York Times*, February 9, 1996, A16.

U.S. National Church Arson Task Force. *Fourth Year Report for the President.* Washington, D.C.: GPO, 2000. <http://www.atf.treas.gov/pub> (accessed June 10, 2003).

——. *Third Year Report for the President.* Washington, D.C.: GPO, 2000. <http://www.atf.treas.gov/pub/gen_pub/arsonrpt3.htm> (accessed September 15, 2003).

Walker, Alice. *Everyday Use.* Edited by Barbara T. Christian. Women Writers: Texts and Contexts. New Brunswick: Rutgers, 1994.

Williams, Melvin D. *Community in a Black Pentecostal Church: An Anthropological Study.* 1974. Prospect Heights, Illinois: Waveland, 1984.

Wilmore, Gayraud S. *Black Religion and Black Radicalism: An Interpretation of the Religious History of Afro-American People.* New York: Orbis, 1973.

INDEX

Abernathy, Ralph David, 68
Abrahams, Roger, 236 (n. 36)
Alcohol, Tobacco, and Firearms, Bureau of (ATF), xi, 38, 43, 45–46, 76
Amen corner, 94, 108–9, 121, 128
Anthony, Mrs. James (Jane) E., 141, 182, 185, 186, 245 (n. 15)
Arson, xii, 13, 17, 38, 42–43, 45–47, 52–54, 60. *See also* Burning, of churches nationwide; Burning, of Greene County churches; Burning, of Little Zion

Baltzell, Thomas, 56
Baptism, 183–90, 248 (nn. 21, 24), 248–49 (nn. 25–26)
Baptist Training Union, 213
Bartlett, John, 240 (n. 7)
Barton, Michael A., xiv, 9, 25, 87, 117, 129, 134–35, 140, 207–29, 233 (preface, n. 2), 245 (n. 12), 250 (n. 43)
Bauman, Richard, 91–92, 165, 234 (n. 7), 239 (n. 47)

Belief, personal: development of in conversion experiences, 161–62, 167–83; study of, 162–67, 247 (n. 1); confirmed through baptism, 183–90; as faith in challenging times, 190–98; heeded in call to preach, 198–202; as foundation for ministry, 202–6. *See also* Prayer; Signs from God
Bell, church, 112–13, 146, 148, 149, 246 (n. 18). *See also* Building: physical structure of Little Zion
Ben-Amos, Dan, 16, 236 (n. 31)
Berger, Harris M., 166
Berry, Mary Frances, 73, 76–77
Boligee, Alabama, xi, xii, 2, 4–5, 38, 39, 42, 43, 44, 45, 47, 62, 75, 76, 80, 81
Boykin, Milton Lee, 67, 72–73
Bragg, David, 56
Bragg, James, 189
Bragg, John, 55
Braggs, Joe, 68

Segregation: in Greene County, 4–5, 10, 14–15, 44, 74–75, 152, 159

Self-reflexivity, 7, 25. *See also* Fieldwork

Sermon: as performed African American tradition, 40–41, 111–12, 123–25, 129–35, 163, 201–6, 216, 217, 223, 237 (n. 40), 244–45 (chap. 4, n. 3). *See also* Call and response; Preaching

Service, church. *See* Worship service

Seward, Adrienne Lanier, 16–17

Sharecropping, 12, 22, 59–60, 61–62, 235 (n. 18), 242 (n. 47)

Shiloh Baptist Church, 174, 175

Shuman, Amy, 15, 16, 236 (n. 31)

Signs from God: voices and visions, 79, 97–99, 102–3, 172–73, 174–75, 179, 181, 191–202, 214–16, 218, 219, 243 (n. 76), 249 (n. 31); in conversion, 161–62, 163, 171–78, 179, 181–82, 214–15

Slave culture, 1, 11–14, 22, 37–38, 57–58, 77, 235 (n. 14), 243 (n. 82)

Small, Dick, xiii, 1, 55, 56, 233 (preface, n. 3)

Smaw, Isaiah Buxton, 56

Smaw, Richard (Dick) I., xiii, 1, 55, 56, 233 (preface, n. 3)

Smaw, William, 56

Smith, Bessie, 116, 179, 182–83, 193, 194–95

Smith, Henry, 171

Smith, Margaret Charles, 3

Smith, Mary V., 47–48, 170–71, 178–80, 184, 248 (n. 20)

Smith, Thomas James, 179–80, 182–83

Smothers, Gladys O., 61, 68, 69, 146–48, 152–53, 154, 155, 156, 159, 246 (nn. 17, 20)

Smothers, Jonas, 52, 68, 146–48, 179

Smothers, Ronald, 241 (n. 10)

Southern, Eileen, 178, 237 (n. 40)

Southern Christian Leadership Conference (SCLC), 52, 64, 71, 75, 80

Special events, at Little Zion, 140–51

Spencer, Garric, 74–75

Spiritual journey, individual. *See* Belief, personal

Spring Hill Baptist Church, 153, 194, 249 (n. 32)

Stephney, Christopher, 221

Sunday school, 24, 116–25

Testimony, 92–93, 118, 134, 161, 163–65, 173, 188, 190, 208, 210, 250 (n. 1). *See also* Narrative, personal

Titon, Jeff Todd, 90, 243–44 (n. 1), 250 (n. 1)

Tradition: at Little Zion, xiii, 28, 30; as defining element of folklife study, 15, 236 (n. 31); Little Zion, and other African American churches, 18, 237 (nn. 39–40); changing, at Little Zion, 89, 94–95, 109, 110, 119, 121–23, 125, 128–29, 130–35, 138–40, 149, 161, 167–70, 181–82, 183–86, 188, 214, 201–2, 215, 221–26, 229; definition of, 106; preserving and transmitting, at Little Zion, 110, 111, 112, 113, 117–18, 124, 202–4; in caring for the church building at Little Zion, 110–15, 246 (n. 17); in transportation to Little Zion church, 115–16, 211–12; in Sunday school at Little Zion, 116–25; in the worship service at Little Zion, 125–40; in special church events at Little Zion, 140–51; at Little Zion School, 151–60

Transcendence, xiv, 92, 93, 137, 163–64, 173, 181, 188, 189, 192, 200, 203

Trelease, Allen W., 13

Turner, Morris, 220

Turner, Victor, 234 (n. 7)

U.S. Commission on Civil Rights, 14, 64, 71, 73–77

U.S. Justice Department, 38, 44–45

Walker, Alice, 246 (n. 21)

Washington, William, 55

Washington Quaker Workcamps (WQW), xii, 5, 81, 243 (n. 79)

Watson, A. P., 167

Watson, Forris, 55

Weddings, 141–45, 245–46 (n. 16). *See also* Marriage

Whitewashing, at Little Zion, 114–15

Williams, Hosea, 68

Williams, Melvin D., 33

Williams, Oscar M., 48, 51, 56, 61, 62–63, 67–70, 78–79, 85–86, 87, 112, 114, 128–29, 130, 146–59 passim, 165–66, 167, 168, 169, 171, 177, 180, 201–2, 205, 207, 219, 220, 233 (preface, n. 2), 246 (n. 18), 248–49 (n. 25), 250 (n. 43)

Wilmore, Gayraud S., 237–38 (n. 40)

Worship service, 125–40, 220, 245 (n. 6). *See also* Call and response; Preaching; Sermon; Sunday school

Young, M. Jane, 234 (n. 9)